# Strategies
# for Winning

# Strategies for Winning

▲

*A Top Coach's Game Plan*
*for Victory in Football*
*and in Life*

## George Allen

**McGRAW-HILL PUBLISHING COMPANY**

New York   St. Louis   San Francisco   Auckland   Bogota   Hamburg
London   Madrid   Mexico   Milan   Montreal   New Delhi
Paris   São Paulo   Singapore   Sydney   Tokyo   Toronto

1 2 3 4 5 6 7 8 9 DOC DOC 8 9 2 1 0 9

ISBN 0-07-001079-X

Book design by Mark Bergeron

# Dedication

▲

TO my best and most loyal team:
   To Etty, my wife, for putting up with all the craziness, the hirings and firings and changing houses; to my sons George, Jr., Gregory and Bruce; and to my daughter, Jennifer, soon to be a published author herself; and to Jenny Lumbroso, the matriarch, for the example she set for all the Allens . . .

   with pride and gratitude for their love and unending support, this book is dedicated.

# Contents

▲

# Foreword

▲

*by Sid Luckman, Chicago, Illinois*
*All-time Bears quarterback*

THE first time I met George Allen, I knew he was a winner. He had so much energy and drive as a young assistant coach. He was innovative in so many areas of football for the Chicago Bears, George Halas could not give him enough work.

I knew George as a young assistant coach with the Bears in 1957. Later he became the head defensive coach, and every year the Bears provided outstanding defenses. The 1963 Bears team won the world championship when his defensive team led the league in ten out of fourteen categories and finished second in four others. They intercepted forty-one passes in fifteen games, including the championship game, and allowed only 144 points. This defense was recognized as one of the greatest in the history of pro football.

Besides coaching the defense, he held several other positions. During his eight years as personnel director, the Bears had four Rookies of the Year. He was the general manager without portfolio, and made all the trades that helped the Bears win. He maneuvered them into having three first-round picks so that they could draft Dick Butkus and Gale Sayers. He drafted and signed Mike Ditka and won a celebrated competition for Ronnie Bull over Lamar Hunt, the Dallas Texans, and the new American Football League.

He made the first international trade when he drafted Ed O'Bradovich in the seventh round and traded Pete Manning of Wake Forest for Jim Finks of Winnipeg in the Canadian Football League. He was Halas's strong right arm, and he must have loved the old man; he worked seven days a week and no one ever heard him complain.

George Allen is one of the few individuals I have known in my life who had the ability to do any job he was assigned. He was an outstanding administrator. He was very well organized, a detail man, a motivator. He would work long hours and be effective the next day because of his personal habits of health and conditioning. He was an innovator in so many ways. He was responsible for the nickel defense still popular today, in which a linebacker is replaced by a fifth defensive back.

He organized a grading system for scouting that is still used today. He told all the scouts at a famous meeting in Pittsburgh that they were not going to sleep that night until they finished the new grading chart for college personnel.

George was totally prepared before he became a head coach. He was successful and won at every level. I think the fact that he coached in high school, as an assistant at the University of Michigan, as a head coach in college for nine years and as an assistant in the NFL for nine more prepared him well for his unique career—fourteen straight winning seasons—as a head coach in professional football.

I have followed his career for years. As the former chairman of the President's Council on Physical Fitness and Sports and Chairman of the National Fitness Foundation, he is doing the same things there: bringing innovation to the programs he develops and motivation to the people with whom he works. After all these years, I am proud to be his friend.

# Acknowledgments

▲

THIS book is truly a team effort, with contributions from sources in all walks of life, in all parts of the country—and even around the globe.

As a coach, I learned long ago the risks of trying to single out the "stars" of the game. For each one mentioned, two were overlooked. Space is short and my memory grows weaker; but those who contributed their time or an idea or an encouraging word to this project, I appreciate them. They know who they are and in my heart, if not in my notes, so do I.

But special thank yous are owed to: Gayle Spade, Tina Harris and Tommy McVean, members of my office staff while the bulk of this work consumed me; John Kilroy and John Carlson, of the Kilroy Center in Los Angeles; Gar Laux, who was helpful in many ways in his years with Chrylser; William Bennett, the former Secretary of

Education, and now the nation's drug czar; Bill Lamothe, of Kellogg's; Admiral James D. Watkins, the chief of Naval Operations.

Also, to Malcolm Forbes, and his president, Caspar Weinberger, the former Secretary of Defense; George Otott, Buck and Mickey Melton; Bill and Ruth Ann Biggs; Fritz and Michelle Hitchock; Tom King, Robert Tish, Bob Hyland, Donald Trump and John O'Brien, for their support; Jurgen Palm, of the German Sports Federation, and Marat V. Gramov, of the U.S.S.R. Committee on Physical Culture and Sport, for their courtesies.

I have enjoyed the company of the country's leading football writers and columnists, among them Mel Durslag, Bob Oates and Jim Murray, in Los Angeles; Cooper Rollow, in Chicago; Len Shapiro, in Washington; Edwin Pope, in Miami; Furman Bisher, in Atlanta; Mickey Herskowitz, in Houston. They were sometimes puzzled by my methods, and disapproving of my tactics, but overall we stirred up some fun.

A final word of gratitude to a remarkably patient and persevering editor, Tom Quinn; to Mickey Herskowitz, for his introductions and suggestions; and to Sid Luckman, one the game's great quarterbacks, for providing the foreword.

# Strategies
# for Winning

# Introduction

▲

*by Mickey Herskowitz*

*Nothing in the world can take the place of persistence. Talent will not; nothing is more common than unsuccessful men with talent. Genius will not; unrewarded genius is almost a proverb. Education will not; the world is full of educated derelicts. Persistence and determination alone are omnipotent. The slogan 'Press On' has solved and always will solve the problems of the human race.*

GEORGE Herbert Allen is one of those born motivators who can persuade you with parables, morals, mottoes and candy-grams. There is a point, a message, an insight to every story he tells.

He recalls a game in 1983 when he was coaching the Chicago Blitz in the new United States Football League. The score was tied at the end of the regulation four quarters. The official incorrectly called the coin toss, giving the other team, the New Jersey Generals, possession to start the sudden-death period. Allen's captain, Stan White, an ex-Detroit Lion, knew the opposing captain from their work together in the Fellowship of Christian Athletes, so he appealed to his sense of fairness: "Damn it, you're a Christian. Tell him the truth. Tell him the truth. Tell him you called tails."

The New Jersey captain looked White in the eye and, without a word, reached down, picked up the ball and walked off the field.

"And you know what happened?" George Allen continues. "We got the ball back, drove into field goal range and won the game."

*1*

The moral was clear: God may be too busy with Lebanon and Central America and the nuclear arms race to keep up with pro football standings, but cheaters never win. Almost never.

Allen once made a speech in his role as chairman of The President's Council on Sports and Physical Fitness to a group of coaches at a bodybuilding convention. Among other morsels of information, he told them, "For all the fancy things you see on the shelves, fruity things and chocolate things and things shaped like stars and loops, the No. 1 cereal in America is still cornflakes." (The message: keep it simple.)

When George coached the Redskins it was his custom to spend a few minutes at the end of every practice working on field goals with the line of scrimmage at the one-yard line. "I don't know of any other coaches who had their kickers work on that," he admitted. "They look on it like kicking an extra point. But *I have seen kickers miss extra points*. So we had Mark Moseley work on it." (The message: take nothing for granted.)

As a voice in the desert coaching a team called the Arizona Wranglers in 1984 (having fled Chicago), George Allen was the most enduring name in the troubled USFL. You had to take seriously any team and any league that had George Allen in it. When he went his own way at the end of the season, the league lost a chunk of whatever credibility it had left. Pro football has never seen Allen's equal as a builder or, more correctly, a rebuilder. The Los Angeles Rams had not posted a winning season in seven years when he arrived; the Redskins hadn't won in fifteen. In those two jobs his teams won ninety-one games and lost twenty-seven. He won with teams that were out of draft choices and short of talent and thought to be too old. What they were never short on was coaching.

He was, when he coached his last game after the '85 season, the only active coach in pro football who had served at least twelve years without a losing season. Yet without fear of correction one may say that George Allen has been fired more than any successful coach in captivity. He has been fired fast and he has been fired slow. He has been fired on an employer's whim and after slow, dangling, twisting months of rumor and front-office sniping. He has been fired on Sundays and holidays and twice by the same owner, Dan Reeves of the Rams—once on Christmas day. (In this category, Allen edges out

Bum Phillips, who was given the boot in Houston on New Year's Eve, an occasion without religious meaning.)

For four years no team in the National Football League would hire him. It was bizarre then and a mystery still. Today, he says, a coach must not only win, he must be compatible. The next step is to require them to post a performance bond. "I've always been a general manager as well as a coach," Allen points out, "and the tendency today is not to give up that much authority."

Through it all—through his exile, his firings, his bitter disappointments—George never wavered in his enthusiasm for the sport or his belief that his ways were right. You could hear it in his voice: the joy of being reborn, of building a team from scratch when he helped launch the new league. "Our first day in camp we didn't even have towels and soap," he said. "It reminded me of when I was at Morningside College in Sioux City, Iowa. I had to seed the practice field so we'd have grass."

At Whittier College in California, a school whose most famous graduate is Richard Nixon, Allen coached the football and baseball teams and taught a class in anatomy. His annual pay was $4,800 a year. When he received a raise to $5,000, he ran home to tell his wife the good news, cautioning her: "We'd better put the whole two hundred in the bank. We're liable to need it."

Allen was a classic worrier, as great coaches often are. Whether he searched for peace, or even needed it, is debatable. During the season he would get so preoccupied that he couldn't remember whether or not he had eaten. He would sit and tap his memory painfully. In despair, he might order a glass of milk and a ham sandwich, just in case.

His temperament demanded that he win. He was known to drive his staff past midnight, then look up and ask, "What have we forgotten?" He is a sharply handsome character who seems unaware that he has a face. He is so tireless, so positive, so much into everything, he makes it easy for others to be jealous of him.

He has been the chairman of the President's Council on Sports and Physical Fitness under Presidents Carter and Reagan. In that role he has taken the lead in creating the National Fitness Foundation.

His critics poke fun at the way he fusses about details, his special strategies, his superstitions, his penchant for worrying. They are not sure how much he won by scheming and manipulation and how much just by outworking his rivals. But he knew how to build and prepare a team and his players knew that he knew.

He is, first and foremost, a masterful motivator, and this book is about motivation.

His teams went to the NFL playoffs seven times and to the Super Bowl once. What he has learned from a lifetime in coaching Allen now passes on to the reader. Here is Allen on motivation:

"Whoever said that you don't need to motivate a pro didn't know how wrong he was. You've got to motivate everybody, veterans and rookies alike. I feel very fortunate that throughout my life, for one reason or another I have been a self-starter. Sometimes just the way you talk to people can motivate them. You know the type of guy I want around me? This kind: If I were recruiting at Navy, I'd look for a fellow who says, 'I'd like to play Army a nine-game schedule. Nobody else but Army.' That's the type of guy I want around me.

"I like signs and other reminders. I just love them. I have a sign on my desk that says 'THE TEAM IS NEVER UP!' I put that there after our first Super Bowl with the Redskins, against Miami. We were flat, hard as that is to imagine. Just before the game I was going to talk to the team and rile them up. I thought the dressing room was subdued. Then I thought to myself, 'I don't have to do that, this is the Super Bowl. It's the biggest game of their lives.' That sign reminds me never to take anything for granted and always to do what you believe. I like to get people to think. That's why I use constant reminders. You've got to say things over and over again, because you only get through to about 40 percent of them the first time. It doesn't bother me that those 40 percent may have to hear the same thing seven times. It's better than the other 60 percent not hearing you at all."

Analyzing George Allen was a favorite pastime in pro football for most of two decades. For a fellow so pleasant and agreeable and so intent on good works, he remains a controversial figure. Once, when his Arizona Wranglers trampled the Oklahoma Outlaws, their coach, Woody Widenhofer, said mysteriously, "He'll catch his lunch some-day." (We interpret this to mean that something George ate would

4

come back to haunt him. It never did. Both his teams went to the playoffs, in the arctic cold of Chicago and the pan-fried heat of Arizona.)

Those who know him well, in fact, would find it hard to like someone who didn't like George Allen. If he has been portrayed on occasion as a ruthless competitor, that impression seems wide of the mark. True, as a coach his was a tireless search for the winning edge and he delighted in finding a loophole in the rules. But this is not the way he comes across in the flesh. He never raises his voice. He is a careful listener. He cares for people to the point of pain.

It is his enthusiasm, his energy, his devotion to positive thinking, his Don Quixote tendency to see the good earth where others see mud, that some of his rivals and critics resent or distrust or disbelieve. But *that* is the real George Allen.

Few are more qualified to analyze him than Jack Pardee. It was Allen who brought Pardee back to the National Football League as a linebacker with the Rams after a bout with cancer had sidelined him a year. Allen made him a coach on the field in Washington. And when George was fired by the Redskins, the guy who replaced him was Jack Pardee. Later they opposed each other in the USFL.

"I think the world of George," says Pardee. "I know he's controversial. But he is a great judge of people. He uses the shotgun approach: he tries to hit everything. Not everybody responds to the same method, so he doesn't use just one. That's why the veterans like him.

"When he first came to the Rams, he called a squad meeting and suggested that we ought to have a special yell, a team cheer. You could see the players looking around, thinking, 'What's with this turkey?' But that's George Allen. He's a great guy and his teams take on his personality."

Pardee still remembers how, in his playing days, Allen would call him after midnight to get a point across, knowing that Jack would not get back to sleep until the message sank in.

In the routine that Allen keeps, the way he does things isn't always synchronized with the ways of the rest of us. As an assistant coach with the Chicago Bears under George Halas, he hauled home with him each night a briefcase that would have bent the back of a burro. To reach his stop in Deerfield, George had his choice of the

5

fast train, which got him there in forty-two minutes, or the slow train, requiring an hour and five minutes. George took the slow train, enabling him to get more work done en route.

Even today, past 60, he lifts weights and runs at least three miles most days. He was one of the special runners for the 1984 Olympic Torch Relay, carrying the torch one kilometer after training for two months, gripping a brick in one hand to condition himself to the added weight.

His former players still recall with affection and amusement scenes of George heading for the practice field, hauling a stack of notebooks under one arm and cans of film under the other. One day, impatient to get to the stadium for an out-of-town workout, he ordered the bus driver to leave when he discovered no one else was ready to go. The only passenger on a forty-eight-seat bus, he may have looked lonely, but it is doubtful that he was. If at times George appears to be talking only to himself, you conclude that the conversations are never dull.

As matters developed, George Allen and his "Over-The-Hill Gang" had their last hurrah in the National Football League on the eighth of December, 1977, at RFK Stadium. Although no one could have imagined the sequence of events that would follow, Allen coached his last regular-season NFL game that day.

The Redskins finished with a nine-and-five record and lost the wild-card berth to the Bears on the basis of net points. The *New York Post* voted him coach of the year. Returning in the off-season to the Rams, George coached two preseason games and was the victim of one of pro football's most impetuous firings, by Carroll Rosenbloom.

All the more poignant, then, is the following story by the late Ernest Cuneo, written on the day in 1977 that a long and colorful NFL chapter ended:

# The National Whirligig
### by Ernst Cuneo

Washington, D.C. Dec. 8, 1977
*(reprinted from: North American Newspaper Alliance)*

OF JIM THORPE,
OF CLASS, AND THE
GEORGE ALLEN REDSKINS

It was halftime at a dreary little Ohio Stadium. The first wisps of snow from the dull gray clouds whirled around the cheerless grand-stands, more than half empty because a wolf-jawed wind was blowing in a blizzard from the Lakes. The Brooklyn Dodgers were playing a pickup Ohio team. It was late November of 1932 and then, as now, Ohio could always pick up quite a team. Hence, an Atlantic Seaboard team was as alert as Dan Boone as soon as it crossed the Alleghenies, because in pro football the Ohio Valley was still the Dark and Bloody ground.

The pros of both teams, however, didn't go into the locker rooms. They pulled up the collars of their sideline jackets, stuffed their numbed hands into the slant-pockets, and pounded their feet on the hard ground to keep warm. They waited to see a feat so unlikely that it is expressed in the American idiom "This I gotta see."

Presently, a 44-year-old man in a football uniform trotted to midfield. In those days, 44 in pro football was Methuselah. Since players played sixty minutes, both offense and defense, the injuries piled up early. Indeed, a player over 35 was flirting with a visit from next-of-kin.

The 44-year-old man was regarded as the greatest of the great: Jim Thorpe. At 44, he still had the athlete slouch of a smooth-muscled Olympic decathlon winner, all the more remarkable since he had won his hardest battle—that against alcoholism. He wasn't a big man, as size runs now. He was about six feet three and 192 pounds.

It had been advertised that Thorpe could drop-kick over one goal from the fifty-yard line, then turn around and drop-kick an-other fifty-yard goal over the other goal. This was a superhuman feat for a man in his prime, let alone 44. For one thing, the football was bigger and heavier then. Not even the pros had ever seen this done, and the bets among themselves were three to one that Thorpe couldn't do it.

Well, he did. With Indian stolidity, he booted one over the west goal, then turned around and booted one over the east goal. That's not the point of the story. The point is that all the pros gave him a tremendous cheer, muffled enough in the snowy stadium, and rushed out to congratulate him. Thorpe was as pleased as a child. The spectators gave him a ho-hum hand. The reason is that they didn't know class when they saw it.

This raises the interesting question of what class is. The arbiter of those times was Damon Runyon. Runyon said it couldn't be defined. It might be the lift of Citation's foot, the snap of Whirl-away's head, the flick of Sugar Ray Robinson's glove, and you'd know it when you saw it, though you couldn't tell why.

But Runyon was wrong. Sir Winston Churchill defined the basis of class. It is the discovery in adversity that man is nothing but a spirit. This is not the spirit of going down fighting. Quite the contrary. On the heart of every real pro is engraved, "Don't die fighting; fight to win."

As the life of a professional football player goes, he is at peak speed from 21 to 26; he is at peak strength from 26 to 31, though he doesn't have quite the electrical reaction. After 31, he is neither at peak speed nor peak strength, but by then his trade has been pounded into him and he can depend upon his skills. But after a few years of this, though his speed and his strength remain constant, his power to absorb punishment and especially to recuperate from it declines rapidly.

And that's when a player or a team shows its class. This year, the oldest team in terms of years and of battering experience is demonstrating unsurpassed class, a demonstration it could not be making were it not in adversity. As one who doesn't know a Washington Redskin player or coach and has no desire to meet one and is indifferent to Redskin fortunes, the fact nevertheless remains that this team of old pros is showing class that no team can show when it is a front runner. As this goes to press, the old pros still have a fighting chance to make the playoffs. Like Dempsey in the great Firpo brawl at the Polo Grounds, they've been decked four times and four times they've gotten up, not only to go on fighting, but fighting to win.

*Not since old Jim Thorpe walked out on the 50-yard line has the National League seen such class—and seldom has it been less appreciated.* It has been called raw courage. This is absolute nonsense.

Raw physical courage is a basic necessity, but class is the courage of the spirit; not merely the taking of the field but the indomitable pitting of the heart against impossible odds. Wellington was great at Waterloo; but Churchill exhibited Britain's class when, with 40 percent of his outnumbered RAF down, he beat Goehring's Luftwaffe in the Battle of Britain.

In smaller measure, the snow has fallen on the headstones of Thorpe and most of the younger pros on the field that snowy Ohio day.

But it is reasonable to suppose that if he were alive today, Jim Thorpe would appreciate the class of the indomitable, old-pro Redskins because *George Allen and his players are strictly Jim Thorpe-type of guys.*

—Mickey Herskowitz

## HOW TO MOTIVATE YOURSELF
### by George Allen

1. Compare yourself with someone of similar age-career-background.
2. Compare yourself with a wealthy person—what has he or she achieved?
3. Remember that someone is always ahead of you: smarter, better looking, faster, stronger. You can't let that pull you down.
4. Work out.
5. Diet.
6. Take a trip—get away from your normal routine.
7. Visit someone less fortunate.
8. Work harder.
9. Pray—give thanks.
10. If you have talent, don't waste it.
11. Know that you have something no one else has.

## HOW I MOTIVATE MYSELF

1. Work extra hard
   a) Stay positive all day.
   b) I enjoy working hard, always have.

*9*

2. Get up early
   a) Best part of the day.
   b) Few people around.
   c) Sets pace for the entire day.

3. Have a good physical workout: one hour of any or all of the following
   a) Jogging.
   b) Weight lifting.
   c) Stretching.
   d) Swimming.
   e) Basketball.

4. After a good workout, read a newspaper; relax.

5. Make a list of goals for the day
   a) It helps keep me organized.
   b) I try not to make the list too long.
   c) I make a duplicate because I like to carry one with me.
   d) I make notes by my bedstand before retiring.

6. Eat a fiber breakfast of natural–raw foods
   a) Carries me through the day until evening.
   b) Raisins, figs, apples, apricots, bananas, oranges.

7. Organize myself away from distractions
   a) Avoid noises and telephones.
   b) Create a space away from kids and people who might misuse my time.
   c) Build motivation into the surroundings with photos, posters, and the like.

8. Play a cassette of inspirational music
   a) Whatever type of music I find stimulating.
   b) I enjoy big bands; plenty of Goodman, Miller, James, Al Hirt, Sinatra, Dorsey.

9. Make sure I get fresh air—not air conditioning
   a) I don't liked to be cooped up in a room with windows that don't open.
   b) I prefer to be near water, with a breeze.
   c) No claustrophobia.

10. Work from a stand-up desk
    a) I use a drafting table.
    b) I work in my garage.

11. Know that I can outwork anyone
    a) Mental attitude.

b) I make it easy for myself to work out.

12. Eat a light lunch.
    a) Saves time.
    b) After a good breakfast, a big meal isn't needed.

13. Visit someone—or a hospital—and spend time with someone less fortunate
    a) Do something each day to help someone else.

## MY PHILOSOPHY OF WINNING

To be successful, you must win. To win, you must WORK HARD.

You must DEDICATE yourself to a far-reaching goal . . . and sacrifice to reach it. You must ENJOY what you do . . . be enthused with your activities, in love with the idea of winning.

You must REACH BEYOND your abilities, recognize that no talent, without hard work, can make you a winner. You must BE HONEST with yourself—and with others . . . There is no easy way to success.

You must treat your body with respect . . . disciplining yourself into SUPERB PHYSICAL CONDITION. You must BE LOYAL . . . to yourself, to your ideals, and to your team or company.

You must become a LEADER, first leading yourself, and then leading others by your example. You must have a complete MENTAL COMMITMENT, overcoming all defeats, relentlessly pursuing total victory.

You must consider winning as essential as eating and sleeping. You must consider success the heartbeat of life.

The people I most admire and who most motivate me are ordinary people who have:

1. Vitality and a sense of accomplishment.
2. The ability to get things done.
3. Tremendous energy.
4. Self-discipline.
5. A willingness to reach beyond their gifts.

*11*

# PEOPLE WHO ARE WINNERS

People who are on time.

People who are in shape.

People who are enthusiastic.

People who are self-disciplined.

People who are committed to a goal.

People who are dedicated to their job.

People who are organized.

People who are tough mentally.

People who enjoy helping others.

People who are innovative.

People who are loyal.

People who enjoy life.

# 1

# The Book of Firsts

▲

*Losers never know why they are losing. They will mention injuries, the officiating, the weather, bad breaks. The big thing is not what happens to us in life, but what we do about what happens to us.*

IN a year when the United States Football League found itself punting from its own end zone, I sat down to finish a book on motivation.

Were the two somehow related? Certainly. The owners, the coaches, the players—virtually everyone connected with the new league—were among the most motivated people I have ever known. They had all the best goals: money, pride, glory, and above all a chance to pioneer, to build.

So what went wrong? Greed, ego, and selfishness ruined it for the owners and everyone else. The irony is that we still don't know if the idea of football in the spring might have worked. In my mind, the concept never received a fair test.

I was part of the experiment as a coach and part owner, and I had the distinction of fielding what amounted to two expansion teams in two cities in two seasons: the Chicago Blitz and the Arizona Wranglers. I challenge anyone to top that record.

I have no regrets about the time, effort, and emotion I invested, only disappointments. From the start I argued that the USFL should grow slowly, resist expansion and allow eight original teams to establish an identity. And shortly I was reading in the papers that George Allen was trying to run the league.

So the USFL opened with twelve teams in March of 1983, and within a year had expanded to eighteen. It simply made no sense. By expanding so quickly, even as weaker clubs were leap-frogging into new locations, a credibility problem was created. We had to spend more money, screen more players, and waste precious time defending ourselves to the press and public.

Too many inexperienced investors expected us to draw big crowds overnight. They never understood that the old guard in the National Football League, the Rooneys and the Maras, went through years and years of losing money. Even when I was with the Chicago Bears in the early 1960s, George Halas was still counting the house. The size of your phone bill sometimes determined whether you had a profitable month or not.

But the USFL had its share of good owners, bright front-office types—many of them out of the NFL—and capable coaches who worked the kind of hours that would have made a Cambodian rice farmer complain.

And I thought the teams had some terrific names: the Blitz, Outlaws, Bandits, Gamblers, Wranglers. When Jack Pardee signed on to coach the Houston team, he asked one of the owners, Jerry Argovitz, how they picked the name Gamblers. Argovitz replied at length, as he often did, that the name was meant to reflect the risk-taking spirit of the city. Also, they were hoping to bring in as an investor the singer Kenny Rogers, whose hit "The Gambler" was one of Jerry's favorites.

"It's a good thing," responded Pardee, "your favorite wasn't 'Coward of the County.' "

A new professional football league is no place for the faint of heart. The first time we held a free-agent camp for the Chicago Blitz, we had to worry about towels and soap, things you take for granted with an established team. We had players who overcame an unending streak of adversity to prove that they were quality people: Trumaine Johnson, Tim Spencer, Greg Landry, Stan White, Karl Lorch, Kevin

Long. We achieved something rare in any league: two runners, Spencer and Long, who gained a thousand yards in back-to-back seasons.

We played and won the opening game of the USFL's first season, over the Washington Federals, in what was billed as a homecoming for George Allen, in the stadium where I had coached the Redskins for seven seasons. It was like Jesse Owens returning to Berlin . . . or Jesse James going back to Missouri.

The network asked me to do a TV spot promoting the game. They wrote a commercial that had me taunting the home team, and I said, "Wait a minute, I can't do that. It'll fire them up. Change it." My players were lined up behind me, laughing. We drew 39,000 spectators in the rain, and beat the Federals, 28–7.

I will never forget charging out of the locker room at game time and finding the stadium people—ushers and vendors and the clean-up crews—lined up to cheer and welcome us back. At half time, I was walking off the field when a network announcer asked me to say a few words. I had never had that happen before.

By the end of the 1983 season, the league was already hurting. Seven teams were either sold or relocated, even as the league was expanding into new cities, hustling fresh money to cut its losses. Saddest of all, the league didn't need to challenge the NFL to succeed. It only needed to show some staying power. The American Football League survived because its owners held on through the first five years.

The USFL owners were an interesting cross-section. Alfred Taubman had the Detroit franchise, the Michigan Panthers, and he was willing to pour in heavy dollars to field a winner. Another sharp owner was Myles Tannenbaum in Philadelphia, who hired Carl Peterson out of the NFL to run his team. Marvin Warner, the principal owner in Birmingham, was a former ambassador to Switzerland.

But the showman was easily Donald Trump, the young New York real estate mogul who might have been the new league's Lamar Hunt if things had turned out differently. He had the money, the clout, and the imagination. He wanted to get things done and he had the market in which to do it.

Of all the owners, Trump seemed best able to afford the early losses. When he bought the New Jersey Generals they had already signed Herschel Walker out of Georgia. Trump went out and added Doug Flutie for $7 million, winning a bidding war in which the other side did not bid. It was hoped that the Boston College hero would do for the USFL what Joe Namath did for the American Football League. Flutie showed a knack for the dramatic rally, and he won a few games for the Generals, mostly by handing off to Walker. But by the end of the year, Trump was petitioning the other owners to help pay Flutie's salary.

No one can accuse the league of not having been aggressive enough. It gave away money, cars, and tickets. And yet the crowds kept getting smaller, until the USFL made its final play before a crowd of six people: the jurors who heard the antitrust suit against the NFL in federal court in New York. It ended with the jury awarding one dollar in damages, tripled under the law.

The future had looked shakier with each season. At one point, John Bassett, who owned the Tampa Bay team and probably had more marketing savvy than any of the others, threatened to bolt and start a new league. Bassett was dying of a brain tumor, and he offered to sell his franchise if a buyer could be found.

The new USFL commissioner, Harry Usher, who had been Peter Ueberroth's second in command at the Olympics, hailed Bassett's change of mind as "a vote of confidence in the future of the league." I am by nature an optimist, but Usher outdid me. He must think buying flight insurance is an act of confidence.

Everywhere you looked, the owners were cutting their office staffs and trying to hold off their creditors. In San Antonio, paychecks bounced like golf balls on a driveway. It was sad, of course, because a lot of good people were hurt and some were going broke.

The league wounded itself by moving out of three of the biggest television markets, Chicago, Boston, and Los Angeles. When the talk started of moving to a fall schedule, we lost the contract with ABC, and it appeared that the league's best hope for television was a guest shot on Candid Camera.

The Bible says there is for all things a season, but you couldn't prove it by the USFL. The decision to expand was a disaster, but the proposal to turn to an autumn season served only to position the league for its suit against the NFL.

It was a failure of the commissioners, first Chet Simmons and then Usher, not to check out the qualifications of the owners thoroughly. Someone in the league would recommend someone else, and that seemed to be the only research anyone did. Anyone who wants to dip a toe into a new pro football league had better be prepared to lose between $3 and $5 million.

One of the smarter moves was made by Jim Joseph, who bailed out after the first year, selling his Arizona franchise to Dr. Ted Dietrich for $7.2 million. Ted, a nationally known heart surgeon, lived and practiced in Phoenix. He gave up a first-place team in Chicago in return for a last-place club in the desert. And the man who bought the Blitz from him defaulted on a letter of credit; to my knowledge, Dietrich never collected a dime.

There was enough irony to go around. One reason I had thrown in with the new league was because I knew Chicago, knew the fans, and thought they would support another team, one coached and managed aggressively.

In the switch, we took roughly half our Chicago roster to Arizona, and wound up beating the Blitz, our old team, 36–0. But the move, which was a financial bomb for Ted Dietrich, would be a near-crippling blow for the league.

We were successful in Phoenix, won the western conference and drew a couple of crowds of just under 40,000. We would have cashed in on the field and at the box office the next season, but his losses on the Chicago deal forced the doctor to merge with the Oklahoma team. That was my cue to leave.

Merging is like bringing another family to live in your house. The chemistry is never there. It may start out all right, but in the history of all sports there never has been a successful merger of two franchises.

For all the havoc and headaches, I am grateful for my two years in the league. It was like discovering Australia; you never knew what you were going to find. Every day I found myself saying, "This is another first." I always said that if I wrote a book about the USFL, that would be the title: "Another First."

We practiced in a blizzard in Chicago once, the players squinting to locate each other as though they were playing at the North Pole. That was a first. And from there we encountered the broiling heat and sandstorms of Arizona. Another first.

*  *  *

When you are in a league that has no history, the minor problems become fascinating. There are no game films. To make a point or to cover a technique, I once used some footage from the 1975 NFL season. I was amazed at the reaction of the players. The uniforms looked baggy and outdated to them, and they would call out, "Who's that running with the ball, Red Grange?" Once, Pat Fisher, an all-pro, jammed someone with a fine tackle and they only wanted to know who the midget was.

We had so many obstacles, so many handicaps, I looked forward to each new day just to see what would happen. Once we went out to the practice field and all our footballs were missing. Another time we went into the meeting room and there was no blackboard, no chalk, no erasers.

In Chicago, to film our practices and games, Doctor Dietrich hired two cameramen who had never filmed football before, had never even been to Chicago. They drove me batty with their habit of eating fried chicken and leaving the bones in my office. I would tell them to send a film to Michigan and it would wind up in Denver. They were the kind of guys who went around looking for a left-handed monkey wrench.

We seldom had to wait long for the next development, and whatever we expected we were infrequently disappointed. In 1983, while still coaching the Blitz, I held a free-agent camp on the West Coast for players who had not been drafted. We held the camp at the University of Southern California beginning at 9 o'clock one morning, making it known that the players should be on time.

Much to our surprise, we had such a large turnout that we closed and locked the gates a few minutes before 9 A.M. About an hour later, a young fellow named Tom Porras came up to me on the field and said he had been late and had missed the quarterback test. He asked if he could be given a tryout at that time.

I asked how he had gotten onto the practice field when the gates had been locked. He explained that he had climbed over the fence, which was about 10 feet high.

"If you wanted a trial so badly that you climbed over that gosh darn fence," I told him, "I'll certainly give you one."

Porras looked so good that we signed him to a contract. He was our back-up quarterback with both the Blitz and the Arizona Wranglers. The moral to his story is that if you want something so badly that nothing can stand in your way, you will almost certainly make it happen.

In Phoenix, the county operated the training complex and only one custodian had the key to the power supply. He went out to happy hour one day and never came back. We were practicing at night then and had no way to turn on the lights, so I had all the players pull up their cars around the field and turn on their headlights so we could practice. Frank Corrall, our kicker, taped a flashlight to his helmet, making it look like a miner's hat, so he could see the ball. I also called him over when I needed to check my clipboard.

We simply took every disadvantage and tried to turn it into an advantage.

Phoenix was an attractive city, but the climate required an entirely new approach. The temperature hit 117 degrees in June and July, and we had to go to night practices as a last resort. They had to move the championship game from a noon kickoff to 9 P.M., and even then it was 106 degrees.

I kept the same schedule as though we were practicing in the daytime, getting up at six in the morning and reaching the office at seven. We put the players on a different timetable. They came in at three, as did the office staff. Everyone else, the trainers and equipment men, had to be there in the morning.

The players hated it, as I knew they would. Everyone had a complaint: "When are we going to see our kids? When we get home they're in bed. When they go to school, we're asleep."

It was like working the graveyard shift at a factory, but we had no alternative. There was no other way to beat the heat. Actually, it turned our season around. We won six straight and made the playoffs.

But I can assure you that it is non-motivating to practice football at night, in the desert, with limited lighting and the dirt always in your face. One night I was bitten by a black widow spider. Another time a rattlesnake slithered across the field. A kid who worked for us, Spanky Crawford, had a pet boa constrictor, so I told him to handle it. We had canvas duffel bags to keep our equipment in, and he got a stick and coaxed the rattler inside the bag. I told him if nobody called for it in thirty days, it was his.

The boa constrictor figured in one of the craziest scenes I have ever experienced as a coach. We had an ongoing situation with the

*19*

players over some minor pilfering. Players being players, they were always picking up a few extra pairs of socks, or T-shirts—on our budget they had to cut a few corners.

Well, Spanky kept his boa at home, and on his day off he would bring it to the office in a kind of aquarium. He would just goof around, wear it around his neck. But our equipment manager, a clever fellow named Tom McVean, noticed that there was no pilfering on the days Spanky showed up with his pet. On those days the players avoided the equipment room. When they walked up to the cage, the first question they asked was, "Where's the snake?" So even when Spanky left it at home, Tom would answer, "Oh, he's around here somewhere."

Once a week, Spanky fed the boa constrictor a little white mouse, which was its only meal. It occurred to Tommy that it might be interesting, possibly even motivating, for the players to observe this ritual, watching the snake strike. I thought I might squeeze some symbolism out of it, the mouse representing the team we were playing that week, which happened to be Houston.

So we set up chairs and invited the players into the equipment room. I made a short speech about how we were going to devour Houston that week, just as the snake was going to devour that mouse. There was another nice touch involved, because the Gamblers had what they called the run-and-shoot offense, designed by their offensive coordinator, Mouse Davis. Their receivers were quick little guys known as The Mouseketeers.

Spanky tossed the mouse into the cage and the first thing it did was dart toward the snake and peck at his head. The snake jumped back. For about five minutes it went that way, and suddenly the players were laughing and applauding and cheering for the mouse. He was the underdog. The mouse was still racing around the cage and the players were yelling at us to spare him. So Spanky took the mouse out and gave him a reprieve.

I waited until the last player had gone, and as I reached the door I turned back and snapped at Spanky, "Don't ever bring that snake in here again. He's a loser."

Later, Spanky explained that the noise and commotion upset the boa, and he must not have been hungry.

There may be a message in here somewhere about mice and men. On the other hand, there may not be.

* * *

I will say this for the United States Football League. The product was better than anyone had a right to expect. Its strength was in the coaching, its weakness in the owners whose assets were borderline. Too many times the owners rained on their own parade.

For all the alternating currents, the frustrations and the moments of comedy, it is a full feeling to know that you have done your best, as most of us did in the USFL. When you have given everything you have of yourself, you can live with the outcome without regret.

Let me repeat a constant theme of mine: you are not going to win all the time. I was fortunate to have a record of winning 71 percent of the time, but there will always be factors no one can control—in football or business or life. If you have given it your all, drained yourself dry, just emptied your tank, you can live with yourself. You might not like it, but over the long run you are going to be consistent, and consistency is the truest form of success.

The 1984 season in Phoenix was the most difficult, challenging, and disrupted of my entire coaching career. When we moved out of Chicago, with one year as an expansion team behind us, we were merged into the new Arizona Wranglers. The "old" Wranglers had finished dead last, so we had to overcome that image in an entirely different environment with a new organization.

No one had gone through that kind of transition before—two expansion teams, back to back, with different players, coaches, trainers, doctors, equipment men, public relations people, and office staff. True, we kept a lot of our Chicago players, but the chemistry was missing in this new location. It was difficult for everyone to get adjusted, especially for the many players who were settled in Chicago and liked the city. As the Chicago Blitz, we had won twelve games and tied for first place, led the USFL in scoring and finished first on defense. We also led the league with forty-two interceptions, including the playoffs. The last time a pro football team had won twelve games in Chicago was in 1939, the year Hitler marched into Poland.

One of the most difficult things I had to do in 1984 was accept the idea that I could not control as many facets of USFL football as I could in the NFL. There were so many different factors and problems to overcome in the new league. Not unless you have been in both situations and had the responsiblity for molding a team can you appreciate how disorienting the changes were.

For example, the officials were different. They were good men trying to do a job, but they were not NFL officials. The players were different, too. They would sometimes make mistakes that cost you a game because of poor judgment.

For example: we lost a game to Denver when we had them stopped, on third-and-25, with just a short minute to play. Our cornerback tried to intercept a pass, interfered with the receiver, and gave them a first down to keep the drive going. On top of that, the pass was so badly thrown it could not have been completed. I never lost games like that in the NFL.

A week earlier, we had been beaten when one of our defensive players rushed the punter to block a kick, when he should have been covering the end man. Our opponent completed a pass for a first down and eventually it led to a touchdown. We lost that game by one point; we lost to Denver by three. I felt tested, all right. I was living on the edge.

Those are meant only as examples of how thin the line is. I'm not critical of our players, who played with all the heart and vigor a coach could ask.

You cannot control what people are going to do, but I have always been able to control myself and my preparation. From a very young age, I was always busy; that was one of the choices you made when you were poor in the midst of the Depression. I've always had the feeling, no matter what I was doing, that I could be putting my time into something else as well. It bothers me to waste even a few minutes.

There is always something you can do to improve yourself. Life is going on all around you. Someone is in a similar situation and will make it. If you are bored, it's your fault for not using your head properly.

As this book is being completed, I have put my coaching career behind me, after 32 years, and moved on to a challenge of new dimensions as Chairman of the National Fitness Foundation.

The job is so different, the hurdles so endless, that I find myself still living and working up to my full capacity. It is called "risk living" when you attempt to raise $40 million from the private sector so that a sports and fitness academy can be built without one dollar of taxpayer money.

I am being tested again in another profession, and I have no doubts, no second thoughts. Most of us take too few risks. We lose account of ourselves and what is most rewarding in life. Success is not always achieved by those who wait placidly. I have never regretted making sacrifices, working seven days a week, a minimum of 100 hours. The most enjoyable times are when you work hard and overcome the odds.

I have been a builder in my career as a coach, beginning at Morningside and Whittier Colleges, then with the Chicago Bears' defense, and on to the L.A. Rams, the Redskins, the Chicago Blitz and the Arizona Wranglers.

Oh, sure, I would be tempted by one more shot at building another team into a winner and going for a championship. I know I said I'm retired, and I am. But I'm not deceased. Like an old-time boxer, start to count to 10 over me and I am liable to get up.

In the meantime, I will enjoy the challenge of improving America's fitness. And when I reminisce about my last seasons in a short-lived league, I will laugh at the parts that were meant to be laughed at and feel pride at what we accomplished as coaches and players. We did some pioneering, and we ranked fairly high in survival training. You can't buy that across a counter.

# 2

# Somewhere, Something Incredible Is Waiting to Happen

▲

*You must keep fighting for what you desire to achieve.*
*Life is a battle. If people expect otherwise, then*
*constant disappointment occurs. The tougher*
*the job the greater the reward.*

I coined that expression, about the reward, in 1966 when I took over as head coach of the Los Angeles Rams. They had not known a winning season in eight years.

I was born motivated. Not everyone is. But I believe motivation can be passed on and acquired, like a vaccine. I believe in the power of words, although they tend to change on us and become tricky or fancy. I remember when the term "pursuit" became so popular in football. Before that we called it chasing 'em. I'm in favor of positive reinforcement, but I liked it more when we just encouraged each other.

With the power of his language, as much as any strategy, Winston Churchill restored the faith of a nation and led a beleaguered Britain through the worst hours of World War II.

Other examples are not so weighty. Harry Wismer, the sportscaster and onetime owner of the New York Titans, later the Jets, used to greet nearly everyone he saw with a hearty "Congratulations." It was Wismer's theory that most people had recently done something they were proud of. Then he would be on his way, waving his cigar at their frequent question, "How did you know?" He did no harm and often made them feel good.

## YOU'RE NEVER TOO YOUNG

The forms of motivation are endless. It is like education. There is no point at which you can have too much. The main thing is to remember that you start over every day. I put lessons of my lifetime into the principles and theories I used on my football teams. They worked. They will work for you.

The summer of my twelfth year I went out looking for a job. I had nothing to offer except the ambition and the need to earn money, because my dad was out of work and not well. The Depression was on and jobs of any kind were scarce. My mother worked part-time at an amusement park, as well as baby-sitting and taking in laundry. My sister, Virginia, was too young to work.

We had no automobile and didn't own our home. I decided there were two jobs I could handle. One was working weekends as a caddy at Tommy Armour's golf club. The other was at Mr. Couch's nursery, planting dahlias at thirty cents an hour, eight hours a day. I quickly realized I had to work longer hours in order to help provide for my family. I asked Mr. Couch if I could increase my schedule to ten hours so I could earn an even three dollars. We couldn't make it on the two dollars and forty cents I was bringing home. It was that close.

The other motivating factor for me was that I learned that if I got up at 5 A.M. I could put my name on the caddy list early, go out in the morning, come back before noon and caddy another 18 holes in the afternoon. If I arrived at the clubhouse later, the list was too long and I could be sure of just one round of caddying.

By working at the Couch's nursery five days a week, ten hours a day, and using my weekends to caddy double shifts, I made enough money—if I didn't lose any golf balls—to help support my family.

As opposed to golf, the nursery work was boring, an unending routine of digging holes and planting dahlias. Still, I tried to plant each one just right so the roots were upward, and I made a point to break up the soil very fine so the bulb would grow. To motivate myself I sang all day. I was always down on my hands and knees because my instinct told me that was the way it had to be done, rather than just dropping a bulb into the ground and covering it with dirt.

My first reward, and recognition, came when Mr. Couch praised the job I had done and said that every dahlia I had planted came up. It appeared they were going to have their best harvest of flowers. Then each plant had to be staked so that the flower had some support.

If you are wondering what this has to do with football, the answer is everything. It also has to do with business and education and politics. I learned the value of hard work very early and became self-disciplined. I also learned that if you wanted something badly enough you could get it. In fact, Mr. Couch told me that he could not afford to raise my hourly rate to 35 cents an hour, but he would allow me to cultivate a piece of his land for a vegetable garden. He even had it plowed for me so all I had to do was get the seeds, plant them, and keep the weeds out. This was a better deal than a nickel raise. I planted corn, potatoes, carrots, beets, turnips, cucumbers, and cantaloupes. By storing some in the basement in baskets filled with dirt, we had fresh vegetables all winter.

This was my first real success, at anything, and it motivated me to continue trying to help my family over the hard times. It was splendid training. I didn't feel sorry for myself, but proud of my jobs. They probably kept me out of trouble. I didn't have enough time or money to smoke or drink. So the lesson has lasted a lifetime. I've always tried to turn every disadvantage into an advantage. Coaches call this making chicken salad out of chicken feathers. Most of the time there is some benefit from every setback, if you approach it properly. That is attitude and that is motivation.

Even today I feel guilty watching television because I'm not improving myself enough. I would rather be part of something happening than watching someone else perform. Of course, you do tend at times to feel a little left out. At a party for Danny Thomas in Beverly Hills, I met Larry Hagman, who plays J.R. Ewing on the series "Dallas." But I had to ask him who he was. I had never heard of him. I can't help it; I get depressed watching television.

## AND YOU'RE NEVER TOO OLD

As men or women grow older, they should broaden their range of friendships downward, chronologically, to experience the stimulation of youth. In addition, as you grow older you will have fewer contemporaries. The more young friends you have, the less likely you are to become isolated.

I have been fortunate all my life because my work has centered around the young. Keep in mind that the players who were the heart of my "Over-the-Hill Gang" in Washington were in their mid-30s, an age considered old only in athletics. I am told that young female swimmers have to guard against feeling jaded at fifteen.

My last two years of coaching, in the United States Football League, coincided with my work as chairman of the President's Council on Physical Fitness and Sports. I had a unique opportunity to work with fitness leaders all over America and around the world.

In this position, I appeared at the White House and presented a set of gold-plated, 25-pound barbells to President Reagan. I also planned to show a series of illustrations, and went to some length to be sure that an easel I would be using faced the president's chair. To my surprise, he remained standing during the entire 25-minute presentation. And he curled the barbells with ease. This indicated to me that for a man in his seventies, the president was in fine shape.

As a footnote to history: a moment of small drama occurred when the president's public relations people worried that the media might take liberties with equipment sometimes referred to as dumbbells. We resolved this problem by insisting that the gift would be referred to at all times as barbells.

## DR. EINSTEIN, I PRESUMED

I have carried with me a memory from the war years that may fit into several categories: age, mental and physical fitness, motivation. As a naval midshipman at Princeton in 1944, I developed one Sunday morning an urge to meet and play a game of checkers with Albert Einstein, who lived in a two-story brick home a few blocks from the campus. I had won the checkers championship in college, but my sudden ambition evoked howls of laughter in the dormitory. There was no way Professor Einstein was going to permit a visit from a complete stranger.

Nevertheless, after church a friend and I, in our dress blues, located the house where the famed mathematician lived and knocked on the door. It was the middle of winter; snow was banked against the house and blanketed the roof. Thick draperies covered the windows, but when I knocked a second time a corner was pulled back and a woman's face appeared, looking at us blankly. She motioned with her hand—I took it to mean that we should wait—and a moment later the door swung open. She asked us what we wanted.

I said, "We're midshipmen, here to see Mr. Einstein."

She said, "Wait, I'll see," and closed the door. We stood on the step, stamping our feet and rubbing our hands against the cold. A few minutes passed and she opened the door and beckoned us into the entry. "Stand here," she said. "He will be down shortly."

It didn't dawn on me then that anything remarkable was happening. But in all likelihood, hearing that two young men in uniform were at his door, the great scientist had allowed us inside his home out of courtesy or curiosity or both.

We strayed a few feet from the entry and began to peer around the living room. Then I was startled by a fearful racket, and I looked up to see Albert Einstein bounding at full speed down the stairs, dressed in a gray sweatshirt and soiled tennis shoes.

He was then 64 and just as I pictured him, the wisps of white hair floating around his head and the full mustache concealing his mouth. He had a pipe in his hand. He was the picture of motivation, pounding down that stairway. That was the way he exercised, running up and down his stairs.

He did not seem upset or surprised, or especially pleased, after we introduced ourselves and said we had just wanted to meet him. Then I said I had a special request. "I'd like to play you a game of checkers."

He said, "No, I'd rather not."

I persisted. Just one game. He looked a little puzzled now. "I don't know what you have heard," he said. "There are many stories about me. But I don't play much checkers. I don't like it much."

I said, "Well, I would just like to be able to say I played you one game."

He said, "I do not even keep a board in my house. Did you bring a board with you?"

I had not. I thought it would look a little odd if I carried a checkers board across the campus to church and into the neighborhood. I didn't want people to think I was crazy, although by then I suppose I had not helped my case.

There was nothing left now except to thank Einstein and say goodbye. I am not sure what inspired him to say what he did next. He may have been impressed with my brashness and felt we should not be sent away empty-handed. Or maybe it was just the uniforms and the falling snow and the passing moment. But he said, and I recall it distinctly, "You boys ought to know, the war will end soon. A great boom," and he spread his hands.

I was glad then, and more so today, that we took that walk. I wonder how many times, out of meekness or inertia, we talk ourselves out of a reward easily attained.

# THE QUALITY OF LEADERSHIP

My definition of motivation in one word: leadership. It doesn't matter who is being led, because each situation requires a different type of leadership. In athletics, you have emotion, excitement, action: You work against a stopwatch; quick decisions and quick communications are essential. In business and in administrative situations, people seldom face two-minute drills during which the entire deal or fiscal year is on the line.

However, I am convinced that a good leader in any profession can become a leader in other fields. The reason is simple: the qualities for leadership don't change.

Of course, even leaders may face rejection. There is no disgrace in being rejected. You can't be shy in looking for a job. You can get pushed around in business or in life, but know which way you are going and get your foot in the door. You can't give up as long as you have an income and a chance to improve. You learn from trial and error.

I never had time to analyze myself, but I began to discover my strengths. I could take any little fragment of information and use it.

This is a gift for the eternal child in each of us, the joy of learning. I strongly urge you to do what you enjoy doing, even if you encounter early roadblocks. Getting fired doesn't mean you are a bad person or unqualified. Most everything worthwhile is difficult, and there is no assurance you can do it. What I want in life is to keep moving and growing, not to be worrying about the future. So keep your head down and work. I am always impressed by people with a capacity to work.

## FEAR OF FAILING

Some people won't apply for a job out of fear of being rejected.

When I got my master's degree, I interviewed for several jobs with no success. Don Canham, the athletic director at the University of Michigan now, was the track coach at the time. He offered me a job as an assistant track coach—probably one of the biggest honors I've ever had because at that time in my career I wasn't well-schooled in track and not qualified for that position. Michigan was the national champion then, and those were the years when Fritz Crisler had his great teams. I never expected to get an offer from the University of Michigan. But I wanted to coach football, even if it was junior varsity, in addition to track. And Canham said no, not at Michigan. Track was a full-time job. So I turned the offer down.

Given my background, my independence hardly seemed justified. I was a good athlete in high school and won nine letters, but I was never a regular in college. The most I weighed was 178. I would be classified, I like to think, as an average athlete whose coaching career was anything but average.

I received permission to use the university's stationery because I had been the line coach of the 150-pound team, and I applied for an assistant's job at every school in the college Blue Book. At that time there were about 850 of them. I sent letters to places I'd never heard of. Out of those letters I got two responses indicating a job might be available.

One was at Trinity University in Hartford, Conn.; the coach there was Dan Jessie. I had heard of Trinity. The other was from Morningside College in Sioux City, Iowa, a school unknown to me

31

and a town whose name was only faintly familiar. I decided to apply at Trinity, but by the time I did the job was filled. That left me with Morningside.

They flew me in from Chicago on what was one of my first plane flights, and I got airsick. I was so sick when I landed that I couldn't even keep the interview. I had to go straight to the Martin Hotel, throw down some medicine, and go to sleep. My only thought was, I really laid an egg on this trip.

The next day I went to the campus and met with the president and a board composed of faculty and business people. At the end of the interviews, the president, Dr. Rodeman, said, "Well, you've answered all our questions."

Then I reached into my pocket, took out a sheet of paper with notes on it, and said, "Do you mind if I ask a few questions?" I had ten or twelve, and I didn't realize that my asking questions would impress them.

I was caught off guard when the president offered me the head coaching job. I pointed out that they had a head coach, Les Davis, and I had not come there to apply for his job. I was told that Davis was going to retire and that the head coaching job was mine on the condition that I was willing to coach track as well. So I had come full circle on the subject of track.

Then someone said, "One thing you haven't asked about is money, and you've been here for two days."

I said, "Well, I'm more interested in beating South Dakota University." That was their big rival, and I knew they had not beaten them in sixteen years; the entire presidency of Dr. Rodeman.

He said, "Well, the job pays $3,900."

I said, "That's okay, but I would like to have an assistant. For one man to turn this around is a big order." Morningside had not won a conference game in two years.

But it quickly became apparent that I would be pretty much on my own. My only hope was that if the baseball coach accepted an offer from a school in Nebraska, they would replace him with someone who had football experience. I told them I would think about it and flew back to Detroit.

I went in to see Fritz Crisler and told him I had been offered the job at Morningside College in Sioux City, Iowa. I had to explain to him where it was. Don Canham's advice was to ask the board to change the name of the school to Morning Star. Crisler treated the question more soberly and told me to take the job before they changed their minds. I had been offered positions at two big-city high schools, but I knew that you could be a good coach in high school and never break out of it.

To start at the college level seemed too promising a chance to pass. I called Morningside and accepted, with one request: if I couldn't have an assistant, would they put up $500 or so, and I would hire someone to help out during two-a-day practices? On that basis, I opened workouts for my first season. Later, the baseball coach did move to Nebraska and I hired a full-time assistant, Bill Pritula.

The president saw the letters I mailed to the athletes, telling them what to and what not to do. He was so motivated he asked me to speak to the faculty. I was 27 years old and smart enough to decline, knowing how my lecture might be received by people who had been there for years and were far more qualified in their jobs than I could be. So he sent the faculty copies of my letter instead.

There was never enough money in the budget to pay my way to coaching clinics, so I would go to the dairies, to Trueblood Construction, to Sam Yokem Office Furniture, and each would donate $50 toward my expenses. The college kicked in another $25 and that made it possible for me to attend the conventions. I would eat at all the exhibits and fill up on hors d'oeuvres. I always sat in the front row at the lectures, and met a lot of coaches that way. One year, 1951, at the old Commodore Hotel in New York, they gave me the job of registration chairman. I thought it was an honor until I found out no one else would accept it. I worked so hard and took it so seriously that I was sick for a week with the flu and a sore throat after I returned to Morningside.

Then I was appointed to the rules committee, the only small-college coach on a panel that included the likes of Lou Little, Columbia; Gen. Bob Neyland, Tennessee; Earl Blaik, Army; and Bobby Dodd, Georgia Tech.

Later, when I had moved on to Whittier College in California, Richard Nixon's alma mater, I got around the fund-raising problem by inviting coaches to Whittier and holding my own clinic. I would bring in Red Sanders and Jess Hill and Jordan Oliver. They would appear for nothing and I would tie the clinic into the Shrine All-Star game, persuading one of the teams to train on our campus.

As many as 500 high school coaches would come in for the day, and we concluded the schedule by going out to watch practice. I talked ten sporting goods companies into showing their wares and charged them $25 each for booths. Then I hired someone to mimeograph my notes from the lectures, and I'd sell them for two dollars through ads in such publications as *Scholastic Coach*. I ran the whole clinic myself—didn't even have a secretary.

In those days I did a little writing on the side for exposure. I wrote a column on West Coast football in a magazine called *Southern Coach and Athlete*, and I did it for free, for the byline. I also contributed to the *Athletic Journal*, which paid $25 for an article. I considered this a good deal until I learned that they paid $75 for a series. After that I cranked out one series after another. I had a cedar desk built in my garage that allowed me to stand up and work.

I always had a pressing need, in those years, to put away a few dollars toward the next day's meals. When I was in graduate school in Michigan I invented a hand stamp that would print formations and defenses, X's and O's. I would sell them in sets—four-, five- and six-man lines, all the formations. Those stamps helped pay my way.

## THE WINDS OF CHANGE

When I coached the Blitz in Chicago, the weather was so bad—no one had ever played football in Chicago in February and March—that our practice field was under snow and the turf was frozen. There was a junior college about an hour away with the only Astroturf field in all of Chicago. It was too icy to drive separate cars over there, so we chartered buses. The wind was blowing off Lake Michigan and the buses were heated against the bitter cold. Coming back, we often hit the late-afternoon traffic jam, and the return trip would sometimes take two hours. After practice everyone would be tired, bundled in sweaters, and the heat from the buses put the entire squad to sleep.

After we arrived at our headquarters, I would hold a team meeting. You can imagine how stimulated the players were by then. It was so cold the ball boys and the equipment man wouldn't come outside; they stayed in a trailer. Some days the wind blew so hard you had to lean into it to keep your balance. We couldn't put the ball down and walk off, it would just blow away. Then it would snow. And here we were practicing for football, asking ourselves, what have we gotten ourselves into?

We had to ask the players to go through these wild conditions for three weeks: bring all your gear with you and try to hit a sled in the winter. But what these hardships did, I kept reminding our players, was to bring us together. Being on that bus, riding to the junior college and back, made us more of a family. So we took something that was time-consuming, hazardous, and possibly demoralizing, and turned it into a plus.

Albert Schweitzer called it the fellowship of pain. If the conditions had been ideal, if our field had been well-equipped and convenient, we would have walked to practice and missed this kind of bonding.

## THE HOME-FIELD ADVANTAGE

For our home opener in Chicago, we drew a decent crowd against Denver on a day of heavy snow. The snow plow had to clear the field before the kickoff so you could see the lines. I caught the groundskeeper at a busy moment and asked him which side was the home team's. He pointed to the near side and said, "Why don't you take that one, it's the closest."

We wound up losing the opener by three points in a blizzard. But in the locker room after the game, the first question the press asked was, why were we on the visitor's side of the field? I said, "We were *what*? I just took the one where the groundskeeper pointed."

Of course, which bench the team sat on had no bearing on the outcome, but it did give me an idea. Our next game was again at Soldier's Field, so I told the team, "As far as I'm concerned, we're still undefeated here as the home team. We were on the visitor's side last time. From now on, we're on the right side, the home side." It may have seemed a slim thread, but it was a way of reminding our players that each week we started over. And that's motivation. We went on to win twelve games that year.

# LOOKING FOR MR. GOOD WORD

In August of 1985, I sat down and dictated a letter to Vince Ferragamo, the quarterback who had just been traded by the Rams to the Buffalo Bills. Ferragamo had been with the team when I was the coach so briefly that summer six years earlier. I felt I knew a little about adversity.

All I did was pass along a few notes I made to myself "concerning your new challenge with the Bills. (1) Don't be discouraged no matter what happens to you or the team; (2) You have everything to gain; (3) Learn to get rid of the ball quickly; (4) Work on setting up quicker; (5) Don't throw the ball unless you are sure; (6) Don't take unnecessary chances; (7) Be positive with your teammates; (8) Don't let the weather bother you; (9) This is a break for you and your family; (10) Work hard on the field; (11) Study hard; (12) Buy your own projector; (13) Make sure you understand everything; (14) No distractions; (15) You're working for a good owner (Ralph Wilson); (16) Take charge in the huddle."

I closed with, "I will be watching and rooting for you and your team this season. I know you will be a success because you are a winner."

I am sure some people would ask, why bother? My answer is, why not? More than any other position in football, quarterback can be the most depressing. The old cliche is true: they get too much credit and too much blame. As a result, they need more reassurance than the other players.

Mel Durslag, the talented columnist for the Los Angeles *Herald Examiner*, wrote a piece about the letter and asked if I thought Vince would heed my advice. I replied, "If I were Vince, I'd pin up the letter where I shave and read it every morning."

Mel replied, "But most guys shave in the bathroom. Is that where you want your prose pasted?"

I replied that it might open a new career for me. "When the coaching staff is listed, it might read, 'So-and-so, offensive line coach; so-and-so, special teams; George Allen, bathroom consultant.' "

## REDSKINS' WEATHER

We were playing the St. Louis Cardinals one year in Washington as a snowstorm blew in, and at a team meeting the night before the game I reminded the players that snow and rain and bad weather didn't bother the Redskins.

I singled out our fine linebacker, Harold McClinton, and told him I wanted him to jump into a snowbank in front of all the Cardinals during the warmups "and let them know that we're tough. Act like a wild Indian."

McClinton was eager to oblige. Unfortunately, the temperature dropped sharply overnight and when Harold made his dive the snow had frozen and turned into solid ice. He bounced back about fifteen feet and sprained his ankle.

On second thought, that might not be a very keen example of motivational psychology.

## THE DRINKING FOUNTAIN

Every day that I have the opportunity, I like to run on the beaches near my home in Southern California. There are three beaches, Hermosa, Manhattan, and Rat Beach. All are popular with the public and attract surfers from throughout the area. My usual route takes me down the hill to the pier and back.

I enjoy running along the shoreline. When the tide is out, I can run on the hard sand, but if the tide is in and the water is high, I have to follow the softer sand, which is harder on the legs and not as enjoyable. Completing the course from the top of the hill to the pier, then back along the bike path and up the hill, is approximately five miles.

When I run, I run without stopping, even if it means going out of my way to avoid a youngster on a skateboard or some other obstacle. I get more out of a run physically if I don't have to stop. But the key to the entire run is the last 400 yards, which are up a very steep hill, roughly sixty degrees. You test yourself more going up that hill than you do in the previous four miles or so.

At the top of the hill, near an elementary school, is a drinking fountain that was donated by the Malaga Cove graduating class of

1975. Every day when I reach the top I try to get a drink from that fountain. For the last two years, the fountain has never worked. All you can get is a slight trickle of water if you press your mouth hard on the spigot and almost suck the water out. That is not very hygienic, so I don't drink there.

One day recently the weather was extremely hot and the humidity very high, which is unusual for Southern California. As I came up to the top of the hill I was a little woozy from the heat and from running hard. I desperately needed water.

A youngster was sitting next to the fountain that hadn't worked in so long, and I asked him, "By the way, have they fixed that fountain?"

He said, "No, it's still broken."

So I went over to the grass and cooled down, doing my stretching exercises. All the while I kept thinking of how much I needed a drink. There are no refreshment stands in the area and I kept thinking what a shame it was that this fountain didn't work.

Except for that flaw, the fountain is a work of art, made of stone and chrome and looking almost like a small pyramid. As I looked at it, I thought about walking over to see if it was working. And then I thought, why should I go over there when it has not operated in two years and the youngster just told me it was still broken?

As I was leaving, I decided to try it anyhow, even though I was sure the effort would be useless. I walked over, turned the handle, and got the surprise of the month. The water shot up like a geyser; the fountain was working 110 percent. I had my drink, and then another, and another. Nothing ever tasted so refreshing.

I think the moral of the story is that even though something has not succeeded, or has failed in the past, or even if someone tells you that it will not work, you do what you believe and try again.

This time, the next time, it just might work.


## THE FISH STORY

When I was a kid, one of my favorite activities was fishing. I used a hand line and would fish in Lake St. Clair and other lakes around Michigan. In the summertime, I would get up and go fishing for most of the day.

One thing I learned that helped me to become a successful fisherman was to use more hooks. I would put on four hooks, all baited, while most of my friends were relying on one or two. Sometimes I pulled in my line and had two fish! One had already caught himself without my being aware of it.

This story applies to everything in life, and its point is very simple: If you want to catch more fish, use more hooks.

# 3

# The Future Is Now

▲

*Thomas Jefferson said, "I like the dreams of the future better than the history of the past." This is exactly how I feel. What I have learned is, forget the past—the future will give you plenty to worry about.*

IF I were starting out today to hire a coaching staff—or to open an office—I would begin by looking for a young, single candidate with about four years of experience who would work day and night, seven days a week, and who wanted to learn. He would want to work so badly that he would be willing to work for nothing. If I could find that individual, I'd have a picture of myself not quite forty years ago.

That person could go up the ladder—in a hurry.

I think that when you like your job so much that you enjoy coming to the office every morning, you are blessed. That's the way I have always been. I would rather do my job, whatever it is, than anything else. I can see no difference between a chair and a man who sits in a chair if he is not accomplishing something. One must accomplish to live. I don't enjoy a long lunch hour. For most of my life I ate right on the job. I would rather spend the time I save working out, or discussing with my staff something that will help us improve.

When I was coaching the Rams, Charlie Maher, a writer with the *Los Angeles Times*, asked if he could follow me around for a week, keeping my hours, for a story on a typical week with George Allen. By Wednesday he figured that we had worked forty hours.

No, you don't have to work my hours to succeed. You only have to work more than your competitor does—or more than you did when you were not succeeding.

Unless you make some progress every day, you are going to get behind, or someone else is going to get ahead of you. To me, what you do with your free time determines how successful you will be and what you will contribute to society. For all my teams, we had a big sign in the weight room that read: "WHAT YOU DO IN THE OFF-SEASON DETERMINES WHAT YOU DO DURING THE SEASON."

That slogan was and is part of my philosophy. When I came to the Washington Redskins there was no off-season program. If you don't do things in the off-season, you are not going to win. In fact, people who think there is an off-season in football, or in any business, are mistaken. If there is an off-season, there is something wrong. The off-season is the time when you improve.

I have always believed that "the future is now," an expression I coined in life as in football. Another part of my philosophy has been to take someone nobody else wants—a so-called problem player—and make him productive. Why? Because we are willing to take the time to solve his problem. This is not a conceit on our part. I learned long ago that you can't judge people by reputation.

Few of the players who came to us as bad actors were actually bad people. They played well for us. And it wasn't a question of what they were paid. Money isn't always the answer. Money doesn't make one happy, although it helps. What most people really want is recognition.

The toughest part of coaching is the individual conferences, going over players' problems. Not football problems. That is the least of it. It's the other worries, the type a man has no control over, that will make him unproductive if you don't help solve them. As a coach, if a player had a problem it became my problem. I wanted to know every detail and see what could be done to relieve it so we could concentrate on winning.

One thing you can't do in any business: you can't let problems lick you, because they will always be there. Every day I try to run up to three miles and work out with weights, just to offset all the nagging problems that arise. If you're not in shape, the problems will defeat you. Each year—or month or week or day—you will encounter new and different problems. If you approach them in the right way you can solve them all. I don't believe that we were put on earth just to have a good time, to laugh and joke. I mean this with all sincerity. I think we were put here to overcome problems. I don't think there are any I can't solve or that we can't solve together. And I don't fear them.

Part of my personality is that I like my players, regulars or not. I am happy for their success. When I talk about them with others, I actually feel emotion, just as if they were members of my family. That was partly my philosophy, but it was also my disposition. I tried to develop a team of people whom I knew. If we prepared them properly, they would win. This I believed. When they made a mistake, or did something wrong, I blamed myself. If they lost, I felt that somehow, subconsciously, I had let them down.

Whoever said that you don't need to motivate a professional didn't know how wrong he was. You have to motivate everybody, veterans and rookies alike. I feel fortunate that throughout my life I have been a self-starter. Not that I didn't have my ups and downs, but the more problems I seemed to have, the more setbacks, the more these things spurred me on. Some people let the least little thing get them down.

When you say that each person is an individual, it sounds like a quote straight from the Book of Great American Cliches. But it runs smack into the old coaching principle that to be fair you must treat everyone alike. All of which recalls Henry Jordan's famous reference to Vince Lombardi: "Coach is fair. He treats us all alike. He treats us all like dogs."

Of course, what worked for one will fail for another. I never tried to motivate a player until I knew something about him. I would begin by just talking, getting his thoughts on different things—on what he hoped to achieve, what he had done in the past, why he did or did not succeed, how he spent his time after practice and in the off-season. Then, after I saw what he did at practice, in meetings, and off the field, I knew if what he said was just bull's wool or in earnest.

43

I firmly believe, and bear with me if I keep repeating it, that just the way you *talk* to people can motivate them. But I don't have much patience with those who won't study or prepare or make sacrifices. That player will not help us win our championship. That employee will not help build your company.

As an example of the type of person I would like to hire, I imagine coaching at the U.S. Naval Academy. I would hope that the man I was interviewing—an assistant coach, or whatever—would say, "I'd like to play Army in a nine-game schedule. Nobody but Army." That is the type of attitude I'd want him to have.

You have heard the saying, "It's all in the head." For most of us, that's where it's the hardest. The mental part of football is more difficult than the physical. Mental preparation never ends, whereas with the physical side you can be on the field an hour and a half or two hours, blow the whistle and you're done. But the mental part goes on and on—when you're eating, when you're sleeping, and when you're walking around.

Trading was a part of the mental game for me, and I enjoyed it. Trading is to coaches what cutting a deal, closing a contract, or making a big sale is to a businessman. This is where you move the chess pieces; it provides a feeling of power, a clash of wits. You have to know what you want and what you are willing to give up, and you have to work hard at it.

A month after I became head coach of the Rams, Vince Lombardi called to offer me a trade: a player he no longer needed in exchange for a second-round draft choice. I knew the player, and for us he would plug a hole. I also knew I couldn't draft anyone in the second round who could give us as much help.

I said to Lombardi, "You got a deal."

There was a silence on the phone. It didn't take a genius to figure out what was going through Vince's mind. He was surprised at how quickly I accepted. It made him feel that he could have gotten more. He figured that as a young coach in my first head job, I wouldn't yet know the market for certain players. I told him to telex the deal to the league office.

Half an hour later Lombardi called back. "I have to change the deal," he said. "My coaches don't think I got enough."

I asked him. "Your *coaches*? I thought you made the decisions in Green Bay. Vince, we made a deal. I took your word on it."

Lombardi said, "No, I can't do it. You have to throw in another draft pick, a fifth."

I told him the deal was off and we hung up the phone. Weeks later, I gave him the choice and the trade was made. I didn't care. I knew the player we were getting would help us, and he did.

The point is, Vince thought he could take advantage of my inexperience. He didn't. I made the trade I would have made in the first place. Experience itself isn't worth a cent unless it's the right type of experience. What is the right type? Being in an organization that knows how to win, knows what to do to win, is completely organized, and has a philosophy and a program.

What counts is having the right kind of individual, not just one with experience. The woods are full of experience, and I say that as a coach who was identified in Washington with a team that won fame as "The Over-the-Hill Gang." We took what started out as a piece of fun, a gentle putdown, and turned it into one of pro football's legends.

There is so much misunderstanding about experience—in industry as well as sports—that it's difficult even to talk about. But let me apply this to football, and the reader can add his or her own projections. In football, 30 is considered old. But not in my playbook. Maybe a 30-year-old isn't as fast as he once was, but he doesn't have to be because he ought to be smarter; he is more likely to be in the right place at the right time.

I don't think you can always be building toward the future. People are constantly looking for a player who is 22 with eight or nine more years ahead of him. In baseball you always hear about the great young pitching staff, where the oldest starter is 24. That has nothing to do with it. How much ability do they have? How much of it are they using? How badly do they want to win? To me, the best years of an athlete's life are after 30, provided he has taken care of himself. I think he appreciates more, he has more leadership, is smarter, more dedicated, and makes more of a contribution to the entire team than he did when he was 24.

Phil Niekro was still winning baseball games, including his 300th, for the Yankees at 46. His "baby" brother, Joe, was going strong at 41. Al Kaline, Henry Aaron, Frank Robinson, Carl Yastrzemski, Gaylord Perry, Tom Seaver, Nolan Ryan—all are notable examples of players who were still winners at or beyond 40. In hockey, Gordie Howe played until he was 50, and had the distinction of being the first professional athlete to play on the same team as his sons, Mark and Marty.

In football, George Blanda had to be cut from his last training camp at 49. He was still throwing touchdown passes when he was 46 before he became a full-time kicker. Charlie Joiner of the Chargers was still outrunning defensive backs at 38. Earl Morrall quarterbacked Miami to a Super Bowl when he was 39.

Where would the Lakers have been without Kareem Abdul-Jabbar when he was pushing 40? Only one player has appeared in an NBA lineup at an age older than Kareem. Bob Cousy, then a coach, put himself on the active list and played a few games at 41. With the pounding your legs take, basketball is the sport least likely to encourage longevity.

Everybody has to have a philosophy. A lot of teams, and companies, don't have one, or if they do it changes every year. You have to believe in certain things, know what you want, and not let criticism from the public and the media bother you. Men like Walter Alston, John Wooden, Emile Francis, Lombardi, Bear Bryant, Tom Landry, Don Shula—I could name dozens—took charge of their programs this way and succeeded. You don't change your philosophy when you lose if it is a sound philosophy and you understand it. If you get disgusted after a losing year and suddenly change, then all those years of building are wiped out.

So winning isn't just getting experienced people or spending money. Has any team in baseball spent more millions than the California Angels, who have never won a pennant? Yet the payroll of the Dallas Cowboys has rarely ranked among the NFL's top ten. The most important thing you need is organization.

One of the results of good organization is that you allow your players to concentrate. This is necessary for good practices and is a large part of winning. You don't want your game plan defeated before you have a chance to execute it. But you can't concentrate with distractions all around. You can't enjoy a lecture or an artist performing if you aren't in the right atmosphere, if you are uncomfortable. It's like taking a night class in a lecture room in which the acoustics aren't good and the seats are uncomfortable: as a result, you don't get much out of it. If I were teaching a class, I'd want a certain seating arrangement. I'd want the students to be stimulated as they walked into the classroom, before I even started lecturing. That's not pampering. That's part of the lecture.

I have to keep coming back to the fact that I like signs and other reminders. I love them. I keep one on my desk even now that says "THE TEAM IS NEVER UP!" I had that one made after the 1973 Super Bowl, when we lost to the Dolphins. We were flat for the Super Bowl, hard as that is to imagine. Just before the game, I was going to talk to the team and stir them up a bit. I thought the dressing room was subdued. Then I thought to myself, "I don't have to do that. This is the *Super Bowl*. This is the biggest game of their lives."

But I was wrong and we lost, 14–7. That sign reminds me never to take anything for granted again. I like to get people to think. That's why I use constant reminders. I think you have to say things over and over again because you only get through to about 40 percent of them the first time. It doesn't bother me that that 40 percent has to listen to the same thing seven times. That's no problem. That's the way it should be. It is better for them to listen to the same message seven times and win, than not to listen once and lose.

We made major changes at our training camp in Washington in 1973, after the Super Bowl. Every season we made changes, but never just for the sake of changing. Everything we did was calculated to help us win. Even things that seem minor can lead to results that are major.

I brought in an agronomist in the spring of 1973 and we went over the procedure of weed killing and sodding and grading. We improved the drainage system at Redskin Park. That may not seem a part of any coaching philosophy, but to me it was. When we came back from our training camp in September, a great practice field was waiting—green grass and no weeds. I didn't want to be killing weeds in September. Tommy McVean, our equipment manager, replaced the padding on the goalposts. I wanted my players to see that everything was freshly painted, everything was new that had to be replaced. It was the start of a new year.

To me such steps are as basic as A-B-C, and always have been.

Some people don't consider that coaching. To me, creating Redskin Park was a major accomplishment. I wanted such a facility because I thought it was important to have a place the players could call home, where we had everything under one roof. When a player went out there, he was getting ready to win. This was our home. When we practiced at Georgetown, we had students and people right off the street milling around. That's not conducive to winning football. At Redskin Park, the players had their own parking lot for ninety cars, where they didn't have to worry about getting a space or being towed. When they reached the park, they knew they could concentrate on football and winning. It helped morale. We had two fields, one with grass and one with Astroturf. Whatever surface we were to play on the next week, that was the one we practiced on. It was that simple. All of this comes under one word: preparation.

Football is a game of emotions, a vigorous, highly competitive contact sport involving desire, discipline, and drive. It is the popping sound of pad against pad. The tension and nervousness of the pregame wait in the locker room is followed by the thrill of charging out onto the field.

Victory is often highlighted by the beauty of an electrifying broken-field run or the precision of a long pass. Defeat is marked by the frustration of missing the winning field goal or dropping a touchdown pass.

I was, throughout my career, an emotional coach, and I am proud to have been so labeled. I put every fiber in my body into every practice and every game. I was sometimes ill after a bad practice. I just couldn't help myself.

Mental attitude, therefore, plays a tremendous role in the success of any professional. An athlete can have great natural ability but will never reach his or her potential unless a proper attitude can be developed. The individual with the right frame of mind will make that natural ability work. I would rather have an athlete, or an employee, with the right attitude and less ability than one who has a ton of ability and a closed or uncaring mind.

Wherever I was, whatever the quality of our team, I tried to make our players realize that one of the great opportunities in life is to take an ordinary job and make something out of it. *We all have ordinary jobs.* Whether a person is a coach or a player or a musician, what counts is to want to do something in life and make a contribution. What a pathetic ambition it must be to go through life content to eat, watch TV, sleep, drink, and drive a car.

I urge anyone taking the test of a first career to get the very best out of what they have within themselves. Not too many people do this in any walk of life. But "I can't" and "I quit" are two phrases that are rarely if ever sanctioned in American society. Even when you believe yourself to be outmanned or overmatched, a will to win and self-confidence can get the job done.

I have found that what applies to a football team applies to good business. After the players learn the fundamentals and the playbook, it is morale that makes the team. To win, there must be a strong sense of togetherness, of group support and purpose. It is this kind of team spirit that wins games and overcomes adversity.

Morale is a mental condition and is characterized by an unfailing ability to overcome odds, to make a comeback. Teams fall behind. Companies lose accounts, suffer financial reverses, are unsettled by market conditions. We tried to create in our players a real love for the game and a spirit of work, determination and loyalty. Convincing an entire squad of often temperamental performers to become one unit, a family, and to forget jealousies or animosities cannot be done fifteen minutes before the kickoff. A coach, a boss, must be getting the team ready all year long.

To many, my approach may appear corny or even naive, but we wanted, encouraged, *demanded* emotion and enthusiasm. To impress the team with the importance of a particular game or to call for an all-out effort or self-sacrifice on their part, we made it a practice to post slogans on the walls of the locker room. Sound childish? Not at all. Most young people will accept challenges and, quite often, they can be challenged with slogans and posters.

Epigrams can be useful, both for content and as a way to train your mind. I seldom finish an airplane flight without scribbling a list of things I need to do, or points I want to make about whatever subject I have at hand.

I believe that in each of us there is a need to strive, to compete, to get in the arena. Any arena. I am not very enamored of the Olympic ideal, that the glory of sport lies not in winning but in taking part. I believe in winning. To encourage anything less, I think, is to tolerate losing.

## DO YOU KNOW THE DEFINITION OF A LOSER?

A loser is someone who:

Plays the piano in a marching band.

Goes to the gourmet shelf in a supermarket and asks for Philadelphia Cream Cheese.

Saves up all his life to buy a cemetery plot and then gets buried at sea.

You get the idea: I believe in winning. But first one has to compete. I rely on sports as a reference because it is the world I know best, the one in which I am the most comfortable. I believe in it as a reflection of the larger world outside. I like the action, the people, the language, the fact that the results are spelled out every day in the box scores and standings. You always know who won or lost (or tied).

Great coaches are usually great motivators. They will go to any length to find a psychological edge over the opposition, or to inspire their players. In Los Angeles, I coached an all-pro tackle named Rosey Grier. Years earlier, he was a youngster, a gentle Goliath trying to break into the lineup of the New York Giants. The coach, Jim Lee Howell, felt that Grier—his given name was Roosevelt—lacked the "killer instinct," and he made it a special project to instill in him this quality.

Howell would tell his team, "You have got to punish your man to make him respect you," and then he would wince when Rosey Grier would help an opposing quarterback to his feet. Howell finally gave up on his Grier campaign after the incident of "The Published Scouting Report" during the pro football season of 1958.

Unnoticed by the coaches, two writers were present when the team's scouts gave the defense a belittling rundown of the next opponent, Philadelphia. This Eagle was "too slow to cover the sweep." Another would "quit if you take him on physically." The comments made great reading in the next day's sports pages, and even better reading when picked up by the papers in Philadelphia.

At a team meeting, Howell sought to turn the situation around. "Those guys are going to come in here Sunday with fire in their eyes, spoiling for blood," he challenged. "So what are *we* going to do about it?" Howell happened to be looking at Grier when he roared the question. Rosey jumped to his feet and said, "Maybe it isn't too late; we could send them a telegram and apologize."

The next year Grier was banished to the Los Angeles Rams; ironically, that trade turned out to be the motivation he needed. Stung by his rejection in New York, he became a mainstay of the Rams' famed defense, "The Fearsome Foursome." He weighed as much as 290 pounds during his career, and it must have been a curious sight off the field to see Rosey practicing his hobby, which was needlepoint. There is no record of anyone ever making fun of it.

Grier was a man of other interests. He was at the side of Robert Kennedy that night in April of 1968, in the kitchen of the Ambassador Hotel in Los Angeles when the young senator was murdered. It was Grier, the ex-football player, who subdued Sirhan Sirhan and took the gun away from him seconds after the shots were fired.

As Grier acquired confidence in his ability as an athlete, he grew as a person. To be successful in any endeavor, some form of confidence, even fake, is essential. We all have our insecurities and they can be useful. Dwight Eisenhower once said that we should "approach any undertaking as if it could be lost in the last minute. This is sports, this is politics, this is business, this is life."

In his memoir, "At Ease," the former war hero and president recalled two fantasies from his Abilene boyhood. In one he was a railroad engineer breaking the record from St. Louis. In the other he set down the next three batters on nine pitches in the last of the ninth inning with the bases loaded, to the thunderous applause of the spectators.

Not a man publicly fond of intellectuals, Eisenhower always said that his main motivation at West Point was football, which "more than any other sport tends to instill in men the feeling that victory comes through hard, almost slavish work, team play, self-confidence, and an enthusiasm that amounts to dedication."

I believe Eisenhower became a legendary general and a revered president not because he knew so much about tactics or the levers of power, but because he understood human nature. He was injured in the Army game against Tufts in 1912, ending his college football career. Through the years, men kept introducing themselves to him as "the tackler from Tufts," and apologizing for it. Ike estimated that Tufts must have had three dozen men on the field that day if everyone who confessed to inflicting the injury had played.

Ike was surely the most athletic of our presidents, although Gerald Ford and Ronald Reagan would not be far behind. Ike was very strong, especially through his chest and arms, a result of gymnastics he took up when he had to stop playing ball. He was also a gambling man, and his early Army years were filled with bets that he could walk across a parade field on his hands, or climb a flagpole, or pick up a chair by one leg at a general's tea. Later, he would play as important a role as any man in making golf an acceptable American passion. Most important, however, was his attitude. Sports was never a stylish image-builder for Eisenhower. Nor was it a vehicle for publicity or social contacts.

This is a point that needs to be emphasized: Do what engages you for your own reasons, not to please or impress other people. If it is right, they will know, and if it is wrong, what they think won't help you anyway.

Younger people today are more likely to be jealous guardians of their right, or need, to express themselves as individuals. It is harder to develop a team feeling, but no less satisfying. We always tried to create an atmosphere of discipline and good humor. The coaching staff subscribed to the old cliche "Firm, fair, friendly." The office doors of our staff were always open to members of the team. If a coach is genuinely interested in the people around him, they will know it and believe in him.

We encouraged players to have respect for each other and to help one another. In other words, a general feeling of mutual admiration and warmth is an important quality of any team. We did not always succeed in this aspect, but we tried. Each individual deserves to be treated with equality and fairness, and nothing will ruin a player's morale quicker than his belief that he is not getting a fair chance.

There is no effort more wasted or misguided than to listen to excuses and alibis. If things go wrong, if you lose, if the job doesn't get done, accept the verdict and move on. I resisted complaints—from myself or my players—about the breaks of the game, the officiating, and grousing of that kind. The sad truth too often is that while you are trying to get back that touchdown you felt was taken away from you, you are likely to lose the next game and the one after that.

Discipline works both ways and is essential to a winning effort. I do not believe in chewing out or embarrassing a player, or an employee, in front of others. There are not many people who enjoy being criticized in front of fifty or sixty people. It is much better to talk to him alone. Everyone should be treated with dignity.

And I will not criticize him for a mistake he made while trying. The only mistakes that should be dealt with quickly and sharply are mistakes of omission or indifference—allowing something to go wrong because someone did not give 100 percent to prevent it from happening. Even then, I made it a point to be rational and to explain what the problem was. I made it clear that I would apply whatever punishment was necessary and appropriate, however, the matter was strictly between the individual and me. If disciplinary action is taken, no one else should have to know about it.

Generally, I have found that, on a team or in an office, the kind of people you have will determine the type of discipline and control used. Coaches, or bosses, will be just as nice or just as tough as their players want or need them to be.

Loyalty is the ingredient that holds all else together, the glue, the adhesive. Hemingway called it the bonding of men. The team player never second-guesses the quarterback, a teammate or a coach. Inside the clubhouse, we always urged our players to "Let what you hear there, see there, and say there . . . STAY THERE!"

The person at the top has to be himself or herself, and not try to imitate someone else. However, I strongly believe that an individual can be spurred on to greater effort with the right handling or direction. The more you encourage or motivate someone, the better he will perform and the more he will produce. So I don't believe in browbeating people. The more productive they feel, the better the relationship they will have with others in the group.

Great competitors have a tremendous, almost obsessive desire to excel, an urge to be the best. They take pride in their performance.

They hurt when they lose. No one ever intentionally sets as his goal being mediocre. The members of a team with an intense pride will always be tough to defeat. They will never fold. Their opponents will have to kill them inch by inch.

It was a tradition of mine in training camp to outline the psychological profiles of "A Champion" and "An Also-Ran." When things were not going well, I sometimes called in a player and reviewed the characteristics with him.

## PROFILE OF A CHAMPION

*Ambition.* desire for high goals. hates to lose. cannot stand failure. puts goals above ability.

*Coachableness.* takes advice and is easy to coach. eager to learn. easy to approach. follows rules and directions.

*Aggression.* a tiger! first-place-belongs-to-me type. asserts himself.

*Leadership.* shows the way and sets a good example. respected by team members. mixes well. others follow his example and take his advice.

*Take-Charge Guy.* takes over when things go wrong. under pressure, he does something about the problem. Often a hero.

*Hard Worker.* one of the first to practice, the last to leave. does extra work. never misses practice. follows instructions.

*Physical Toughness.* develops toughness by hard work. in great condition. keeps training rules and trains year around.

*Mental Toughness.* never gives in to his feelings. has never-give-up attitude. ignores heat, cold, pain.

## PROFILE OF AN ALSO-RAN

*No Drive.* does not care whether he wins or loses. goes with the tide.

*Know-It-All.* never listens and will not accept new ideas. rebel, griper, works by himself.

*Mouse.* never talks back. high on self-abasement. always kicking himself. introvert, generally.

*Follower.* will go with crowd, generally behind them. never tries to lead.

*Watcher.* Caspar Milquetoast. if there is an accident, he watches or runs away. worried about what people think.

*Corner-Cutter.* ducks practice. cuts out tough practice. always has excuses. lots of absences from practice.

*Hypochondriac.* a muscle grabber—always has an injury. never works out consistently.

*Complainer.* gives up easily. easily distracted from the job at hand. will look good when competition is not of high caliber and will look bad in the big game.

*Quitter.* cannot stick til the end. easily distracted. starts many jobs, finishes few. unreliable.

# 4

# We Have
# But One Objective . . .
# to Win

▲

*One person with a belief is equal to a force of ninety-nine who only have interests.*

MOTIVATION is a kind of vitamin for the mind. It comes in many forms, in different strengths, some easier to swallow than others. You can't be motivated without believing in something: yourself, your faith, your boss, your job or team or cause.

Letters went out to 200 people—business figures, entertainers, politicians, athletes, some of them my former players and friends—asking them to talk about whatever it was that motivated them. Some were moved by the power of words, others by an act or a challenge. All agreed on the essential nature of motivation. All said they had it. But many could not say how or why. In selecting which replies to print, the emphasis was not on whether the thought was deep or the remarks clever. What we wanted was a range of reactions.

It is clear from the replies that a certain kind of individual needs to be motivated by others. I found this to be the overwhelming case in coaching. I can assure you that few people will slam themselves at somebody else's body without a little urging. But there are individuals who can be described as inner-directed, who draw upon their own strengths. Both ways work, as these letters will show.

### MUHAMMAD ALI, former heavyweight boxing champion:

"When I was a kid in Louisville I had a job sacking groceries. I found a second-hand but really sharp bicycle I just had to have. It was blue and beautiful. I didn't make much money at the grocery but I finally saved up enough to get that second-hand bike. I parked it behind the store, proud and happy. I worked hard for it. Then somebody stole it. Just about broke my heart. I walked all over Louisville that summer, looking for that bicycle. I walked and looked, looked and walked. Never found it to this day. But every time I got into a ring, I looked across at the other fighter and I told myself, "Hey, that's the guy that stole my bicycle!"

### SPARKY ANDERSON, manager, Detroit Tigers:

"In the spring of 1984, I waited for everyone in the clubhouse to get totally dressed. Then I asked everyone to look at each other. I said, 'The name across your uniform is Detroit. Starting this year that is a special name. This is a very good team now and we will be respected by everyone. It also will be a very hard club to make, so I hope all of you are ready to work. Because you're going to win it this year. Don't wait for me to win one game. It is going to be in your hands. Handle it with great determination. I want to prove to you, you can be champions.'

"I think with Kirk Gibson, I just kept talking with him—kept telling him that in time he was going to be a great player 'if you are willing to go through the hard times. It won't be easy because you have not played much baseball. But I see it in you. Don't ever give up—no matter how tough it gets.' In 1984 Gibson produced, and it did all come together."

(Note: The Tigers got off to the fastest start in fifty years, won thirty-five of their first forty games, led the American League wire to wire and won the World Series.)

**TRACY AUSTIN, championship tennis player:**

"Motivation played a crucial role in my success in the 1981 U.S. Open. I had been off the circuit for five months at the beginning of that year because of a back injury. That was the longest amount of time I didn't play tennis as far back as I could remember. It was a very frustrating time for me and I was eager to get back. I got the physical part back first, but then I had to work on my concentration and mental toughness. That was a big change, because that area was always my strength before the injury. That summer I worked extremely hard on both aspects, physical and mental.

"I was playing Martina Navratilova in the finals of the finals of the U.S. Open and was getting demolished. The first set was over before I realized what was happening. Here it was on national television and it wasn't even a match. I began to think of all the hard work and extra hours I had put in that summer, and got mad. I started to concentrate on one point at a time, blocked out all other thought and tried super hard on every point. I won the last two sets in a tiebreaker, 7–6. The determination and motivation to come back from the injury and from being so down in the match was what pulled me through. I was motivated to work extra hard during the summer to play well again. And that in turn motivated me to want to win that final match because I was determined and felt I deserved it.

"I remember motivation being a factor in my career way back when I was fourteen years old. I was playing in the semifinals of an 18-and-under tournament against a friend who was three years older than I was. I had never beaten her before and we took (lessons) from the same coach. He was at the tournament and I remember him going over and talking to her before the match. I figured he would come over and talk to me also and remain neutral. He didn't.

"Needless to say, before the match even started I was fuming. I couldn't believe he could be that mean and I was going to show him I could win without his advice (or support). It was a long three-set match and very hot. She was bigger and stronger so I started to tire. But all I needed to pump me up was to look over at him (our coach) and remember his favoritism. When I won, he went straight over to console her. I felt sorry for her because we were from the same club and his giving her instructions before the match had backfired. He made me so mad that I was motivated to win."

**GENE AUTRY, western singer, actor, owner of the California Angels:**

"I was working as a telegrapher for the Frisco Railroad line in Chelsea, Oklahoma—that was pretty much my ambition—and I had my feet propped up on the counter, picking on a guitar and singing along to pass the time. Then a customer walked in, wearing a topcoat and a hat. My feet hit the floor, but he said to keep singing, the music wouldn't bother him. He had a newspaper column to file to New York—he was visiting his sister in Chelsea—and he walked over to the desk and sat down to correct it.

"After awhile he got up, handed me his copy and said he liked my voice. Said he thought I ought to go to New York and try to catch on with one of the recording companies. I looked at the bottom of the last page of his copy, and the name read 'Will Rogers.' I had thought about it from time to time—trying to break in on the radio or in records. But that was all the motivation I needed. I used my railroad pass to get to New York and took three months off to make the rounds of the recording companies on what was called Tin Pan Alley. Then it all fell into place."

**WILLIAM J. BENNETT, former secretary of education:**

"I attended Gonzaga High School in Washington, D.C., where I was, I confess, an indifferent student, more interested in playing football than academics. On the strength of my athletic abilities I was offered a scholarship to Williams College, a small but highly respected liberal arts college in Massachusetts. I had every intention of spending my time at Williams much as I had at Gonzaga, by playing football and studying just enough to get by. I looked forward to a lucrative career in business and advertising. Then something unexpected happened.

"In those days—not really so many years ago—most American colleges and universities required all undergraduates to take specific courses in humanities. Williams was no exception. Although initially I regarded these courses as nuisances, I soon changed my mind. In these courses I encountered some gifted teachers who, by the force of their enthusiasm, intellect, and commitment, engaged me in a confrontation with great works of literature, philosophy, and history. At first I resisted making the effort required to learn what they had to teach. But my professors persisted. They demonstrated to me that ideas matter, and that they have the power to move the human soul just as they can change the course of history.

"Someone once said 'Once you've read Dostoyevski, nothing is ever the same again.' At Williams College I read not only Dostoyevski, but also Aristotle, Plato, Shakespeare, Henry James, George Eliot, and many others. I changed my major to philosophy, and went on to earn a doctorate degree in the discipline. Instead of pursuing a career in business or advertising, I became an educator."

**LARRY BIRD, Boston Celtics' two-time MVP:**

"We used to shoot free throws at six in the morning, before classes, in high school. There was this one friend of mine, my best friend at the time, and he would never show up. We were in the regionals that year and he missed three 1-and-1 situations in a row. We lost in overtime. I never said a word to him; I just looked. He knew what I was thinking. I don't think I've talked to him since that day.

"I was no genius, but I did my homework and went to class. Sooner or later, it's the same thing in basketball. The same guy who didn't do his homework wound up missing the free throws. I see some of them sometimes when I'm home. Most of them have trouble keeping jobs.

"Me, I was going to be a construction guy and pour cement. Then, during the summer between my junior and senior years, I grew four inches. I'd say my vision, my court awareness and my height are God-given. Everything else I've worked my butt off for."

**EARL ("RED") BLAIK, retired Army football coach:**

"On Friday morning at 5:30 A.M., I was called to the training room —a most important summons because it was the day before the 1948 Army-Navy game. This was the year the Cadets returned to a victorious season after the undefeated years of 1944–46 and the hiatus of 1947. The '48 team was undefeated as they prepared for a Navy team that was given little chance against us.

"When I entered the training room the stench sickened me; four doctors were dispensing paregoric from gallon bottles, and the entire squad was showing degrees of vomiting. The impact of the entire mess sickened me—and without, as yet, considering how they might affect the game the next day.

"The squad was to leave West Point at 10:00 A.M. by bus after attending first class. Instead of class, the head of the medical department ordered them to bed.

"Any opportunity to depart West Point was a must for The Corps, and the football squad sent a delegation of their first-team players to plead that they must leave for Philadelphia. All were suffering degrees of sickness from food poisoning caused by rancid turkey dressing served at dinner the previous night. They would not get well in one day. One curious symptom of the illness was the fact that the palms of their hands turned a greenish color.

"It was decided the Cadets would do better by going ahead to our destination, the Manufacturers Club in Philadelphia. We took the Penn Railroad from Newark, canceled practice, then bedded the squad when we got to the club. The mood was grim. Prior to the mass food poisoning we had lost Stuart and Hank Foldberg, two great players, and Gil Stephenson, with injuries. No mention was made to the press, and the decision not to make public our distress gave the sports writers considerable material after the game and the following week. Personally, I was given many lashes and publicly condemned.

"The game turned into a rear-guard action, with the Navy forcing the Cadets to call upon the kind of motivation reserved for a catastrophe. A game that was considered a certain win for Army ended in a 21–21 tie. Few recall that Army was fortunate to field a team that day, and the tie serves as the only blemish on a 9–0–1 record—but not in my book.

"Recently, I had occasion to ask General Scott, the superintendent of the Air Force Academy, if he recalled that game. As a halfback, he had great speed and would have been a key player in the game. I was curious about what his recollection would be. He said the players kept looking at their hands, at the green palms, and they knew they would be forced to motivate themselves to play, let alone play well. When Scott tried to turn on his speed and move into high gear, he felt as though he was running in mud. He could not get untracked, a helpless feeling still vivid to him today.

"Exactly what motivated them I cannot say. Training and tradition, most probably. It wasn't a victory on the scoreboard and the details are hardly pleasant, but it sticks in my mind as an example of motivation overcoming hardship."

**PAUL BLOCH, Rogers and Cowens, Vice President, Public Relations:**

"When I was in the sixth grade, I was playing on the varsity basketball team at a private military school and I very much wanted to play on the first team; however, there were at least seven better players than myself on the team. We played a game against an academy in Anaheim, California, and I was so motivated to help the team that I got off the bench and played well over my head. I made three baskets in a row at least twenty-five feet from the basket to put us back in the game, and keep the score close. Although we finally lost, no memory of my youth is stronger than that one, or the lesson I learned that day.

"When I was 12, I wanted to enter a tennis tournament at camp, but had hardly played at all and sat it out. Working very hard and playing only part-time in the course of one year, I picked up the game fairly well. I went back to the camp where I first picked up a racket a year before and ended up playing in the finals of the 'A' tournament. I lost in the final set, 8–6, to a terrific player who had been competing for about six years. I was so motivated that nothing stopped me from getting to those finals, including an injury to my right foot.

"In business, those early roots and discipline that you gain from your family are important in whatever you do. I was willing to work long hours in order to afford the lifestyle that would make me the happiest, as well as putting myself in a position where I can help others less fortunate. It is important in the success factor to be able to give something back to those who helped you and those who need help."

**JOHN R. BLOCK, former secretary of agriculture:**

"Personally, the Boston Marathon exemplifies an experience which demanded motivation. For the inexperienced marathon runner even to qualify is the ultimate in achievement. I had previously run in Grandma's Marathon in Duluth, Minnesota, with the time of three hours and seventeen minutes, but to qualify for Boston I had to shave eight minutes off my time.

"Complete dedication and commitment were necessary to prepare for the qualifying marathon held in Central, Illinois. I was motivated not by any single individual but because I had established a personal goal for myself and nothing would stop me in my drive to succeed. For me the day that I qualified for the Boston Marathon was a bigger thrill than actually going there and running the race itself."

**GEORGE BUSH, president of the United States:**

"I think back to my days as a navy combat pilot in World War II. Our squadron was a team. Close-in flying required a lot of teamwork, too, but the motivation had to be there.

"The motivation came from being on a team with a dedicated group of people, all of whom believed 100 percent in the mission. The mission—to help end the war. The ultimate goal was clear, our role as pilots was clear, and the common bond of dedication to country and the willingness to risk one's life for country—all came about because we were motivated."

**KENNETH H. COOPER, M.D., M.P.H., founder of the Cooper Clinic:**

"What encouraged me to continue in this field (the motivation to concentrate on wellness rather than disease) has been the tremendous number of letters from appreciative people. The testimonials, the daily contact with patients and hearing their stories, are all extremely motivational to me. During the early years I had considerable difficulty from the medical society accepting my restricted type of medicine and, even more important, accepting my desire to do maximum-performance treadmill stress-testing. During these difficult years, the constant encouragement received from people all over the world convinced me that what I was doing was right. If you had asked me to predict in 1970 the success and acceptability of The Aerobics Center and The Aerobics Program, I would have missed a thousandfold."

**DONNA DE VARONA, assistant to the president, ABC Sports, Inc:**

"While in grade school, I tried many times to become actively involved in competitive sports events and was denied. The football and Little League baseball teams were organized for little boys only.

"I made a concerted effort in the third grade to organize a group of girls to cheer the young boys on, but I'd leave the playing field feeling frustrated, angry and empty. Finally, after much protest, I was able to persuade the young boys to let me play during recess in the sandlot baseball games. But again, after school hours, when the game of baseball was organized into what we now know as Little League, young girls were left out of the game.

"This time I didn't become a cheerleader. Instead, I spent my allowance money on bubble gum so I could bribe my way into the dugout. Once inside, I learned which bat each player preferred, how many sticks of gum each player chewed during the game, and who preferred butter on his popcorn. I was not alone in my quest to become the official batgirl of the Walnut Creek Little League Team. I had strong competition: the younger brother of one of my brother's teammates.

"Fortunately, one day as I was hustling bats, Henry J. Kaiser, the sponsor of the team, came out to watch his son play, and was impressed by my determination. A week later a Little League baseball uniform—pinstripes and all—arrived at my doorstep. That day the mailman gave me my first official recognition and I became the batgirl for the team.

"At the end of the season the usual sports banquet paid tribute to the batter with the highest average, the pitcher with the best record and the fielder with the most hustle. But that night they also paid tribute to the batgirl, 'Lizzie the Loudmouth Lizzard' (my nickname), for being the most animated supporter.

"The following year the head coach called me to ask if I was coming back to assume my old position. For a year the trophy they had given me had stood on a desk at the foot of my bed and, although I cherished the recognition, I told the coach no. He was flabbergasted. I explained that I couldn't bear to sit on the sidelines anymore and that, although I'd learned a lot, someday I wanted to find a place where I would at least be given the chance to fail or achieve, but most of all be allowed to play the game.

"That summer I found an age-group swimming program, and three years later represented the United States in swimming on the Olympic Team."

**ELIZABETH DOLE, secretary of labor:**

"I believe the motivating factor for my life in public service can best be summed up by the following remarks made by Woodrow Wilson to his fellow citizens as he called them to community service:

" 'Someday when we are all dead, men will come and point at the distant upland with a great shout of joy and triumph and thank God that there were men and women who understood to lead in the struggle. What difference does it make if ourselves do not reach the uplands? We have given our lives to the enterprise. The world is made happier and humankind better because we have lived.' "

**TED FRITSCH, special-teams coach, Atlanta Falcons:**

"I never had any problems motivation-wise, which I feel stems from the relationship I developed with my father. My dad was an all-pro fullback and placekicker with the Green Bay Packers from 1942 to 1951. I didn't see my dad play, but lived with him as a high school and college coach. Once I realized how important football really was to him, I knew I wanted to be a part of it. My biggest desire or drive was to make my dad proud of me. I guess all that I did, in whatever I did (in any sport or endeavor), that was the motivating force behind my efforts to succeed.

"I guess I became self-motivated after that, because as time went on and I got older, I wanted to be the best in whatever I did. (That was) another important trait I got from my dad. It's impossible to be the best at everything one tries, but you develop a sense of mastering some things better than others.

"Coming from St. Norbert College, a small school of 1600 students, I was given no chance to make the grade as an NFL player. The head coach at the time didn't do much to get me a look; he seemed to be more interested in two other players. So it became important to me to prove myself. I knew my dad would be proud of me if I could crack that forty-man roster. I worked and studied all through training camp, hoping my efforts would win out. I came into camp a little small at 238 pounds, but the best deep snapper they had. I took a lot of pride in my snapping ability and spent a lot of time perfecting my ace in the hole. I made that forty-man cut!

"After being part of the team for three years, I suffered an injury in 1975 which forced me to sit out the season. It was a big disappointment. But I knew I could turn this around to my advantage. I was not a starter, and a knee injury could end my career. I wanted to come back bigger and stronger, with no signs of that knee injury. So there I was in 1976, primed and ready to go and back in training camp for the Falcons, only to be traded to the Washington Redskins one week before the season opens. I guess being the new guy—the need to prove myself again—to be accepted by my peers—being surrounded by tradition and the type of coach George Allen was, were all motivating factors for me to be a part of the Redskins' success.

"I think the game I remember the most was my first as a Redskin. It set the tone for me. We opened the season with the Giants, one of our divisional rivals. The game was close the whole way. Our quarterback, Billy Kilmer, goes down in the fourth quarter and is replaced by a then outspoken and unproven Joe Theismann. The game started to get away from us. But in came "Band-Aid" Billy. He ignited a spark and, with the last-minute drive covering some sixty yards, we scored to win the game.

"Being around such great players as Diron Talbert, Kilmer, Len Hauss, Ron McDole, Bill Brundige, Pat Fisher, Chris Hanburger, Kenny Houston, and special-teamers like Rusty Tillman, Pete Wysocki, Bob Brunette and Eddie Brown was motivation enough to stick around for as long as I could. To win the play-offs was always our goal. The special-team Superstar Charts which were hung downstairs near the locker room were enough to keep me at a peak each week. I became totally committed to giving my best both in practice and on Sunday. To be the best at what I did was very important to me.

"In another game against the Giants, in 1978, we were in overtime and tied at 13. I threw a cross-body block on a punt return and broke five ribs in the process. I was unconscious for several minutes and had to be helped off the field. The winning drive was going on and there I was on the bench. I knew I had to take a practice snap or two because we would be attempting the winning field goal soon and I had to go in for the kick. When I tried to bend over the ball, I couldn't breathe. I remember telling Theismann in the huddle to hurry the set because I didn't know how long I could take it. The snap was there and Moseley was true and we won, 16–13. I spent three days in the hospital and finished the season without missing a game.

"There was something about "Redskins Weather"—that Redskin magic that Coach Allen always seemed to bring across to his players. Somehow, someway, he showed us how to win, how to work, and how to prepare. Not everyone enjoyed his methods, but Allen made them winners.

"That spirit remains with me today as I serve as special-teams coach with Atlanta Falcons."

## DAN GABLE, wrestling coach, University of Iowa:

"There was a tragic incident involving the murder-rape of my sister. I was 15 years old at the time and consequently I had to use this event to try to help my life for the future. I figured instead of moping around about it, feeling sorry for what took place, I would help utilize what took place for my own personal gain and, as well, for my parents. I basically vowed that whatever I was going to do, it would have made her very proud of her younger brother. Plus, now that I was the only child, I felt I had an obligation to become closer and to give my parents more personal satisfaction. At the time my sister was four years older than myself.

"The summer after my high school senior year I was working out with a top collegiate athlete in wrestling and he literally wiped the mat up with me. He hurt me so bad that I actually fled to the corner of another room and bawled like a baby. I can remember that incident so well, and telling myself that this was never going to happen again. Even though I had been a successful high school wrestler, to adapt to college meant becoming more intense and dedicating myself that much more for future competition. I vowed at this time that I would never get out of condition for wrestling again until I retired from the sport.

Once in college, I used the top wrestlers from across the country to help motivate me. There was a big rivalry between the Iowas and the Oklahomas in collegiate wrestling. Well, the word "Oklahoman" or "Okie" was what made me get out of bed early and make me work hard at my sport during those particular years.

"Once I graduated from college I realized again that I would need new motivational tools. Then I turned to who were the best in wrestling and, of course, that was the Soviets or Russians. One incident involved a national coach, Bill Wick. He said to me that whenever you think your practice session is done and you are ready to go to the showers, think about your opponent before you do so. Think about that Russian that you are going against; wonder whether he is still training. Then because of that, if you see him still working or training, go out and run an extra mile or two, or practice a little longer. I thought about that after every practice, and it kept me there longer when I normally would have been done.

"When I was growing up I read, 'The Heart of a Champion' by Bob Richards, and it spurred me on because of the great number of fascinating stories within its pages. One (athlete) in particular really impressed me. His name was Emil Zatopek from Czechoslovakia. I always use in my own training and coaching a statement he made in the book: 'When practice is over for the team or for everyone else, that's when my practice just begins.'

"I've always looked for motivating factors in my life, and especially now in coaching. Right now it's simple, because if we win our tenth national championship in a row, the University of Iowa wrestling program will be the sole leader in NCAA sports history in terms of consecutive national championships won.

"My real motivation in coaching, though, doesn't involve records. It involves individuals. From a coaching point of view, I get very close to my athletes and because of that I get extra incentive to bring the best out of them. I even go beyond the athletes that I coach; I look to their parents, because that is what I go back to in my own life. Athletes in college and in high school do not always realize the importance of what they are doing and, because of that, I look to their parents and try to make them proud. They get more out of it at that time of their lives than the actual athletes.

"My own personal philosophy of training and conditioning is that no matter how hard and how scientific one gets, he can never reach his 100 percent potential mark in physical and mental capacities. Consequently, perfection is impossible. But striving for it is what it is all about."

**ROMAN GABRIEL, former NFL quarterback and college coach:**

"There have been so many examples of motivation along the way, but one that stands out happened in 1966, our first year together with the L.A. Rams. Bill Munson and I were sitting in your office listening to your approach on making the Rams winners. You spoke for about thirty minutes and then asked Bill and me if we had any questions. We had always been told, not asked, our opinions in the past, so we did not respond. I'll never forget your response. You said, 'Even if you do not have any questions, ask what color the walls are, so at least I'll know you want to improve.'

"We all tend to retain those things that have a bearing on our lives. That experience has stayed with me and has been instrumental in all the successes that I have been a part of: when we listen and ask questions, we learn."

**J. PETER GRACE, chairman, W.R. Grace & Co.:**

"In 1945 I found myself head of W.R. Grace & Co. when my father, the late Joseph P. Grace, and his chief assistant both became ill. While we were posting profits, the company had what I call 'minus momentum.' Most of our earnings were dependent upon Latin American operations and shipping, and—because the political climate in South America was very unstable—the future had a lot of question marks.

"I decided we had to diversify, and narrowed the choice down to the chemical business. Many members of our board of directors were highly skeptical—it was, after all, a radical move away from the company's origins and into an entirely new business. But I was convinced that, unless we changed direction, we might not survive as a company. In 1952 the board convened for a vote of confidence in me, and I survived by one vote.

"Today, more than half our earnings come from the chemical side, and all the business we owned when I became president in 1945 has been divested. With hindsight—when your vision is 20/20—it was a good decision.

"The second example is more recent. In March of 1982, President Reagan asked me to chair the President's Private Sector Survey on Cost Control (PPSS), to study all the agencies and departments in the federal government and make recommendations on how each could operate more efficiently.

"It was an honor to be chosen, but the survey was born out of necessity as the federal deficit was (and is) ballooning out of all proportion to our children's and grandchildren's ability to repay it.

"We came up with 2,478 recommendations which, if implemented, would save the federal government—and us taxpayers—$424.4 billion over three years. To promote the survey's findings, I joined with Jack Anderson, the syndicated columnist, to form Citizens Against Waste (CAW). CAW's mission is to inform and persuade the American people that we have to vote the big spenders out of Congress and continue to streamline government operations using the private sector as a role model. My motivation in all of this springs from my promise to the president that I would see the PPSS project through, and from the fact that our future prosperity depends upon it."

**CARY GRANT, actor:**

"I was once involved with a fellow in a deal I really couldn't understand, and I tried to puzzle it out. I was talking to a friend of mine, Norton Simon, a very sensible and knowledgeable businessman. I told him about this proposal, this position in which I found myself.

"He said, 'I don't know how I can help you get out of it, but I can show you how to understand it. Consider the motivation.'

"I said, 'What do you mean?'

"He said, 'Well, what was your motivation for getting into this deal, and what was his motivation?' He added that when I could answer that question, I ought to be able to unravel the problem.

"It was one of the best pieces of advice I ever received. The deal was a bad one. And I went to the friend who brought it to me and we both got out. Later, we went into several other investments.

"A lot of people never know why they do something. What motivates you to invite someone to dinner? (Had I done that less, I might not have been married so many times.) Is it to repay a favor? Or to ask one? Or just to be seen? It never hurts to ask, I have learned, what motivates me to do this thing?"

**DOROTHY HAMILL, gold medalist, Olympic figure skating:**

"One day in the Olympic Village (at Innsbruck), I was handed a copy of the International edition of *Time* magazine. I was on the cover. We had always had a subscription to *Time*, and I had read cover stories about politicians and film stars, kings and space explorers. It was difficult to comprehend that I was now reading about myself.

"Telegrams addressed to me had been pouring in to the village. Gradually I realized these were all from complete strangers who had taken the time to wish me luck. I was overwhelmed by it. Suddenly I was carrying more than my own personal hopes and fears. I felt that in a sense I was no longer Dorothy Hamill—I was the United States. The medal was not mine to lose; I was representing the hopes and dreams of thousands of people I had never even met.

"Finally . . . I was standing out at center ice, taking deep breaths and trying to still the thudding of my heart. My knees were trembling slightly. I felt enormous pressure on me as I waited what seemed like hours for my music to start. I tried to block everything out except the skating.

"And then I was skating, and I had never felt as good as I did at that moment. I felt I possessed endless strength and I knew instinctively that I was not going to fail. Finally, it had all come together."

### DAVID R. HANNAH, director of Athletes in Action:

"When my oldest son, Eric, was a freshman in high school he was only five feet tall and weighed 100 pounds. Through a commitment to work hard, train, and lift weights, he is developing into what I think will be one of the top kickers in high school before he finishes his career.

"Eric has faced an unusual amount of adversity physically. He has worked hard and overcame much of it because of a strong, positive motivation and willingness to work hard. He has a herniated disc as a result of an automobile accident. He continued to kick at Capo Valley High School in constant pain. At the end of the season he had missed only one kick, and that was with 104-degree temperature."

### BOB HOPE, entertainer:

"Motivation played a crucial role in my success in Chicago, when I was standing in front of the Woods Theater, starving. I owed about $400 just in coffee and doughnuts. But I stuck it out. A friend of mine came along, asked me what I was doing. I told him I was starving and he took me to a booking agent. He gave me one day's work at the West Anglewood Theater, out in South Chicago. And from there I never stopped.

"So my motivation was food. It took quite a while to get there, but I finally made it."

**GORDIE HOWE, ice hockey hall of famer:**

"I grew up in Saskatoon, Saskatchewan, where every able-bodied boy played ice hockey on an outdoor rink in temperatures that often dropped to thirty and forty below. We would get up at five o'clock to play before school, and skate down the frozen road to the rink at Avenue F because it had a heated shack.

"At age 9 I couldn't skate too well, so they made me the goalie. I worked hard to improve because I could see right away there was an advantage in being a forward over a goalie. I didn't get to see all the game, but I got my turn in the shack.

"We had no gear, so we wore rubber boots and used tennis balls for pucks. I stuck magazines and mail-order catalogs in my socks for shin pads. A neighbor lady would warm up the tennis balls for us in her oven. We used to compete for marshmallows—that wasn't so bad when your diet was oatmeal three times a day.

"School was difficult for me. I was quiet and bashful to the point of pain, and the lessons were hard for me. Years later, my mother would tell the story of how I failed the third grade, and she sat down with me and asked if I had ever gone to the teacher for help. I replied, 'No, Mum. I don't want to bother her.' And then we both had a good cry.

"Hockey was my way out, but I never dreamed I would play it past the age of 50 and wind up on the same team with my two sons, Mark and Marty. Almost from the first time I saw him play, I knew Wayne Gretzky would break my records. But that's one he won't get: he won't play with his two sons for six years."

**MIKE HULL, former NFL player, assistant U.S. attorney:**

"When I came to the Redskins in 1971 after three very difficult years with the Bears, I considered myself mistreated, misunderstood, and ineffective. When told I had been traded, I considered retiring and going to law school full time. I came to Washington with a skeptical attitude, motivated not to destroy myself in an effort to be a decent professional football player, and knowing an education would provide lasting rewards. I didn't think I wanted to play anymore.

"But I met George Allen, absorbed his ideas on developing yourself to the full extent of your abilities, and became motivated again.

I began really caring about playing. I never imagined we'd win a championship or that I would play on a Super Bowl team; those things were not factors in my motivation. I wanted to prove to myself, and others, that I could make a good football team. And beyond that I wanted to do my best; I was motivated by the need to make the best possible use of my abilities. As a football player, as a human being, I didn't want to waste myself.

"Without that motivation I would have left football in 1971, just three years after being the sixteenth player picked in the draft; I would have had to admit to myself that I had not measured up. Instead, I ended playing four more years, in several playoff games, the championship game and the Super Bowl—experiences I will always treasure.

"I suppose what was truly unique about our Redskins was the diversity of personalities we had on that team. I don't think I could ever define what motivated Wilbur or Talbert or Larry Brown or Jefferson or Jurgenson or any of the other fine athletes we had on that team. But I can say with confidence that collectively, especially during the 1972 year, we were all doing our best to stick together as a team. We were motivated by the goal of a championship that was in our reach, but day to day, injury to injury, hour to hour of pounding, blood and sweat, our primary motive was to excel and accomplish something excellent as athletes. Most of us were rejects. You (Coach Allen) always said, 'You've got something to prove, men.'

"In 1974 I had pinched a nerve in my neck, paralyzed my left arm, broken my nose, and generally wiped myself out on a tackle in the Philly game. We were going to play the Cowboys the next week. I was in traction for a couple of days and feeling was coming back to my arm. I returned to practice with a brace on my neck, face guard altered to protect my nose.

"Now, I was just a special-teamer. But Coach Allen considered the special teams a vital part of the game; indeed, we had won many games over the years on his innovative approach to the 'teams.' The doctor had said that I shouldn't play, that if I did I would have to be cautious (if that is possible on a kick-off team). All Coach Allen said was, 'We need you. I'd rather have you out there at half-speed than someone who hasn't been on the field for me.' He easily could have let me pass the game. I wasn't a billboard player, and folks wouldn't have noticed. I wanted to make the effort; when all indicators said hold back, I wanted to again test myself when I knew I was hurting. I saw my teammates do it every week.

"I played in the game. And although I was strapped together like a mummy, I managed to do something significant. Beyond getting through the game without any permanent injury, I made a key block that no doubt knocked down, in a domino effect at the line, about five of the Cowboy coverers on one of our first returns. Kenny Houston caught the ball, found nobody on his left side because I'd put them out of action, and breezed on in for a touchdown. It was very satisfying, and to this day serves as a reminder that you can get things done when all about you think otherwise.

"Without a doubt, the accomplishment most directly related to my motivation to do my best was the completion of three years of law school at Georgetown, passing the bar in Washington, D.C., and now working as an assistant U.S. attorney in D.C.

"It has been a long and arduous task. I started law school part time in California in 1971 and really didn't finish until 1979. Eight years of focus on one key goal: getting my degree. I started completely over, in a completely new profession. And I continue each day, all the time, trying to do my best as a human being. That's my motive, my goal."

## LAMAR HUNT, owner, Kansas City Chiefs:

"One of the outstanding examples (of motivation) I can recall was the occasion of the first preseason game the Chiefs ever played against an NFL team—our 1967 win over the Chicago Bears, 66–24.

"We had played and lost the first Super Bowl the year before and had seen the AFL and the Chiefs maligned because of that result. There was a buildup in the minds of our coaches and players as we approached a new season determined to erase the stigma. On that August night in Kansas City, we were a team on fire—a group that for that one night couldn't be stopped. The result was the largest defeat in the history of the Chicago Bears, not very important in many ways except in the hearts of those who participated.

"Years later, when he retired, our fine tight end Fred Arbanas told the press that this one game would remain as the most memorable of his career. This is an indication of the intensity of that night, because Fred had a great career at Michigan State and in the pros

75

started in two Super Bowls. And yet one preseason game was his most memorable."

## ROBERT HYLAND, broadcaster:

"The source of my motivation was my father, Dr. Robert Hyland, the 'surgeon general of major league baseball.' My father was a great doctor and much of his career involved helping athletes perform at their best. He taught by example and the precept that there was only one way to do things—with total commitment and dedication. He was my No. 1 hero and inspiration, and he introduced me to other heroes throughout the sporting world: Babe Ruth, Lou Gehrig and Ty Cobb from baseball, and football greats Ernie Nevers and Red Grange. These great athletes personified his competitive spirit. His example inspired me through the years to work the long hours (often 2 A.M. to 5 P.M.) required to build a truly great radio station."

## ROY JEFFERSON, staff representative, NFL Players Association:

"After being chosen All-Pro in 1968 and 1969, I was traded to the Baltimore Colts. Even though I had accomplished many individual honors, being traded deflated my ego somewhat. My motivation stemmed from the fact that I was on a new team in a new system; and for me to prove to myself and my new teammates that I could continue excelling at the level I was accustomed to was my motivation. Baltimore won the Super Bowl that year and I had one of my better years as a receiver and was chosen to play in the Pro-Bowl. You can never rest on past accomplishments; motivation is a continuous process— day to day, week to week, year to year.

"I lived my first 11 years on this earth in different 'projects,' federal housing projects, in Oakland, California. I was the oldest of seven children and a bicycle was a luxury we could not afford.

"I got a job as a paper boy delivering the *Oakland Tribune*, and six months later I had the only bike I was ever to own until George Allen had Montgomery Ward supply the whole Redskins team with a bike. Of course, my motivation for getting a job was to earn enough money for a bike, but I increased my route 50 percent in six months and *won* a bike."

**DAVEY JOHNSON, manager, 1986 World Champion New York Mets:**

"I was recruited out of high school, in San Antonio, by Tom Chandler, the Texas A&M baseball coach. After dinner, he moved aside the dishes and handed me a letter of intent. I read it and discovered what I thought was a small oversight. I said, 'Coach, this scholarship is just for one year. You promised me four.'

"Coach Chandler leaned across the table and said, 'Dave, that's the trouble with the youth of today. They all want security instead of an opportunity.'

"I picked up the pen and said, 'Coach, where do I sign?'

"I played baseball and basketball at A&M and we missed a championship in each sport by one game. After my sophomore year I signed with Baltimore, and I remembered what Coach Chandler had said about wanting an opportunity.

"As a rookie second baseman in 1965, I was trying to break into an infield that had Luis Aparicio at short and Brooks Robinson at third. Between them they had eighteen Golden Gloves. But every day they were out there taking hundreds of grounders. One day I said, 'You guys can catch a ground ball. Why don't you work on your hitting?'

"And Brooks said, 'That's why we can catch 'em. We work at it.' I learned another lesson right there. After that, I made myself into a pretty fair fielder."

**DICK KAZMAIER, 1951 Heisman Trophy winner:**

"Since I never planned to live my life as an athlete, as a professional, I set my sights at Princeton on getting the best education I could. Anything else was a bonus. But football gave me values that were essential to a career in business: How to handle losses as well as wins. How to commit yourself to a goal . . . with dedication and discipline and the recognition of something bigger and deeper than one's self.

"And what I think of as the reward of giving your all. In my senior year we played against Brown on a snowy day. Two inches or so covered the field and it was nearly impossible to pass. So I had to run, and I carried the ball thirty-five or thirty-six times, more than I had ever run in any other game. I was just physically exhausted.

77

Leaving the locker room and walking back to my dorm, I was so drained, so deflated, I just cried all the way back.

"It isn't often in your life that you cry out of the sheer emotion of having given everything you had."

**JACK KEMP, former U.S. Congressman, former pro quarterback, secretary of H.U.D.:**

"When I started out in life I wanted to be a pro football player. It was all I ever thought about. When I first began Occidental College I was five-ten and 165 pounds. One day the coach, Payton Jordan, called me into his office and told me, 'Out of all the people on this team, I really think you have it, have something inside you, and I want you to work—work just like you were a pro football player.' When I left that office, I would have run through a brick wall for Coach Jordan.

"Several years later, we had a class reunion and the whole team was there. And I began talking to the players, trading stories about our professional careers, and I began to tell them how I was inspired to pursue pro ball. And you know, I found out that the coach had told every player on the team the same thing—that if they worked hard enough and sacrificed enough, they could make the pros.

"I was furious! For only a minute. Then I realized that Coach Jordan had made every one of us a little bit better, had helped us to struggle a little bit harder, to reach our potential."

**LARRY KING, radio and television host:**

"Early in life my father motivated me a great deal, but when he died I really drifted. I was only 11. But looking back I can see what a lack of motivation did to hurt me. I was different at school—tended to be a goof-off, etc.

"Later, I think I used a lot of self-motivation in broadcasting. I really *wanted* to be successful. I was (and am) very ambitious. There is a puzzle here. Why do some people seem to do it from some inner concept, while most need the help of others?"

**BOB KNIGHT, basketball coach, Indiana University:**

"My dad was without any question the most honest person that I have ever met in my life. From him I learned early that you simply

78

did what you were supposed to do and did it to the best of your ability, being totally honest with everyone whether it was to your benefit or not to do so. Out of this basic approach to life I learned that it was necessary, in a decision-making position, to decide on courses of action based on what you thought was right, not what would be popular. In doing so it was just not possible to worry about criticism that might come your way.

"There have been two quotations that I have kept in my office for as long as I have been coaching. They are:

" 'I desire so to conduct the affairs of this administration, that if at the end, when I come to lay down the reins of power, I have lost every other friend on earth, I shall have at least one friend left, and that friend shall be down inside me.'—Abraham Lincoln

" 'By your own soul learn to live, and if man thwart you pay no heed, if man hate you have no care, sing your song, dream your dream, pray your prayer, by your own soul learn to live.'—Anonymous"

**TOM LANDRY, former coach, Dallas Cowboys:**

"You have read where coaches have been quoted as saying, 'Winning isn't everything; it's the only thing.' I don't believe that is true. I do believe that trying to win is everything. I've seen many outstanding winners in professional football who never played in a Super Bowl or won their conference. One of our favorite slogans is, 'A winner never stops trying.'

"We recognize that God has given us the talent to become an athlete, even though some have more talent than others. I've discovered that it isn't how much talent you have that makes you successful, it is the ability to use all the talent you have—it is the ability to reach your full potential.

"Winning then became a state of mind. Most of the athletes who fail to become winners are those whose fears and anxieties prevent them from reaching their potential. I overcame my fears and anxieties by a commitment to something greater than winning a football game. Apostle Paul explained my discovery in I Corinthians better than I can: 'In a race, everyone runs but only one person gets first prize. So run your race to win.'

"To win the contest you must deny yourselves many things that would keep you from doing your best. An athlete goes to all this

**79**

trouble just to win a ribbon or a silver cup, but we do it for a heavenly reward that never disappears. So I run straight to the goal with purpose in every step. I fight to win. I'm not just shadow boxing or playing around. Like an athlete, I punish my body, treating it roughly, training it to do what it should, not what it wants to do. Otherwise, I fear that after enlisting others for the race, I myself might be declared unfit and ordered to stand aside.

"There are many ways to become a winner. I believe it is more important to first become a winner in life; then it is a lot easier to become a winner on the playing field."

### DR. SAMMY LEE, former diving champion:

"1945, as a retired national diving champion, I attended a diving exhibition. The national diving champion at the moment was a young diver who won national championships during 1944 and 1945. He said 'Sammy Lee, you were certainly lucky that I was not diving when you won your national championships in 1942. Your diving scores were so low I would have won easily. Besides, you are much too short and do not have a pretty enough body.'

"Up to that moment I was content with being a national diving champion of the past, but his remarks needled me into saying, 'Do you know what you just did? You have motivated me into seeing that you will never be national champion again, because when I finish medical school in one year, I will destroy you.' I knocked him off a year later with the highest point total in the history of high diving in that era. He never made our Olympic diving team.

"While a junior at Occidental College, my pre-med adviser told me he would not recommend me for medical school because I was too sports oriented. He also feared that I would be the first Oxy graduate to flunk out of medical school. He told me that I should take up cooking and have a chop suey restaurant like my parents had (a small mom-and-pop place that seated about twenty people). I told him my parents had not worked like slaves to see me become a cook, and that all his tests did not mean a damned thing because there was no test made that measured motivation and desire.

"When my father died a few months later, he said he would recommend me for medical school out of respect for my dad's dying wish, but against his better judgment. When I was honored with a

Sammy Lee Day at Occidental College as the school's first gold medalist in any Olympics and a Doctor of Medicine, his face turned red when I told the students the advice I had received from my pre-med adviser."

## CARL LEWIS, winner of four Olympic gold medals, 1984:

"When I was nine and just getting interested in the long jump, I walked across my front yard and measured Bob Beamon's record— 29 feet, 2½ inches. When you walk it off on your own lawn, it's huge. It's just like jumping over two middle-size cars. I thought, 'How could any human do that?'

"Over the years, I kept walking it off. It began to get closer and closer. I've gone over twenty-eight feet many times. When I finally cleared thirty in the National Sports Festival in 1982, it was disallowed. An official ruled that my toe had broken the plane at the end of the board.

"When I jump, my mind is a blank. You can *feel*, but you don't have time to cherish it. In the air, you don't actually have time to say, 'Gosh, this feels good, let's land.' That's the only sad part to me—you can't cherish it while you're doing it. You have to get over that fear of falling. It's the nightmare almost everyone has: falling out of bed, floating through space, wondering if you'll ever land. I'm not over that fear yet. But if you use it right, fear can motivate you.

"I am not so much moved by winning as by a challenge. I know some people disapprove of what I do, how I express what I feel. Some react by being emotional. Some are low-keyed. I'm having fun and I don't try to hide it."

## NANCY LIEBERMAN, women's pro basketball star:

"When I was a kid in Queens, New York, my parents were breaking up. I started playing basketball to get out of the house and away from the tension. My brother was the bookworm, the student. Me, I loved sports. It made me mad when I couldn't play on the boys' teams.

"When I enrolled at Old Dominion (in Virginia) on a basketball scholarship, the coach kept dragging me to Rotary Club breakfasts my freshman year, trying to sell tickets. I always knew I had to help market the sport, and myself. In 1981, I played against men in the NBA summer league for the Lakers. Pat Riley had called and I didn't ask why they wanted me, although I'm sure the idea was to push the attendance. I just wanted the chance.

"The other players were hacked off at my being there. I understood. They needed to make an impression. Most of them were fighting for a job. And I was going to take ten or twelve minutes of their playing time. Whenever we split the squad for practice, shirts and skins, the opposing team always grumbled because they had to take their tops off. After four days, I decided to put an end to it. I said, 'Okay, we'll be the skins today.' And I yanked off my jersey. Underneath I had on a bathing suit. After that, I was treated like one of the guys. I scored in double figures a few times and in one game had fourteen assists.

"I have my fantasies. I'm also a realist. Men are fifty years ahead of us physically. But someday a girl will come along with the ability I have, or an Anne Meyers or a Cheryl Miller, who is six-four, and she will play in the NBA."

**ART LINKLETTER, radio and television host.**

"I was the radio director of the San Francisco World's Fair in 1939. I was called in by the director and summarily fired because of a personal prejudice that had built up in his mind because of my youthfulness and my origins in Southern California rather than in San Francisco. It was a bitter and surprising blow and came at a key moment in my life, since I was teetering between a career as an executive producer and as a performer.

"Rather than be diminished by this crushing defeat, I determined to use it as a launching pad for a future that would not depend upon one man's decision. I packed up my desk, went home, and announced to my wife that I would never work for any organization again, but would become an independent free-lance performer and producer, depending on my agility and talent to get ahead.

"I have never worked for anybody but myself in the forty-five years that have passed, and I have had one of the most exciting and interesting lives imaginable. My attitude is best expressed by Coach John Wooden's philosophy: 'Things turn out best for the people who make the best of the way things turn out.' Life is uncertain and not always fair, and this approach has been a great help to me through the years."

*82*

**MICKEY MANTLE, New York Yankees' hall of famer:**

"I never thought about *not* playing baseball. I'm not bragging, but I think I was born to play ball. That's the truth. My dad had it planned out. He named me before I was born—after Mickey Cochrane. He thought that was a ball player's name.

"If I could, I'd still be playing ball. I still have dreams about playing. The same dreams. There's the one where I'm making a comeback: I get a base hit and I run to first, hard as I can, but I can't make it. They always just nip me.

"But this is the worst one: I get to the ballpark late and as I jump out of a cab I hear them calling my name on the P A system. I try to get in and all the gates are locked. Then I see a hole under a fence and I can see Casey Stengel looking for me, all of 'em, Billy Martin and Whitey Ford and Yogi Berra. I try to crawl through the hole and I get stuck at the hips and that's when I wake up, sweating."

**EDWIN MEESE III, former attorney general of the United States:**

"When the president nominated me to serve as attorney general of the United States, I began what turned out to be a long battle to obtain confirmation by the United States Senate.

"Those who launched political attacks against the nomination were able to delay the proceedings for over a year.

"Nevertheless, the privilege of serving the president and the country, and the president's confidence in me, provided the motivation for me and my family to continue this effort and ultimately to win confirmation."

**DONN D. MOOMAW, minister, Bel Air Presbyterian Church, and All-American football player:**

"The greatest motivation I knew in my early life was having Red Sanders as my coach at UCLA. He was not a Knute Rockne type. He was quiet, but he believed in his men. He never gave a pregame or halftime pep talk. After the players had all dressed for the game, we would assemble in the briefing room. No one talked—we thought, we prayed, we rehearsed our roles. Coach Sanders would stand before us with his arms folded. He was a terrifying figure, a little man with a scar on his cheek and a frown on his face. He would survey the team one player at a time. To some he would give the look of support and encouragement. To others, the look of scorn and suspicion, as if you were not going to make it unless you changed radically—you can do it, but . . . well, we'll see today.

"He knew men. He admired 100 percent commitment. He demanded it. He got the best out of all of us. Then when it was time to leave the locker room and enter the playing field, he would break the silence with these words only: 'Put on your helmets.' The game began with each player giving his all—for the school, the team, one's own self and, of course, the coach."

**MARK MOSELEY, kicker, Washington Redskins:**

"Motivation is a tough word to define, because I try to be motivated in everything that I do. If I'm not, then I don't even attempt it. The one most motivated time of my life has been channeled into a desire to change certain laws dealing with the parole of criminals. My sister Pam was murdered by a man who was out on parole just six weeks when he raped and murdered her. I have been tremendously motivated ever since to work on legislation here in Washington that will change some of the laws dealing with parole. The result is that we are seeing progress being made toward eliminating parole for such cases as rape, murder and kidnapping."

**JACK NICKLAUS, golfer, entrepreneur:**

"Throughout my life I have been motivated by simply wanting to be the best at what I did. I don't really know what instilled that desire in me, but it has always shaped my aspirations."

**RICHARD M. NIXON, 37th president of the United States:**

"On a Wednesday morning (in 1960) it became clear that I had played out the toughest and closest fight of my political life—and lost. To make matters more difficult, I had lost by the political equivalent of a nose.

"On that rather gloomy morning I received a wire from a leading Southland sportsman. More than a message of condolence, it was a real tonic, because my friend recalled for me the postgame advice given one of the Stanford players after their stunning defeat by Alabama in the 1935 Rose Bowl game. After 'Bama's Dixie Howell and Don Hutson had routed the Indians, a Stanford prof emphasized:

" 'Defeats are poison to some men. Great men have become mediocre because of the inability to accept and abide by a defeat. If you should achieve any kind of success and develop superior qualities as a man, chances are it will be because of the manner in which you met the defeats that will come to you just as they come to all men.' "

## SANDRA DAY O'CONNOR, U.S. Supreme Court justice:

"I grew up on a cattle ranch in a remote and barren part of the Southwest. In that environment, it was necessary to rely on one's own skills and resources to manage the day-to-day necessities of existence. If repairs were to be made, we made them ourselves. If something were to be built, we built it. If a person or an animal became ill, we tried to cure them as best we could.

"My father was intelligent and resourceful. I learned a great deal about the need for self-reliance and for learning about all things from him and from my mother."

## AKEEM OLAJUWON, Houston Rockets basketball star:

"Pride. I need no one to inspire me or to push me, only to explain things clearly. I have always felt it was not up to anyone else to make me give my best. I felt this way when I was a soccer player in Nigeria. Had I not been big, had I not come to the United States and played basketball for the University of Houston, I would have gone to college in my country and been successful at something else."

## JACK PARDEE, former pro football player and coach:

"I was coming off an all-pro season as a linebacker with the Rams, with a new baby and a new house, and I had the world by the tail. Then I woke up one morning and learned that I had cancer.

"I will always believe that I owe my life to a story in the paper about Jim Umbricht, a Houston pitcher who had died of cancer. I read the story of how he came back from his operation to pitch again in the big leagues, but they had caught it too late. I thought about the mole on my arm and my wife, Phyllis, insisted that I make an appointment with the doctor.

"I guess the worst part is when you learn that you actually have it. It isn't a word that sits very softly on your ear. Cancer. I entered the hospital on a date I can't forget. It was Monday, April 19, 1964. It was my twenty-eighth birthday. They operated the next morning. By the end of the week, the doctor came in and told me he had just received the lab reports and the lymph nodes were clear.

"The amount of tissue removed from my right forearm was four inches in diameter. It left a hole that looked like the impression left by a baseball sunk in mud. In time it smoothed out, but I lost the use of my arm for a while. It took physical therapy seven days a week for six weeks to regain the use of it. I had to learn to comb my hair lefthanded.

"I was out of football for a year, and then George Allen brought me back. I played another ten years and went to the Super Bowl with the Redskins. I never thought of my illness as a negative experience. I learned a lot about life. You learn to sort out the important from the unimportant things when you don't know how long you might be around.

"In the years since then, I have been active with the American Cancer Society and I made a lot of speeches about the need for early detection. In a way, my story has helped others. And I would have to say it toughened me for a career in coaching.

"When I retired as a player, I was the youngest coach on George Allen's staff with the Redskins. The way the pecking order was, I figured by the time I got a head coaching job I would be 80 years old. So I accepted an offer from the World Football League, with a team that wound up in Orlando.

"We went to camp in July and the paychecks started bouncing on September sixth. I told our staff that it was going to be the best year of coaching we would ever have, and it was. There were no stars and no prima donnas on that team. Everybody got the same; the quarterback, the kickoff returner and the backup guard all got the same: a gift certificate from McDonald's and sometimes a share of the gate receipts. Once we went to Michigan and came back with $200 each. It was great. I bought toilet paper for the locker room out of my own pocket and we won the championship. I couldn't afford to keep that job, but it was great."

**DONALD E. PETERSEN, chairman of the board, Ford Motor Company:**

"As I look back, I can think of no one incident that was compelling. I have always believed that the motivations I have stem from the support and encouragement I received from my parents during my school years. The importance of education was stressed from my earliest memory, and I was encouraged to believe that I could do anything I chose to do."

**T. BOONE PICKENS, JR., president, Mesa Petroleum Co.:**

"In my early years, I admired Lou Boudreau, who played basketball at the University of Illinois and baseball for the Cleveland Indians. Lou was too short to be a basketball player, but he played anyway and he was good. As a baseball player his hands were too small and he didn't have a strong arm, but they always picked him for the All-Star team. He didn't always have a high batting average, but when he hit the ball it was often at a key moment. I wanted to be like Lou because he got the most out of what he had to work with, and he was cool under pressure. I never met him, but would like just to tell him he inspired me at a certain point in my life.

"In business, my goal is not to come up with one motivational pitch for my employees, but to motivate continually. This can be done through giving people a challenge, giving praise when it is due, as well as through financial incentive. At Mesa, such a package centers on giving them ownership in the company through a stock-purchase plan. In this way they are motivated for both the short- and long-term."

**THOMAS RICE, director of development, Morningside College:**

"During a visit to our development office in September of 1985, you (George Allen) challenged Fred Erbes and me to organize an annual fund raising campaign involving nationally recognized Morningside alumni and friends. Your acceptance of the honorary chairmanship provided the necessary impetus for us to accomplish our goal.

"It is now clear to me why you were such a successful coach.

You motivated us to dream and be creative to help bring higher education opportunities to more young adults."

## EDDIE ROBINSON, football coach, Grambling:

"The 1985 season was my most memorable year of coaching (note: Coach Robinson passed Paul "Bear" Bryant in total victories). The team and the coaching staff have worked extremely hard.

"I feel that God has blessed me and that I have been the luckiest man in the world. All my career I have been associated with great athletes, outstanding assistant coaches, and an understanding and helpful administration.

"You (George Allen) and others know I did not do it by myself. I owe so much to so many. Each player who blocked and tackled for us from 1941 to 1985 must share in this accomplishment."

## SUGAR RAY ROBINSON, boxing champion:

"I had more than 200 fights, started out as a lightweight, then a welterweight, then a light heavyweight. When I walked into the ring, I was always prepared and in shape to give it my very best. I felt I owed it to my fans, my family, and America. My goal now is to try to help others."

## PETE ROZELLE, commissioner, National Football League:

"The strength of the league over its sixty-five years has been the unity of its clubs. When NFL club presidents have been motivated to accomplish a goal for the overall good of the league, they have settled for nothing short of that mark. This motivation on the part of each individual club—to strive for that which benefits the entire league—has enabled the NFL to attain the measured success it has in the sports and entertainment field."

## WILLIE SHOEMAKER, jockey:

"Desire is the most important factor in the success of any professional athlete. Without it the degree of success is limited.

"I have the *desire*."

**MARY DECKER SLANEY, women's distance runner and world record holder:**

"Motivation to run is very, very simple—I love it! I've never had a problem motivating myself to train or compete. I feel I was born to run. It feels so good and so natural.

"Now, competitiveness . . . I've got tons of it. I'm very competitive, love to be good. No—I love to be the best. When I ask myself what motivates me, I come up empty. What motivates me to want to be the best, I think, are other people. I love to prove people wrong. I love to make them eat their words, without having to say a word. People that doubt me, criticize me, throw whatever obstacles they can find in my way, just make me more determined to work hard. *Never* give in!

"What makes it all so special for me is that I really and truly do love to run. I've got examples that could fill a book.

"I was 12 years old; the farthest I had ever run in training was twelve miles. I had been running less than one year and I entered the Palos Verdes marathon. Just two days before the race, a parent (who thought he knew it all) told me I had no hope of finishing. Well, the last six miles were the toughest, and all I did was think of what that man had said. I won the women's race in 3.09.27, and to that date it was the fastest marathon by a woman.

"Injuries! Always, I heard, 'She will never run again, a flash in the pan, a child prodigy, burnt out, etc . . .' Every time I have a setback it makes me even more determined to come back stronger and better than before.

"The latest, and probably the best known, was the fall at the '84 Olympics. The press, critics, other athletes thought they had buried me so deeply with criticism that I would never rally. The hip injury from the Olympics threw more doubt. But I can tell you all, those people who made up stories, who wished I was through, who called me a cry baby, who didn't like the truth as I saw it, they all fueled my fire—they helped give me the spark to have my best performance, my best season to date, in 1985. I had told them, showed them, what was in my heart without saying a word.

"Then, when Zola (Budd) said she had cut over too soon, it made so many so-called experts look stupid. The issue was dropped. The fact that Zola and I do not dislike each other, we speak, we are friendly, makes the people that tried to build this big hate thing look even more ridiculous.

"Anyway, I'm a very self-motivated person—with a little extra fuel thrown in from time to time, which helps create some big fires!"

**ROGER STAUBAUCH, former Dallas Cowboys quarterback.**

"Near the end of the 1960s, I used my navy leaves to work out with the Cowboys in training camp. I drove myself hour after hour, trying to improve with each snap. One day Don Meredith, who was about to retire, turned to Craig Morton and kidded him, 'Old Roger's gonna get your job, Curly.'

I was not quite sure what to make of this horseplay. I asked a writer who covered the team, 'Do they always kid around like that?' He said they did. I shook my head. 'I don't think I could be that friendly,' I said, 'with a guy whose job I was trying to take.'

"So, yes, motivation was a big part of my making the Dallas football team. I wanted to at least give it a good shot at making the pros, and this goal motivated me to keep working out and throwing the ball whenever possible while I was in the navy. I was ready when my opportunity came."

**JAMES STEWART, actor:**

"My father believed that motivation was created by hard work. He ran a hardware store in Indiana, Pennsylvania, that had been in his family for eighty years.

"He was just getting started in taking over the store from his father, who was retiring, when World War I came along. He left the men who were with him in the store to run the business, and he joined the army and was in France for two years.

"He returned and immediately got back into the hardware business and, with hard work, made it bigger than ever. Then, one night, came the fire, which destroyed most of the store. However, he never for a minute let the fire stop him. For a year and a half he worked diligently and built the store back up to its place as the best hardware store in the town of Indiana. He believed in hard work and I do too."

**IRVING STONE, best-selling author:**

"Why biography and the biographical novel? There the motivation is clear. I had been writing since I was 9 years old, short stories, and when I resigned from the economics faculty at Berkeley on May 1, 1926, I went to Europe to write full-time. I wrote some nineteen full-length plays and thirty-one one-act plays in the course of a year and a half. Nobody told me you can't do that. Later, I learned that Henrik Ibsen matured a play in his mind for two years before he set a word down on paper. Ah, youth! I was only 23 years old.

"From the beginning, I had wanted to be a short-story writer, and then matured into wanting to be a book writer. That motivation is clear in my mind. In late 1926 or early 1927, I was exchanging English and French lessons with a young student at the Sorbonne. When we finished our interchange of dialects late one afternoon, he said to me, 'Come down with me to the Rosenberg Galleries. They are having a fine exhibition of Van Gogh's canvases.'

"I replied, 'Thank you, no. I'm just back from Italy, where I froze to death huddling over braziers in the Pitti and Uffizi galleries, and I have come to the conclusion that painting is not for me.'

"He said, 'I have heard that you Americans are good sports, and if you are bored, I will pour enough French wine into you to wipe out the boredom.'

"In the Rosenberg Galleries, which were quite small, only a little larger than my present studio, I found hanging next to each other eighty of Vincent Van Gogh's blazing canvases from Arles, St. Remy and Auvers-sur-Oise. It was the deepest emotional reaction I had ever had to art since completing *The Brothers Karamazov*. I wandered around the room a number of times, staring at these magnificent canvases for a period of a couple hours. My French friend, seeing the state of euphoria in which I had entered, left quietly.

"When I got out to the sidewalk and gazed up at the sky, unseeing, I said to myself; 'Who is this man who can do this to me? Unravel the mysteries of the universe, take the veils away from my eyes so that all organic matter, the earth, the plants and animals and humans who grow on it, and the sky, all pour into the sun and that force is poured back from the sun through the air and into men and animals and trees and plants, all as a unified force.

"Fascinated, I checked to see what had been written about Vincent Van Gogh. There was a small French monograph, perhaps sixty pages and technical in nature, and a biography by a Dutch art historian who had never left his very comfortable leather chair in his beautiful library to go on the trail of Van Gogh. He had simply been writing about the technique of Van Gogh's painting.

"When I returned to New York shortly thereafter, although I knew I was too young (about 25) to write a book about Vincent Van Gogh, and that it should be written by a mature novelist, I realized that nobody else was going to do it and that I simply had to tell Vincent's story. For a period of a year I spent all my evenings up at the public library at 42nd Street and Fifth Avenue in New York City, reading the three volumes of letters to Vincent's brother, Theo, who was his only true and lasting and loving friend. By the end of another year I knew I would have to go back to Europe on the very trail of Vincent Van Gogh and write the story of his life.

"At that time I was earning a living writing suspense or murder stories for *Detective Dragnet* at a penny a word. I sat down on a Monday morning and wrote my first story, and by Saturday night I had written six. Five of the stories sold, giving me $200 for the six months I knew I would need in Europe.

"I walked across Belgium, Holland and France, living in all of the homes that Van Gogh had lived in, and even writing in his mother's wrangle room in Brabant. In Arles, I lived in the home of Dr. Rey, who took care of Vincent over the unfortunate ear incident; and in St. Remy I lived in the medical superintendent's home until I asked him if I could live and work in Vincent's cell. It was unoccupied, and so the doctor gave me permission to do so. In Auvers-sur-Oise I slept in the very bed, in the very room in the same hotel where Vincent had died in 1890. That was how close I got to him.

"While I spent six years attending the University of California and USC, getting a master's there, there was no such thing as classes in the art and science of research. I had to train myself. Perhaps that was good, because now I needed to research not only Van Gogh and the postimpressionists, but also the impressionists who preceded him. When I had all of my material assembled and was ready to sit down at my desk in Greenwich Village and begin writing the book, my early desire to become a novelist overtook me. I also saw that the biographical form could never match the intense and soul-wrenching drama of Vincent's life. The motivation to make it a novel came from my early training at the university, where I read straight through the great European novelists, such as Dostoevsky and Balzac. Van Gogh's life was a great human story, and I thought it ought to be dramatized under a proscenium so that the reader would become not a viewer of this piece up on a stage, but would rise, go up to the stage and become a principal in the drama.

"Parenthetically, the novel of Vincent Van Gogh, *Lust for Life*, which is now in eighty languages and every country where they have a printing press, was rejected for three years by every leading publisher in New York and Boston. Their grounds? 'How do you expect us to sell a book about an unknown Dutch painter (Vincent was known to perhaps three or four hundred Americans in 1931 when I finished the manuscript) to the American public in the middle of a Depression?'

"In 1933, when I was going down to Arkansas to research the first bread riot in America, my then fiancée and now wife of fifty-one years, Jean, took the manuscript over to Maxwell Aley, who was the editor at Longmans Green, a small Catholic publishing house and a branch of the great firm of London. They had published only one novel before this, Rose Wilder Lane's *Let the Hurricane Roar*, and since they had made a nice sum of money out of that, Mr. Aley was able to persuade the owner, Mr. Mills, to take a gambling chance on *Lust for Life*. His grandchildren are still earning royalties for that book.

"My motivation again: to write great human stories."

**GENE TENACE, former big-league catcher:**

"I played on teams that were in the World Series four times and won all four. That may not be a record, but I bet this is: I may have been the only player who ever offered to play for dog food.

"One year, in Oakland, we were $1,000 apart (in negotiations) and I had filed for arbitration. The day before the case was to be heard, I was working out at a health club when Charlie Finley called. He was at a hotel a half-hour away. He asked me to meet him.

"I walked into the hotel's dining room and there was Finley, sitting in an area that had been roped off. His secretary was with him and he was surrounded by phones. I sat down and he hands me a contract and the thousand isn't in there. I said I was going to leave.

Charlie said, 'Look, you know what problems the club had last year. Let's not go through that again.'

"Then the phone rings and he gets up to take the call in another room. While he was gone, his secretary said, 'Gene, I know how you can get that thousand out of him.'

"I'm thinking, well, they're working together. And then she says, 'You have a Saint Bernard, don't you?' I nodded. She said, 'Tell him you'll take his offer if he gives you a year's supply of dog food.'

"I'm still thinking. A year's supply of dog food doesn't sound like $1,000, but with a Saint Bernard you never know. They'll eat all day. So I say, 'Carol, that's not a bad idea.' Finley comes back and he slides the same contract across the table. I said, 'Tell you what, Charlie. I'll sign this if you agree to give me a year's supply of food for my dog.' He says, 'It's a deal.'

"I take out my pen and start to write my name and he lunges across the table and grabs my wrist. 'What kind of dog you got?'

"I say, 'Saint Bernard,' and without a word he grabs the contract, rolls it up, sticks it in his coat pocket and pulls out another contract. This one has the extra thousand in it.

"I'm not sure how he did it or what we felt for him, but I give Finley credit for those great Oakland teams in the early '70s. Reggie, Sal Bando, Joe Rudo, Rollie Fingers. It was sad watching that club break up. But somehow we thrived on the turmoil and Finley sensed it. He did a lot for the game. He was a unique guy."


**DANNY THOMAS, entertainer:**

"I honestly never pursued or prayed for fame or fortune. I came from an immigrant family, people who tried to make a living from day to day, and I just grew up like that. I remember the lyrics from a song written by Jimmy Wetherley entitled 'The Gentler Times,' which included these lines: 'When there was less to give people seemed to give much more; they were more concerned with how to live than what they were living for . . .'

"The only real motivation I ever felt was when I traveled around the country and saw sick children dying of catastrophic diseases. I just knew that something more could be done for them than what was being done. That motivated me toward the building and main-tenance of the world's only complete pediatric research center, St.

Jude Children's Hospital in Memphis, Tennessee, fighting leukemia and cancer and other tragic children's diseases the world over."

## JULIAN THOMPSON, training, reserve and special forces, Royal Marines:

"One of the first tasks I was required to undertake on joining my commando in the Middle East was to lay ambush outside the wire of our camp to catch intruders. The camp had been constructed in World War II some years before, and had a minefield belt around it. Some mines had subsequently been lifted, others had not, and the marking fences had long been removed, rusted away, or fallen into the sand. There was no means of telling where the minefield had been. All the men in my patrol knew that there was a distinct possibility of being injured on a mine. The task was not, therefore, very popular and they regarded the company commander who had planned it as foolish.

"Nevertheless, as Royal Marines they were sufficiently well-motivated to carry out the order, and so with some trepidation we crept out into the minefield and set up the ambush. We succeeded in shooting an intruder. At daybreak we carried his body to a jeep summoned for the purpose—which promptly lost a wheel blown up on an anti-personnel mine. After that, ambushes in the minefield were no more."

## MIKE TYSON, heavyweight boxing contender:

"I was a hyperactive kid, living in a rough neighborhood in Brooklyn. To try to stay out of trouble, I kept a pigeon coop on the roof of the apartments where I lived. But there was always somebody looking to pick a fight, to push people around, always family problems, yours or theirs.

"At 11 I was a truant and at 13 I was sent to a school for delinquent boys. There I was befriended by a guard, an ex-boxer who taught me how to fight. More important, he introduced me to Cus D'Amato, the trainer who had developed Floyd Patterson and Jose Torres as champions.

"Cus became my legal guardian and laid the groundwork for my career as a fighter. He was great for me because he didn't believe in bringing along a young guy too fast, ruining him or getting him hurt by throwing him in against far superior fighters. It had been his life-long goal, his crusade, to clean up boxing. I had won my first eleven matches when Cus died in November of 1985. I dedicated No. 12 to his memory. Cus D'Amato taught me more than just how to box. He taught me about life, and that even in the saddest times life goes on."

**DICK VERMEIL, former coach, Philadelphia Eagles:**

"I was doing the color commentary on the game for CBS the day George Allen was inducted into the Redskins' Hall of Fame. It was a personal thrill for me to watch him be introduced. Not many people in that stadium can even come close to realizing or understanding the magnitude of a day like that for a coach such as George. What he gave of himself was so much more than anyone else would be willing to give, and places him in a very select group. That's why the Hall of Fame honor was so fitting.

"It pleases me to know that I was a very small part of that career. What George didn't know is how much of a contribution he made to mine."

**ADMIRAL JAMES D. WATKINS, former chief of naval operations, Secretary of Energy:**

"This is a story about one of our aircraft carriers, USS *Independence*, and her very special deployment of 1983–84. This particular cruise epitomizes your navy—and the special motivation which takes men from all across this great nation and molds them into a crew. While the cruise of USS *Independence* was not unique from the aspect of time from home and family, it *was* unique in the number of significant front-page events which occurred.

"USS *Independence* left home port in Norfolk, Virginia, in October 1983, bound for the Eastern Mediterranean on what was supposed to be a rather routine deployment. Like any newly assembled team, she needed a while to perfect the mechanics of the 'crew concept.'

"As it turned out, there was very little time to put the team into top-notch working order before being called into action—and action it certainly was. Only a few days out of her home port, acting on the request of Eastern Caribbean nations to move naval forces to the vicinity of Grenada, we (in Washington) transmitted a 'turn starboard' signal to 'Indy.' That was her only advance warning of what turned out to be one of the greatest team efforts I have seen in years.

"What happened next is now history. The Grenada operation removed a Marxist government which had only days before taken over the island nation after a bloody coup. The Indy's crew and air wing magnificently performed the first sustained combat sorties executed by an aircraft carrier since the Vietnam conflict. As an aside, perhaps the *best* example of this special crew and its motivation and spirit was the enormous lines formed by the crew members to donate blood for those, both military and civilian, who had been injured during the fighting.

"Eight days after leaving Grenada, Indy sailed into the Eastern Mediterranean—and the Lebanon crises. Upon arrival, the combat-proven crew assumed the support mission for Lebanon. This mission was complicated by the terrorist bombing and resultant tragic loss of 241 brave marines and sailors only a few weeks earlier.

"During the days ahead, which stretched to weeks and then months, Indy flew reconnaissance flights over Beirut. Once again, Indy was called upon when those reconnaissance flights were fired upon by Syrian-backed forces. Firing upon our aircraft was clearly an intolerable situation; action to silence those offensive forces had to be taken. Again, the ship's performance was flawless.

"Twice during one deployment, USS *Independence* faced combat; twice her crew and airwing proved themselves. Yet this is not the end of Indy's story, for several weeks later she left the Eastern Mediterranean not for home, but for the frigid waters of the Norwegian Sea. After tropic and subtropic operations, Indy went north to a Norwegian midwinter to participate in a large NATO exercise.

"Finally, after 176 days away from home port, 158 of which were spent continuously at sea, *Independence* came home to Norfolk in April 1984. As Indy was entering the harbor approaches, I arrived aboard that wonderful ship to talk to the crew. I will never forget the reception I received, for after all that time away from home, Indy still was ready and willing to go the additional mile. When I touched down on that flight deck, that great crew was lined up, in perfect, sharp dress uniforms, looking every bit the professionals they were . . . and they were *cheering*. Even after 176 days, they would have gone out and done it all over, right then, if asked by this nation.

"I have no simple answer for what turns a group of men into a spirited and motivated crew. One thing is certain—the crew I met aboard Indy last year was truly the epitome of a team, led by a coach we call 'captain' who is a lot like George Allen."


**MAX WINTER, former president, Minnesota Vikings:**

"Some thirty-eight years ago a friend of mine met me on the street and asked me to join him in a venture to purchase a defunct basketball franchise held by Detroit, which later was to become the NBA. The asking price was $15,000. We received the franchise along with twelve dirty jerseys, plus the first draft choice.

"Because of the 10,000-plus lakes in Minnesota, the team was named the Minnesota Lakers. With our first draft choice we selected George Mikan, who, with such other fine players as Jim Pollard of Stanford, catapulted us to six titles in seven years and the most valuable franchise in basketball.

"At that time I met Bert Bell, then commissioner of the National Football League. I asked for a franchise in the NFL and he insisted that I could do justice to only one team. My choice was football, so I went to my basketball partners and two years later they sold the team and moved it to Los Angeles, where the franchise became more successful and more renowned.

"My motivation was not wealth, but an interest in getting involved in sports, with its appeal to the eternal child in each of us. For my share of that original $15,000 investment, I became a major stockholder and president of the Vikings, a team that reached the Super Bowl four times."


**DAVID WOLPER, film producer:**

"Motivation and goal setting I consider to be a secret of my success. I've always set a goal at a distance: sometimes months, sometimes years, and sometimes five years. Setting and reaching those goals is where motivation comes into play. The desire to reach the goal that I set for myself and accomplishing it is one of the great moments of a person's life."

**JOHN WOODEN, retired UCLA basketball coach:**

"Although I believe that either consciously or subconsciously there is a motive for everything we do, the importance of it at that particular time will determine the amount we are motivated to succeed.

"However, emotions must be kept under control or activity without achievment will result. Wanting something too much can be almost as detrimental to the accomplishment as wanting it too little. Consistency of near-peak performance is desirable, but for every peak there is a valley, so do not get too high.

"We are all different to some degree. While the fear of failure may motivate improved effort in some, it may cause inaction in others. Just as the use of the whip may cause some horses to run faster, others may sulk or balk. As a coach I would think I had failed in my preparation if my team needed artificial motivation at game time to get them to put forth their best effort. If they are taught to realize that failure to prepare is preparing to fail, they will be motivated.

"Self-motivation to do your best is all that really matters."

# 5

# No Detail Is
# too Small

▲

*What are we doing that is getting us closer to our
objective—WINNING!*

THIS chapter is for anyone who ever wanted to be his or her own
boss, for those who have that job and plan to keep it, and for
those with ambition to get ahead, to run an office or a company or
coach a team. And for those big enough not to stand in that person's
way.

In 1965, as a young assistant coach with the Chicago Bears, I
wrote George Halas a twenty-page letter, typed and bound in a folder.
Halas was the owner, coach and founder of the Bears, a legend well
before then, the man who practically blew up the first football to
launch the professional game. My letter described what I thought we
needed to do to improve, and how I felt about our relationships—
mine, his, the team's.

I refer to that letter, these twenty years later, not to pat myself
on the back but to show how powerfully motivated the innocent or
committed can be. I mailed the letter while Halas was on vacation
in Arizona. I took the precaution of having it typed on a confidential
basis, by an agency outside our office. The excerpts I quote now are
exactly as I wrote them at the time:

February 15, 1965

Mr. George S. Halas
Arizona Biltmore
Phoenix, Arizona

Dear Coach:

The meeting which you held on February 12, concerning the subject "How To Keep From Going Out of Style," impressed me deeply. First, allow me to compliment you on the concept, content and thorough presentation of the meeting. Secondly, the entire subject matter so intrigued me that I felt compelled to review all of my notes compiled over the last several years and formulate them into writing. It is with the utmost respect and with deep humility that I write this letter, cognizant of the contribution you have made to professional football.

As Alfred P. Sloan, chairman of General Motors, stated to one of his vice presidents, "When a boss and his assistant *agree* on everything, the assistant is not needed." As your defensive assistant, I feel that I can best contribute to you and to the Bears by constructively bringing out those points wherein I feel improvement can be made in our organization and function. Were I to agree with every policy, statement, proposition or strategies of yours, I would simply be a "yes" man and have little, if any, usefulness to you and to the team. To better organize my thoughts and to express the overall purpose of my letter, I have developed the points here in a sequence which I term "Program for Growth."

To grow in the future, an analysis of the present must be made; therefore, the first of my suggestions will outline those things which I feel are incorrect or need improvement in the *present* management of the team. Next, I will develop a series of suggestions for those programs which I feel should be developed for the best *future* prospects of the team. Finally, for my own personal growth and future, I will present those points with which I, frankly, am concerned, together with proposed solutions of my *personal* problems. Please keep in mind that, throughout this letter, everything I am presenting is done so for the good of the club and to improve my own relationship with the club and nothing is intended to offend anyone on a personal basis.

*Present Situation Analysis*

Outlined below are those areas which I think present critical and imperative problems to the Club as a whole. These problems require immediate attention, clear and positive decision.

A. *Morale*

1. Players

Team morale was recently at a low ebb. The untimely deaths of Farrington and Gallimore (two players killed in a car accident) combined with the severe injuries incurred during the season and the resulting losing season of the team have caused player morale to sink. Players have made remarks to the effect of "What difference does it make? What kind of extra bonus, gift, etc., did we get for being champions? They can't treat us any worse for being losers."

Action required—expression of confidence in team and players and extra incentive spelled out as suggested below.

2. Coaches

As after any losing season, coach morale is low. With family and future at stake, every coach is naturally concerned about his status for the forthcoming season.

Action required—expression of confidence in present staff; announcement of salary raises, where deserved; announcement of incentive for next year and coaches' retirement plan. (see below)

3. Office Force

Lack of adequate office space and facilities, even including poor washroom equipment, have caused office staff morale to bottom out. More space is required to properly house people to get their jobs done; better rest room facilities are required for sanitation purposes and more conference rooms are necessary to work with meetings, players and prospects.

Action required—new and expanded quarters.

B. *Organization of Administrative & Coaching Staff*

Like Topsy, the Bears just grew. With no offense intended toward present management, the growth of the NFL has been so rapid with expansion preceding financial rewards for the club, there has been little opportunity to organize the Bears' administrative and coaching staff on a conventional basis. Problems of the seasons, together with the burden of growth, have forced a "make-do" organization upon us. For example, many clubs use a line and staff organization for coaching staffs whereby all assistant coaches report through channels to the Head Coach and responsibility for lower echelon coaches belongs to the Head Offensive Coach and Head Defensive Coach, respectively.

Action required—

1. Responsibilities of each unit coach should be more clearly and concisely defined, together with a strictly-adhered-to policy of reporting to immediate supervisors.

2. Expansion of administrative staff to include a full-time public relations director so as to be on a comparable basis with other clubs in the league and to compete with (a potential) AFL club coming into Chicago.

3. Expansion of coaching staff to include an assistant to me to concentrate on annual draft and player recruitment.

C. *Coaches Retirement Plan*

Three NFL clubs have printed Coach Retirement Plans which have been in effect for years. At the recent NCAA meeting, two additional clubs made announcement of Coach Retirement Plans. This brings the total to five. The Bears have no such plan. To boost morale and to compete on a par with other teams in the NFL and the AFL, such a plan is immediate and imperative.

Action required—finalize a retirement plan for coaches at once and announce same.

D. *Training Camp*

Several problems present themselves in the Bears' training camp which, for player and coach morale, better team performance and overall efficiency, should be corrected. These problems are:

1. Player contracts—A constant source of irritation are those players who for one reason or another have not signed before camp. Missed practices, inattention at meetings and grumbling make for inefficient coaching.

2. Excessive confinement—Resentment to training camp and to management has been incurred because of too rigid a control over private lives of coaches and players.

3. Too many meetings—Coaches and players have expressed dissatisfaction with excessive meetings. No one objects to nec-

essary team or unit meetings, but those that could be combined or eliminated would improve overall performance.

Action required—

1. Institute a policy whereby *no* player is allowed to attend training camp unsigned. Should a player be unsigned for as much as three training days, he automatically plays his contract option.

2. Schedule definite off-time for players and coaches to visit families at least one weekend and every other week. Cancel last week of training at DeKalb to allow coaches to do advance planning and players to arrange housing.

   To my knowledge, we are the *only* team that works right up to the final day before opening training camp. Many times we are even in the office the Saturday afternoon when camp opens the following Monday. This is due to poor organization and much wasted time over the winter months.

   We need a stated policy that all coaches will have at least *one* week vacation prior to the opening of rookie training camp.

3. Eliminate 20 percent of all meetings scheduled last year and shorten the balance. Establish maximum time limit of one hour for any meeting.

E. *Incentive Program*

Upon winning NFL division title, the New York Giants awarded players and coaches a week's vacation in San Juan. This action expressed real appreciation of management. Similar awards have been given by other championship winners, among whom are Green Bay, Cleveland and Baltimore. Such awards have been *above share* of proceeds of championship game.

Action required—advise players and coaches that Bears will award one-week, all-expense vacation for all players and coaches and their wives to Mexico in January if Bears win championship. Approximate cost: $700 per couple.

F. *Film Analysis*

More productive use of game films could be had were more detailed analysis available. Excerpts of films could be combined to provide excellent training material.

Action required—one man should be added to the staff of Mr. Driscoll to spend full time on excerpting and analyzing game films. Additional budget should be provided for equipment, including projectors, splicers and darkroom.

The above problem areas are considered by me to be of a critical nature, and, for the good of the club, decisions on these questions should be of prime priority. Solutions suggested are not yet purported to be the only correct ones, but are given in good spirit to assist management in arriving at fair and equitable solutions to the problems at hand.

Competition in the NFL has become so intense, and the onward march of the AFL forces me to project my thoughts forward and sketch those actions which I feel should be undertaken during the course of the next two years if we are to remain a contender and are to continue playing to sellout crowds. While several of the actions proposed require considerable expenditures, others are programmed to economize and thereby afford all.

Here are listed those projects which I personally feel should be considered, approved and scheduled for incorporation into action as soon as possible to assure the continued growth of team, coaches and management:

A. *Profit-Sharing Plan*

In business today one of the most rewarding incentives to corporations and to executives alike is the adoption of a profit-sharing plan. The company benefits to the greatest extent, since the greatest share of extra profits remain in the company. Paul Calvin, Jr., chairman of Motorola, attributes much of the recent growth of their company to the success of their profit-sharing plan. It is suggested that the Bears establish a program whereby 10 percent of the club's pre-tax profits are divided among coaches and administrative personnel based on a formula to be determined, where service to the club and salary levels are considered. Such a plan would provide the following benefits for the club:

1. Reduce administrative expenses including paper, pencils, long distance phone calls, local calls and unnecessary overtime.

2. Reduce team expenses including travel, supplies, equipment, uniforms, where waste always exists.

3. Develop a more loyal bond between coaches, administrative staff and the club, since every penny saved would affect each

individual and every person would feel that he could not tolerate waste and extravagance in others, since such would affect his personal income.

Such a program would help all individuals in the club since it would offer them:

   a. Part ownership in a growing, healthy enterprise with all the attendant benefits of pride of ownership.

   b. A real sense of management responsibility and with it the feeling of being more than just a "hired hand."

   c. A sense of security that a monthly check alone cannot afford. Such a program would provide Bears employees with the opportunity to realize a portion of the "Great American Dream."

### B. *Combined Scouting Pool*

Scouting today is an expensive proposition. No longer can an NFL club find real football talent in obscure small colleges with which other clubs are unfamiliar. Our draft record in drafting players will stand up to any club in America as far as results are concerned. Under today's conditions, with both leagues beating the bushes to interest talent, we stand to lose a great deal if we do not either expand our scouting forces tremendously or form a scouting combine with several other clubs. I feel the very existence of the Bears as a major football club 10 years from now will depend on how effectively and how efficiently we pool and organize our scouting forces *now*.

### C. *Player Grievance Committee*

General MacArthur once wrote, "A good soldier always gripes." Like soldiers, good football players grumble and moan, sometimes justifiably but more often as a relief against the pressures of competitive sport. Today, there is no channel of communication whereby a player with a real or even an imaginary grievance can express himself, be heard and obtain action. I believe it is crucial to team spirit, morale of players and coaches to institute some device by which players can express their dissatisfaction and receive a decision. I suggest that there be formed a Player Grievances Committee composed of George Halas, Jr., Luke Johnsos and myself. This committee would have to be authorized and empowered to act for the club, and decisions made by it would bind the club. The

*107*

committee would meet every two weeks from the start of training camp until the end of the season, and any player could appear and express his grievance. It would be understood that anything proposed or discussed at such meetings would in *no way* cast any reflection upon the player. Such a program would greatly improve player morale and should be authorized and announced as quickly as possible.

## D. *Strategic Experimental Lab*

Over the 40-year history of the NFL, the Bears have been the greatest single contributor to the game in new and exciting formations and innovations: the "T" formation, use of movies and others. Today our strategy is static, and we are so busy defending against the talent and offenses of the other clubs that little consideration has been given to the development of any basic new strategy. All of our coaches have ideas for new and different offenses yet untried. I propose we contract with one or more colleges or semi-pro clubs, whereby we provide new plays for both offense and defense in exchange for exclusive professional use of game films. Upon trial and refinement, such new plays could then be sprung in professional games, still containing the element of surprise but with the confidence of having pre-tested their effectiveness.

## E. *Development of Separate Special Teams*

Competition in the NFL today is so balanced that special teams often determine victory or defeat. Last season's performance of our opponents' special teams confirm this fact. In my opinion, the Bears should make every effort to further develop our special team, utilizing special talent and special plays, and encouraging in the special team members a sense of pride and accomplishment. Consider what Paul Dietzel did at LSU with his "Chinese Bandits" —a special team made up of scrubs but with an "Esprit de Corps" that won ball games. Our special team should be comprised of men who do not play on either offense or defense but who continually practice and develop plays for:

1. Kickoff returns

2. Punt returns

3. Kickoffs

4. Punt coverage

Such a team should have its *own captain* and its members should be welded by constantly working together into a machine-like unit.

## F. *Numbers Defense*

I have mentioned this several times, but never have had a chance to sit down with you. This is a system of defensive stunts worked interchangeably between two units. . .

## G. *Expanded Taxi Squad*

More use could be made of the current taxi squad by expanding it to approximately 15 members . . . my idea here is to have a special coach assigned to this squad and instruct them religiously in the offense and defense of the next week's opponents, having them run that opponent's plays on Thursday and Friday of each week. Here again, latent talent might be uncovered, but more important . . . we would be much better prepared to win.

## H. *Physical Fitness Program*

In my contract is a statement that I am to stay in "good physical condition." Since I have been with the Bears I have joined a health club during the off season to achieve that objective. It costs me eight dollars per workout, and I would like to work out three times per week but, frankly, cannot afford this.

The Bears should make a deal with the Chicago Athletic Club whereby the coaching staff has a physical fitness program especially designed for our needs.

This could be another first for the Bears and improve the efficiency of the coaching staff.

## I. *Free-Agent Camp*

A special tryout camp for free agents will become more important than it has been in the past. We have been successful in locating free agents without accepting a large quantity. We generally don't bring in over four or five per year. Rosy Taylor, Joe Wendroyski and Jim Purnell are the most recent additions.

The "Free-Agent Camp" could be held in conjunction with the arrival of the quarterbacks at Soldiers Field. A period of two to three days would be the maximum amount of time needed . . . Twenty-five players would be the limit. All of our coaches should take part in this three-day camp.

Those who show potential could be farmed out to a nearby team under contract for the following year. Those who indicate immediate ability would be brought to Rensselaer. All of those players could be signed to reasonable contracts and, in most cases, no bonus. I feel sure we could pick up additional talent that would offset any losses to the drafting competition with the AFL.

**J.** *Farm Club*

. . . It is to our advantage to have a farm club or clubs to develop our draft talent in cases where more seasoning is needed.

**K.** *Postseason and Preseason Games*

Coaching staff should be encouraged to coach in such games as the Senior Bowl, Hula Bowl, etc. This would allow us to evaluate talent in these games for future acquisition by trades.

**L.** *Windy City Bowl Game*

. . . Because of its central location, Chicago should have a bowl game of its own. Members of the Bears staff would select the players from among all those *not* drafted. The game could be tied in with Boys Club charity.

**M.** *Bears Clinics*

. . . The Bears, in conjunction with a Chicago business, would hold clinics for youngsters. Bear players living in Chicago and one coach in charge would visit key areas of the city. The public relations image would be greatly increased.

**N.** *Player Employment Advisory Council*

To help sign new talent and to keep contracts in line, an off-season job program is needed. I suggest we form an advisory council of high-ranking, civic-minded business leaders to counsel and advise players on future business careers . . .

**O.** *Practice Headquarters*

There is no doubt we need a new stadium in Chicago. How long this will take, no one knows for sure.

The meeting room and accommodations we have for defensive teams are undesirable. I don't even have a decent blackboard to use. We should form a committee to research . . . the possibility of purchasing some already existing buildings: a school, country club, recreation center. The Bears could have their own training quarters, practice field, meeting rooms, etc., under one roof.

This would save money, moving problems and improve the entire organization.

In professional football there is no such thing as standing still. We must either progress and become better or we will deteriorate. The Bears must go forward, and I feel the above-mentioned progress will help carry us to title after title.

Coach, this is my eighth year with the Chicago Bears . . . I have been proud to represent the organization. (But) do you realize that never once have you sat down and discussed my personal growth pattern with me?

Therefore, I have listed below those items with which I feel unsatisfied, discontented or unsure; not with any idea of applying pressure, but in an effort to relieve my inner frustration and in the hope that solutions can be given me to further my sense of value to the club.

I fully realize that you have given me my big break in being with the Bears, and I shall be forever grateful. However, I believe I have delivered on every assignment you have given me. In addition, I am continually taking on extra projects to try and improve our football program without your asking me.

Among those improvements which I feel responsible for having introduced to the Bears, I am most proud of the following:

1. Coached a defensive team which in three seasons placed first in 21 separate departments and second in nine others. No other professional team in recent years has compiled such a defensive record.

2. Developed 18 entirely new forms and charts for defensive preparation. No other team has analyzed opponents' probable offensive plays to this extent.

3. Developed a system for evaluating scouts and evaluating possible draft choices. This system has been responsible for drafting better players than many clubs with full-time personnel directors, assisted by up to five times as many scouts as we are.

4. Developed a unique training film program for the Bears, using excerpts of actual game films coupled with sequence film of proper

fundamentals. This was adapted from a system used by me in college coaching jobs commencing in 1948.

A laborious and time-consuming task, but worthwhile in my opinion. Even the most highly reputed defensive coach in pro football has not developed so technical and productive a method of training.

Every person has his share of problems, and mine are not exclusive. I love my work with the Bears and want to grow with them. However, there are some personal problems for which I feel I must get answers in order for me to perform efficiently. I have listed them as follows:

1. Potential positions open to me on the Bear staff and where I stand in the long-range future plans.

2. I personally feel the need for more financial incentive and would like to become more firmly entrenched in the club corporation. At age 42, I'm at my peak earning capacity. With three youngsters to be in college at the same time, followed by a fourth, I face an expenditure in eight years of from $3,000 to $9,000 per year ... My total college expenses will run in the neighborhood of $48,000 ...

To accomplish these objectives I feel compelled to request more freedom in regard to taking advantage of outside money-making opportunities, which include:

1. Holding football clinics when invited.

2. Training program for Canadian club (a means of paying vacation expenses).

3. Completing a prior contract (before Bears) to write a technical football book.

4. Accepting (a) request to produce training slides for youngsters from a non-profit organization, which would be of more value to the Bears in public relations than my $500 fee.

5. Other endorsements and opportunities as they present themselves.

3. The need for improvement in personal relationship with you. Realizing that you do not intend to offend and, further, with the pressure of your busy schedule, I nevertheless feel that a concentrated effort should be made to eliminate some of those things with

which I have become utterly frustrated. Among those I feel deeply about are:

1. Lack of accuracy in keeping appointments.

2. Continual delays in meeting with you and Muggs (Halas, Jr.) to solve problems.

3. Procrastination in receiving decisions.

4. Expressed but unrealized promises for income-expansion opportunities in other fields.

5. Seemingly, there is a penalty for doing things that pertain to football that in other organizations are encouraged.

Coach, while I realize that this is a long and detailed letter, I have poured into this every ounce of my being to state all of the items which I feel will be good for the Bears and for me. I hope the contents will be received in the same spirit with which they have been organized and that we can build a better club—together.

Sincerely,
George Allen

cc. George Halas, Jr.
P.S. (Typed by outside confidential secretarial service.)

Of course, it was not so much a letter as a blueprint. Rereading those thoughts after twenty years, I experienced some of the same feelings I had then: impatience, eagerness, the disturbing knowledge that the Bears were going to slip badly if we didn't take quick and sweeping action . . . and not wanting to go down with them.

From his hotel in Phoenix, Halas called to tell me he had received my letter and would discuss it with me later. He never did. But in the next five years, 90 percent of the suggestions I made were adopted by the Bears—and most of the National Football League.

I believe any dissatisfied employees, if they feel they have earned the right to speak out, should put their opinions and arguments in writing. It is important, however, that what you present is not simply a recital of complaints and slights. Solutions ought to be offered for your problems, and those of the company. If you are sincere and honest in what you submit, and your letter is not accepted in that spirit, you are probably in the wrong company. Of course, I would not recommend that you take this step unless you are prepared to accept the consequences and move on if no relief is in sight. Staying in a job that stifles your growth is unfair to you and your bosses. It is what I call an error. And an error becomes a mistake only when you refuse to correct it.

A year after I mailed my "Program for Growth" to George Halas, I was hired as the head coach of the Los Angeles Rams. I did not leave the Bears under the happiest of conditions. I was still under contract to the Bears, and Halas filed a suit that was intended to show I had no legal right to accept an offer from the Rams. He won the suit and then gave me my release. It was never Halas's objective to deny me a chance to become a head coach—although I believe I had become valuable enough that he resented my leaving. He simply had a point to make, partly legal and partly personal.

I admired George Halas, then and now, and feel a debt to him as the first major influence on me as a professional coach. I learned from him. But I also believe I had every right to express those things I felt so strongly. In addition to coaching the defense, I had the duties of the general manager and the personnel director, without the titles or compensation. Each day I took a local train into the city from my home outside of Chicago instead of the express, so I could spend the extra forty-five minutes on the work I always packed into my briefcase.

Now let me tell you about George Halas, who was motivated enough to help establish a small venture that became a colossal industry. He was one of the men who posed with one foot on the running board of a car in a showroom in Canton, Ohio, the day professional football was born. He was the owner, coach and starting end for the Staley Starchmakers, later the Chicago Bears. He moved the team from Decatur after he was *given* the franchise by the man who owned the starchworks.

Halas was of another era, a world of gaslights and high collars and cobblestone streets. "In Chicago," he said, "we used the Logan Square baseball park. With a morning and afternoon practice, a lunch break was necessary. So every day I had a box lunch prepared—a sandwich, a couple of apples and, at noon, a milkman in a horse-drawn rig would stop by and leave bottles of milk. The sandwich was maybe a dime, the apples a nickel, the milk another dime."

Hail to the Redskins  *(Nate Fine Photo)*

This championship poster motivated the Redskins *(Nate Fine Photo)*

Coach Allen awards a TV set to defensive star of week, Joel Lavender *(Nate Fine Photo)*

A fishbowl view of the Redskins in a pregame huddle   (*From the author's collection*)

Let it snow, applauds
Coach Allen   (*Paul Fine
Photo*)

Third down and that much to go   (*From the author's collection*)

A microphone can be motivating, too   (*From the author's collection*)

George Allen in a pensive
mood   (*From the author's
collection*)

A halftime chalk talk   (*Paul Fine Photo*)

Checking defensive charts with captain Chris Hanburger (55) and assistant coach Bill Hickman (*Nate Fine Photo*)

IF IT WERE SIMPLY A MATTER OF COMPARING TALENT, THE WASHINGTON REDSKINS MIGHT NOT EVEN SHOW UP AT BUSCH STADIUM FOR SUNDAY'S 3 PM GAME WITH THE FOOTBALL CARDINALS. IF THE TWO TEAMS WERE JUST GOING TO SLUG IT OUT, HEAD-TO-HEAD, TOE-TO-TOE, THE REDSKINS WOULD BE SENT HOME IN A HEAP, ASKING DIRECTIONS TO THEIR TEPEE.

A blowup of a clipping from a St. Louis paper makes the bulletin board; the Redskins knocked the Cards out of the playoffs (1977)  (*Nate Fine Photo*)

Allen and owners Jack Kent Cooke (left) and Edward Bennett Williams celebrate a win over the Jets and Joe Namath in 1972   (*Nate Fine Photo*)

Greeting fans in a three-piece suit   (*From the author's collection*)

George Allen with son Greg and daughter Jennifer after a March of Dimes
5-and-10-K run   (*From the author's collection*)

Arm wrestling with Miami's Don Shula   (*DCS Enterprises*)

Coach Allen was the principal speaker the night Marcus Allen received the Heisman Trophy; with previous winners Mike Garrett (left) and O.J. Simpson (right)   (*Arthur J. Corr, Photographers*)

Coaching Muhammad Ali   (*From the author's collection*)

As head of the National Fitness Foundation, Allen presents famed UCLA basketball coach John Wooden the "Healthy American" award   (*From the author's collection*)

With friends Tommy Lasorda and Sparky Anderson  (*From the author's collection*)

Watching Ronald Reagan keeping fit   (*The White House*)

Lifting weights with another lefthander, then Vice President George Bush   (*The White House*)

Allen Family portrait: from left, Bruce, Jennifer, Greg, Ettie, Coach, George, Jr. (*From the author's collection*)

Leading locker room cheers after a 31–30 upset of the unbeaten Vikings; responding are Bob Brunet (26), team chaplain Tom Skinner (center), and Edward Bennett Williams (far right) (*Paul Fine Photo*)

The sign says it all (*Paul Fine Photo*)

That was in 1925, and in all the years since then, it isn't likely that any owner or coach ever got more for a quarter, or more from his players, than George Halas.

*Irascible, wily, flinty*: these were the words so often used to describe him. Yet when he died in 1983, at the age of 88, it was possible to see him as a kind of Barry Fitzgerald figure—the benign if flustered priest of so many movies.

Of course, that description would never square with the impressions of people who suffered the famed Halas temper. He could be cheap and cold and puritanical, and he did not mince his thoughts. Once a barber asked him how he wanted his hair trimmed. "Silently," he said.

Chicago writer Mike Royko once argued a different view: "If he is as bad as people say, why hasn't he been elected to public office?"

The truth is that you don't survive all those years, all those seasons, all those games, by being soft. Surface impressions are easy and fleeting. What counts is the long sweep of time and the verdict of those who get up close. In 1968, the New York Football Writers gave Halas a plaque. The inscription said it was for long and meritorious service to pro football. All he had done to deserve it was to give a half-century of blood and sweat and one-track devotion to a game he helped create.

It was fascinating to hear Halas talk about the creation. The date was September 17, 1920. It was fortunate that the cars of that time were equipped with running boards, because Ralph Hay's showroom had only two chairs. "We all found seats," Halas remembered, "and in something like ten minutes we organized the league and elected Jim Thorpe president."

They also announced that each club had paid a membership fee of $100. That was strictly public-relations hype. "We intended," said Halas, "to give our new organization a facade of financial stability. I can assure you that no money changed hands."

His thinking did not change dramatically over the years. He liked it better when apples were a nickel. But under Halas, the Bears were the most personalized of teams, owned and coached by one man, a dual role he held for exactly forty years. He was a jealous custodian of his work, unretiring three times to return to coaching. In the early years he was also the right end, captain, press agent, ticket seller, trainer, groundskeeper, and general factotum.

You have to understand Halas in that light to see how he could be unsympathetic at times to other people's ideas of how hard they were working.

He wrote out all the publicity releases in longhand and trotted them around to the newspapers. As executive pressures increased, he passed on the job to the team's quarterback, compensating him with an extra $25 a week.

If this doesn't exactly give you a sense of the growth of pro football, it ought to tell you what has happened to the newspaper business. "There were seven or eight dailies in Chicago then," Halas said, "so eventually I hired a sportswriter off one of the papers to do the work. The first eight-column streamer the Bears ever got was in the *Tribune* in midseason, 1925. I was overwhelmed at the attention and was effusive in my thanks to Don Maxwell, at that time the sports editor. But Don shut me off with, 'I did it for the paper, not the Bears. Monday morning is a dull day for news. The Bears simply provided us with a change of pace.' "

His forty years as coach of the Bears broke down into four separate ten-year terms: 1920 to '29, 1933 to '42, 1946 to '55, and 1958 to '67. In the spring of 1920, he recruited players off the campuses of the Midwest with a package offer that included a year-around job at the Staley starchworks and a share of the gate receipts from the team's games.

It was a brute of a game they played. In a game against Rock Island, a Staley lineman named George Trafton tackled a halfback named Fred Chicken—not the most athletic name I ever heard—and slammed him into the stands, breaking his leg. The crowd turned ugly, with Trafton attracting several threats. After the game, the Staley trainer slipped a sweatshirt over Trafton's head to conceal his jersey number. Halas watched with admiration as Trafton, arms pumping, ran down the highway in the direction of the city line, a Rock Island mob fading in his wake.

The next time the teams met, Halas shrewdly handed Trafton an envelope containing their share of the gate receipts. "Do me a favor, George," Halas said. "Keep this for me until we get back to the hotel." Figured Halas: "If the Rock Island fans started looking for trouble, Trafton would be running for his life, whereas I would have nothing to run for except the money."

In 1925, pro football took its first giant step toward respectability when Halas signed Red Grange on the day after Grange had played his last college game for Illinois. "He was the product," Halas once wrote, "of an era that idolized its sports champions. And he had the champion's knack of turning in his greatest performances in the clutch."

Grange had been delivered to the Bears by his manager, a wildly colorful promoter named C.C. ("Cash and Carry") Pyle. It was Pyle who arranged a two-month barnstorming tour that exposed Grange and the Bears in twenty games to crowds totaling more than 360,000. Splitting the proceeds with their rookie halfback, the Bears cleared $100,000 from the tour—their first real profit.

It was this kind of era: In Florida, where the land boom was under way, an army of carpenters erected a 30,000-seat wooden stadium in Coral Gables forty-eight hours before Grange and his teammates were to meet a squad of local all-stars. The next day the stadium was torn down.

Halas had shared the coaching duties and the team's ownership with his quarterback, Dutch Sternaman. In 1930, they resolved a difference of opinion by bringing in a new coach, Ralph Jones, who introduced a new wrinkle, the T-formation with a man in motion. But pro football was a trifle too insecure in 1933 to suit Ralph Jones, and he quit on a championship team. (The Bears had defeated Portsmouth in the 1932 title game, held indoors on a field eighty yards long, on a disputed touchdown pass from Bronko Nagurski to Red Grange.)

Between seasons Halas bought out Sternaman, looked around for the best coach he could find, and hired himself. The Bears repeated in 1933, a goofy year featuring blocked punts, trick plays, Nagurski jump passes, and a tackle by Grange that saved them in the first playoff between divisional winners, over the Giants.

Vengeance was New York's in 1934. The Giants handed the Bears their first loss after thirteen consecutive victories in the famous "Tennis Shoe Game." The Giants donned sneakers at half time, roared from behind on a frozen field, and thumped the Bears, 30–13.

That may have been the best of all Halas teams. After one win, an elated Halas, in a rare burst of extravagance, treated his players to a party at a posh Chicago restaurant. Around midnight the manager stopped by Halas's table to ask if everything was satisfactory. Halas assured him it was, then asked, idly, how much of a bill his boys had run up.

"About $800," the manager replied.

Instantly Halas leaped to his feet. "Eight hundred dollars!" he cried. "That's enough. Shut off the drinks. These men are athletes!"

Grange retired at the close of the 1934 season, and Halas noted sadly: "It was the end of an era. Up to 1934, football had been essentially a running game. Thorpe was a runner. So were Grange, Feathers, Nagurski, Nevers, and Hinkle. Now Arnie Herber and Don Hutson were warming up in Green Bay. An exciting new era dominated by great passers and receivers was at hand."

Two changes cleared the way for the passing game. The ball was slimmed down by an inch and a half, from a plump twenty-three inches around the middle. Halas himself had led the move to permit passing from anywhere behind the line of scrimmage, instead of five yards back.

In 1935, another landmark decision helped reestablish the sport's future. Bert Bell proposed a draft of college seniors, with teams selecting in the reverse order of their finish. Halas went along with the plan, as did all the owners, because the draft was a big, bold step toward achieving competitive balance. "It was good for the league," he said. "We voted that way once. I doubt that you could do that today."

Halas had been the first to work twelve months a year at football, the first to practice daily, to scout, to make game movies, to make a deal for a major player (Ed Healey, for $100, from Rock Island). In 1939 he became the first owner to trade a player for a first draft pick. The pick was Pittsburgh's and he used it to acquire the passing quarterback he craved, Sid Luckman, out of Columbia.

With Luckman running the Chicago T, the Bears reached their dynastic peak in 1940, drowning the Washington Redskins 73–0 in that year's championship game. The Redskins trailed by only a touchdown when an end named Charlie Malone, wide open, dropped a pass from Sammy Baugh in the end zone.

Later, Baugh was asked if the score might have been different if that pass had been caught. "Yes," the taciturn Texan said. "It would have been 73 to 6."

The Bears repeated in 1941, the hard way—forcing the Packers into a playoff by defeating the Cardinals on the last day of the season. The date was December 7, 1941. The elated Chicago players trooped into the dressing room to learn the Japanese had bombed Pearl Harbor. With the established players drifting off to war, to be replaced by the very young and the very old, the Bears won eleven games in a row in 1942, only to lose to Washington in the title game. Bronko Nagurski, five years retired, came out of legend to double at fullback and tackle. The Bears finished the season, however, without George Halas, who joined the navy.

Two smart moves by Halas helped the Bears make the postwar adjustment in 1946. First, he reminded the veterans that some would be rusty and none would be cut because of it. Then he waived all rules. No curfews. No bed checks. "You've had to take a lot of orders over the last few years," he said. "You probably have had enough discipline and regimentation to last a lifetime—I know I have. So all rules are off. You're on your own. It's up to you individually to get in shape."

Sid Luckman was the hero as the Bears won it all. He went in for one play on defense against the Rams and intercepted a Bob Waterfield pass. He carried the ball once against the Giants in the title game and ran nineteen yards for the winning touchdown.

That was their fourth championship since Columbia Sid joined the team in 1939. And this one was a little special; it would be their last for seventeen years. Over the next four seasons, the Bears compiled the best record in the NFL, yet finished second in the West each year. The Cleveland Browns had begun their domination of the league. For Halas, the rest of the decade was memorable largely for what he called "the worst player deal of my life." For $50,000 and two draft picks that didn't pan out, he sent a rookie quarterback named Bobby Layne to the New York Bulldogs.

In 1956, Halas stepped aside as coach in favor of an old crony, Paddy Driscoll. In Chicago, it was treated not as a retirement, but as an abdication. Now it was 1958 and time for another Halas comeback. This one would be his last hurrah.

The Bears had responded with instant titles in 1933 and 1946 when Halas returned to the coaching lines. But the game had changed. The era of free substitution had taken hold. Television riches were around the corner.

But by 1963, the Bears had given Halas, at 68, his sixth championship season. We won it with Billy Wade at quarterback and a defense I had designed. We beat the Giants in the title game, 14–10, with the defense setting up both touchdowns on interceptions by Larry Morris and Ed O'Bradovich.

Halas would stay around long enough to coach Gale Sayers and Dick Butkus, but on May 27, 1968, he made his peace with the calendar. Tough-fibered as ever but 73 and hurting, he retired for the fourth—and last—time.

A painful arthritic hip forced him to make that decision, a hip he had injured half a century before while playing right field in a brief career with the New York Yankees. At midseason of 1919 he was sent to the minors, and his job went to an obscure character named Babe Ruth. Halas had fond memories of that year, and of the day he hit two long drives off Walter Johnson.

"Walter Johnson was in his prime," said Halas. "What a fast ball! Nobody ever threw a ball harder. But that day I hit two balls over the fence off him. They were this much foul." He held his hands about a foot apart. "If they had been fair, they would have been home runs."

There was no humor in his farewell statement, but no one could miss the irony. Halas, who had indeed prowled the sidelines like a restless bear, said he could no longer pursue the officials to argue his case. "I suppose," he said on that day in 1968, "I began to realize this in one of our final games last season, when I started rushing after the referee who was pacing off a penalty, and it suddenly dawned on me that I was not gaining on him."

That was a frustrating discovery for a man who, all his life, had never lost ground.

## FIVE REASONS FOR SETTING GOALS!

1. *Saves Time*—Allows me to do first things first. Worst thing, I've always felt, is to waste time. If you waste time, you're wasting your life.

2. *Keeps You Organized*—Helps you to put things in the right perspective. I try to do too many things at once. Always have and always will—it's hard for me to change.

3. *It's Motivating*—Setting realistic goals that can be visualized and

measured is very motivating to me. Keeps me going and prevents stagnation. I constantly need new challenges to motivate myself.

4. *Confidence Builder*—Provides me with a method of knowing where I am going or trying to go. This is also a form of motivation, but different. Everyone needs constant assurance that they are doing a good job.

5. *Importance*—Setting goals allows me to do things that are important to *me*, not someone else. I have a tendency to get too involved in things that are time-consuming and not that urgent or important.

## THE TEAM PLAYER'S BILL OF RIGHTS

I. You have the right to know what is expected of you.

II. You have the right to judge your own behavior.

III. You have the right to offer no reasons or excuses justifying your behavior.

IV. You have the right to change your mind.

V. You have the right to make occasional errors.

VI. You have the right to say "I don't know."

VII. You have the right to be consulted on decisions that affect you.

VIII. You have the right to say "I don't understand."

IX. You have the right to refuse unreasonable demands.

X. You have the right not to feel guilt.

XI. You have a responsibility to be in shape to enjoy the right to the Bill of Rights.

# 6

# The Eight-Day Week

▲

*Talent alone is not enough. I had some of the most
talented players, but they didn't work hard. I like
people who are enthusiastic if it rains; they can find
something positive in a storm.*

DURING Christmas week two years ago, Etty and I were having
dinner with friends, Mel and Lorraine Durslag and Al and Carole
Davis. Mel could not resist telling this story—either on my behalf or
at my expense, I am not sure which.

I was still coaching and operating the Chicago Blitz in the USFL,
and Mel placed a call to our offices expecting to have to go through
two or three people to reach me.

"The phone rang," said Mel, "and I asked if they would please
put me through to Coach George Allen. The switchboard operator
answered, 'You're talking to him.' "

While Davis broke up, Durslag eased into the punch line: "When
I asked George what he was doing answering the phones, he said,
'The more things you can do, the more valuable you are.' "

It is the proud boast of Davis that he has held just about every
position in pro football, from a scout with the Chargers to owner of
the Raiders. But I doubt that he can beat my resume when it comes
to all-around utility.

Still, for all the odd jobs I handled there, I did not exactly come to the USFL as a debutante. When I took over the Rams as head coach in 1966, after they had endured seven consecutive losing seasons, I was in for some surprises. Everyone in the NFL thinks they know the other clubs' problems and organization. The truth is, they do not, no matter how close they may be to that franchise.

I found out that the Rams job was even more difficult than I had anticipated. As a result, I came up with the axiom "The Tougher The Job, The Greater The Reward." It is a simple principle to absorb: Tough job—great reward. Easy job—no reward.

Anyone who achieves much must sacrifice much. Anyone who would accomplish little must sacrifice very little. Achievement of any kind is the result of hard work and good preparation.

## HOW TO MOTIVATE IN MEETINGS

As a head coach, my prime responsibility was to get things done through my assistants, my players and staff. I learned early in my career that, however sound my ideas might be, they became effective only as they were transmitted to my team to achieve the desired action.

I once thought I was communicating to others very well in a brief span of two weeks on a new job as head coach at Whittier College. I wanted an easy game (spelled w-i-n) before we swung into the regular season's schedule. I asked our assistant athletic director, Bob Clift, to schedule an extra game to be played at home, a chance to show off the team and my new system to the home fans and alumni. We booked a team called Sub-Pac, supposedly a service team based on a submarine out at sea. I was so naive that I thought these guys must surface every day to work out, and they would have sea legs. There was no way they could work on their kicking game at sea—ball handling, kicking, absolutely not.

To make a long story short, Sub-Pac defeated us 51–0 and I lost three players for the season, including my captain, Ed Vanderhaven. We had only seven lettermen to start the year.

I didn't do a good job of communicating to my team or the athletic director what I wanted as an opener. I learned a lesson that I remember even today. I tried to accomplish too much with a new team in a short period of time, and I did not obtain enough information on my opponent. I also did not communicate to Bob Clift that I wanted this early-season game to be a team we would defeat. It was really, in my mind, a practice game, where I would play everyone and set a confident tone for the season. As it turned out, Sub-Pac had never seen a submarine and had been practicing since early summer. They were as close to a professional team as you could get in 1951, lining up against tiny, inexperienced Whittier College. Later in the summer they played the L.A. Rams and gave them a stiff battle for one half.

The true purpose of my communication never got through to anyone. From then on, I always tried to ask myself what I really wanted to accomplish, and then checked every detail.

## How I Tried to Communicate

In college at the University of Michigan, I took courses in public speaking, organization and administration, and minored in English. I wrote a master's thesis rather than taking the easier road, which would have been to take six hours of audit. I realized early in my career that the ability to communicate was a vital tool to coaching and teaching. Clark Shaugnessy, who invented the T-formation, was a brilliant coach, but ineffective as a communicator. Communication is more important than knowledge.

George Halas, the father of pro football, did not have Shaugnessy's great knowledge, but he had enough, and he was an excellent communicator and motivator with his own methods.

I analyzed every coach I met, went to clinics and studied the very best. The ones who were successful over a long period of time could communicate: Fritz Crisler, Col. Earl Blaik, Lynn Waldorf, Frank Leahy, Don Faurot, Red Sanders, Lou Little, Carl Snavley, Bennie Oosterbaan, Bernie Bierman, Bud Wilkinson, Sid Gillman, Paul Brown, Woody Hayes, Bo Schembechler, Joe Paterno, Vince Dooley, Paul Bryant, and Eddie Robinson. Each one had his own style; that didn't necessarily mean just words, but his *attitude* and *action* taken.

## What Is the Purpose of the Meeting?

I tried to ask myself this question: what do you really want to accomplish? This is the key question to ask before every meeting, every session you attend. I always tried to find out what the audience expected. What do they want? What do they need?

Before every team meeting I did research on what I wanted to say. It might be an example I could use in which the L.A. Dodgers and Tommy Lasorda did something in the way of motivation that paid off. It could also be an example in which the New York Giants or Jets did *not*, and I used this to illustrate a point. I would mention by name the experiences of such athletes as Wayne Gretzky, Pete Rose, Jack Morris, Larry Bird, Doctor J. (Julius Erving), Joe Montana, Ernie Holmes, Sugar Ray Robinson. This required research to bring out a positive or negative point. I had one administrative assistant who would cut clippings and record anything along these lines and keep a file for me. I asked my secretary to do the same when reading the sports section.

I always tried to say something that stirred their interest and that they could relate to the team or their position.

Jack Pardee, who played and coached in the pros and in late 1986 was named head coach at the University of Houston, was asked how George Allen could get away with having such long meetings. His answer was, "He keeps them interesting. I look forward to each one."

I tried to draw on my years of experience to hold a meeting. I prepared for each one with charts, diagrams, statistics, research, film clips, special guests. I invited stars from other sports, political leaders, and business figures: hockey greats Jean Beliveau and Gordie Howe, Tommy John of the Dodgers, John Wayne, Wilt Chamberlain, Ronald Reagan (before he became president), Washington Mayor Walter Washington, President Nixon. I continued this practice in Washington and Los Angeles, in Chicago and Phoenix. Once, when things were going badly in Phoenix, I asked a former Redskins player, Charlie Harraway, to speak to the team.

What I attempted to do was take their own interests into focus and build on that. We had great meetings because there was real value and leadership for life as well as for football. After the meeting I would ask Billy Kilmer, Joe Theismann, Sonny Jurgensen, Roman Gabriel, Deacon Jones, Mark Moseley, Bill Brundige, George Stark to sum up my remarks. Then I would ask Charlie Taylor or Greg Landry or Stan White or Joe Ehrman if the summation was correct.

This kept everyone alert, and at times the comments were hilarious.

I called players up to the blackboard and asked them to spell certain words, or the names of one of our next opponents' linemen or linebackers—someone we had to block, someone special to contain. I gave them $10 bills if they could spell difficult names. One time Manny Sistrunk won $20 for spelling Cincinnatti and Mississippi. There was a reason for such names.

Does this approach sound schoolboyish, undignified, adolescent? Maybe so. *But it worked*.

Personally, I was keyed up for every meeting. I sometimes had to take Maalox for my stomach. I always walked in at the exact time the meeting was to start. I did not stand there waiting for them; you lose your effectiveness if you are too early for the meeting. Sometimes I videotaped the meeting to check myself out. One time after a loss, I brought Jhoone Rhee, a karate expert with whom I had been studying, and I broke two boards with my hand and five with my feet. The players all roared. I also cut my hand and broke a small bone in it.

## Make the Message Simple and Direct

Try to make every message simple and direct. Don't become involved and complicated. Many times I wrote on the board four rules to whip Dallas. Then I would talk about each rule and have them mark these in their notebooks.

## Be Sincere—Be Yourself

I usually had a warm regard for my players and staff if they deserved it. I never had a player who wasn't a good football player. I never had an assistant coach who wasn't a worker. Your years of experience, tone of voice and body language all have an effect on your ability to communicate. I was always sincere, not an actor. I have been told that Edward Bennett Williams becomes an actor in the courtroom and, of course, an effective one. *Everyone has to be himself*. I'm an emotional coach, so the tone of my voice was controlled by my feelings. Sometimes these expressions and your voice are more important than the message. Billy Graham grades high in this area.

# HOW I STAYED MOTIVATED AFTER THE NFL

First, I discovered that there is more to my life and my family than the National Football League. After I left, I realized that just because you have a franchise in the NFL doesn't mean you're a professional. My son Bruce put together a team and organization with a payroll of $2.1 million, and I know damn well that we could whip some of those so-called professional franchises that have been in business for years—the business of losing. Look at the Houston Oilers, the Atlanta Falcons, the Detroit Lions, the Tampa Bay Buccaneers, some with huge fortunes behind them.

I found out that some of the NFL organizations don't know why they are losing. If you asked a club official, the answer was injuries, bad breaks, players not playing up to potential, officials, scheduling, leadership within the team. I really got a kick out of these answers. Who are you going to blame? If a team like the Saints hasn't had a winning team in its history, in eighteen years, who are you going to blame? You can't blame the players. They change every year. Until 1987, the Giants hadn't had a good football team since 1963, after which Coach Allie Sherman was fired. You might say that Wellington Mara should have been considered for an Oscar for futility in a city where the fans still supported him 100 percent.

After I was fired by the Rams in 1978, after two preseason games, I never again received a firm offer to coach a team in the National Football League. I have been asked why in interviews beyond number, by friends and former players, by strangers on the street. I have usually shrugged off the question. The answer is too complicated to squeeze between hello and goodbye. I did not return to the NFL because I am incapable of being a puppet coach.

In any job I ever accepted, starting with the first one at Morningside College, I knew instinctively that I had to make all decisions that related to what takes place on the field, just as Landry and Shula have done. I say this without conceit: I have always run the show because I know of no other way to make everyone give more of himself than he wants. And this is the essence of good coaching. Of good management. Of good leadership.

I don't want this to come across as sour grapes. But today, in an era when TV revenues guarantee every owner a profit before they tee up the first kickoff, when the name George Allen is mentioned —or someone like me—the first fear is that he will rock the boat. Make people work six or seven days a week. Call them at midnight with a problem. *Allen is hard to get along with because he demands that everyone earn his pay check.*

That reputation does not embarrass me. Everyone connected with the team is a part of winning and losing, not just the coach. When we win, they win; when we lose, they lose. I have always taken the position that any year you did not make the playoffs, the entire organization should be ashamed, including the switchboard operators. Some owners resented the fact that I would not go to a party if my team lost. Nor did I want my players on TV shows for losers.

I was in my Los Angeles office when Pete Retzlaff, the general manager of the Philadelphia Eagles, called and said he was going to trade big Bob Brown. I asked what he wanted. He said Irv Cross, Harold Jackson, and Jake Carrolla. I said I was interested, but I hated to trade Irv Cross because I had no replacement for him. Pete said, "We want him to coach more than to play."

I said I would call him back in ten minutes. When I did, I said, "Here is what I'll do—I'll trade Irv Cross, Harold Jackson (who had been on my cab squad) and Don Chuy for Brown and Jimmy Nettles," a defensive back to replace Cross. We made the deal. I wanted Brown because we had to have someone who could handle Bubba Smith of Baltimore, then the team to beat in our division. Again, this important trade is an example of making fast decisions, knowing what you want, but also what you are willing to give up.

We defeated Baltimore in the opener, on the road, after the Colts had just been to the Super Bowl. Don Shula said later he would have given the Eagles a better deal than mine. The difference was, I acted without hesitation. I later made the deal for Tom Moore, who in 1966 broke the Rams' record for most receptions (60) by a halfback. We broke the club's seven-year losing streak and won eight games that first year. I eventually gave Lombardi the second round pick, a lineman named Arndt and a taxi squad quarterback. None of the players drafted, including the second round pick, ever helped Green Bay very much.

One thing indecision does is bring on fatigue. Always trying to make the right decision is impossible. Do what you believe, do what you want, and work hard to make that decision the correct one.

The more I study people, the more I am convinced that the difference between one man and another—between the successful and the unsuccessful, between the great person and the ordinary is:

1. The energy level
2. Bulldog determination
3. A purpose; a game plan
4. Basing everything on winning and how badly you want to win

With these four qualities you will be successful; without these four, no matter how much ability you possess you will not make it.

## USING HUMOR IN COACHING

Doing research for a book can be rewarding in unexpected ways. If an author really tries to do a complete job, he learns more than the reader. This project sent me rummaging through several stacks of old notebooks I have kept stored in a utility room in the basement of my home. They were stored in and on an old bookcase I made myself when I couldn't afford to buy one. It is made out of unfinished lumber with five shelves and is six feet tall. I must have saved about 100 books, pamphlets, and notebooks in it, all from college.

Among the things I rediscovered about myself was that I rarely throw anything away. I once made up a notebook, 5-by-8 inches and labeled it, "Lessons Learned the Hard Way." What surprised me the most is that I had summarized each year and was very candid about my shortcomings. It was a review of my nine years as a head coach in college: three years at Morningside College in Sioux City, Iowa, and six years at Whittier College in Whittier, California.

This notebook gave me a better understanding of how I was as a young coach starting out, that I realized my mistakes and put them in writing. Both of those jobs were rebuilding assignments. Morningside was playing in the North Central Conference versus all state schools except one, which was a big disadvantage for Morningside. Whittier had only eight lettermen returning and played Fresno State,

San Diego State, San Francisco State, Chico State, and strong service teams, so we were usually outmanned.

I think everyone should keep a personal outline of his or her early career, whether business, teaching, or coaching. It has motivated me to go ahead to do something bigger and better. I didn't think I was that organized.

When I was coaching at Morningside College, we were always trying to compare teams by comparing scores and figures. This was a motivation piece for my team as well as a humorous incident to relax the players. It can be done with any business situation or figures, it doesn't have to be football. In five easy steps, I can prove to you that Morningside College is four touchdowns better than Oklahoma:

1. Iowa State drops a 21–0 decision to the Sooners.
2. Iowa State dumps the Iowa State Teachers 26–8; thus Oklahoma is thirty-nine points the master.
3. South Dakota State dumps Iowa State Teachers (Northern Iowa) 34–13, so you may figure that State is just eighteen points inferior to Oklahoma.
4. Augustana College drops a one-touchdown decision to South Dakota State; thus they are four touchdowns inferior to the Oklahoma Sooners.
5. The payoff has my Morningside team downing Augustana by eight touchdowns. They automatically move to the head of the class with a four-touchdown advantage over Oklahoma.

I'd always end up by saying there are other ways to figure this, I know, but let's just do it the easy way.

Over the years I have been an astute judge of talent, whether it be that of a player or assistant coach or front office employee. I never used a form or a computer or called around the league to find out more information.

## NINE WAYS TO JUDGE TALENT

1. Appearance: look at three films.
   • I want to see them at their worst.

- I want to see them at their very best.
- I want to see an average game performance; this is all I need.

2. Experience
3. Record (going back to high school)
   - winner
   - loser
4. Attitude
   - seriousness
   - study off-field
5. Intelligence (street smarts)
6. Practice habits
   - notebooks
   - bring a film along
7. Personal habits
   - weight
   - smoking, drinking
8. How badly do they want to succeed?
9. Answer to No. 8 (in two questions):
   1) Why do you want to play for the Rams, or Redskins?
   2) If there were a mosquito on my desk, how would you capture it?
      a) Here is the flypaper.
      b) Here is the fly swatter.
      c) Here is an ax.

# RULES FOR MAKING A TRADE

1. Do we need that player to strengthen a certain position?
2. Is he a smart football player? This doesn't have anything to do with his grades in college—is he football smart?
3. Does he have character?
4. Is he a team player? Is there chemistry with the others?
5. Injury record. Does he have a weight problem?
6. Is he a good practice player?
7. Can he counter someone?
8. How much do we have to give up for him: player, choice, salary?

9. If we need him and don't get him, will we have to play against him in our division?

10. How long can he play? One year, two years, three years, longer?

11. Would he like to play for our team?

Here are five coaching behaviors that have had a strong influence on achievement by my teams:

1. The coach and his staff's ability to present information and procedures.

2. Enthusiasm for coaching players and *hard work*.

3. The use of educational materials, teaching devices, and visual aids to make meetings more effective.

4. A businesslike manner on and off the field.

5. Allowing opportunities for members of the team to contribute ideas for practice and the game plan.

The above rules and guidelines have helped me to win at every level:

- Won 194 football games.
- Only pro coach to have two backs each rush for 1000 yards in consecutive seasons.
- Only coach to take four different teams to the playoffs.
- Won while rebuilding two NFL franchises.
- Won at Chicago and Arizona in the USFL. Won Western Conference title and led league both years on defense.
- Only coach in NFL history who has coached more than 10 years and never had a losing season.
- Highest winning percentage of any coach who has coached more than 10 years, 70.6%.

# 7

# The Art of Concentration

▲

*Try not to do too many things at once; know what you*
*want, the No. 1 thing today and tomorrow. Persevere*
*and get it done. Too often we make things more*
*complicated than they are.*

CONCENTRATE on one thing at a time. This is something I
have found to be essential whether in sports or business. Some
teams, some businesses, some people, don't even realize their minds
are wandering. They're always hurrying to do something else, always
thinking about the next thing they have to do.

For example, you are in an important meeting and it is close to
high noon and someone mentions lunch. What difference does it make
if you are late for lunch—or if you miss lunch altogether? Most everyone is eating more calories than he needs anyway. The important
thing is to concentrate on the moment and have a good, productive
meeting.

Another example: I used to get together with my players before
taking a trip for a road game, and someone in the front office would
say, "The buses are waiting." My reaction was, "Let them wait. We
are in an important meeting preparing for the Dallas Cowboys. Let's

only think of having a good meeting." Again, this type of distraction breaks concentration and defeats your chances to succeed.

There are some people who have many things started, most left undone, nothing completed. They are confused and busy because they are always thinking about something else or hurrying to the next project or assignment. They never complete one job before going to the next.

My theory was, let's have a good meeting; let's have a good practice. *Think of nothing else except what we are doing now*. This was always my approach in everything. It is easy to say but difficult to achieve.

## CONCENTRATION IS LIKE A EUPHORIC STATE OF MIND

The seemingly simple act of being fully absorbed in a challenging task is now being compared to the extravagantly euphoric states similar to the "runner's high."

Basketball players, composers, dancers, chess masters, rock climbers, surgeons, and others were asked to describe in detail those times when they had outdone themselves. One of the elements invariably present in these descriptions was full absorption in the activity at hand, an attention that was finely attuned to the shifting demands of the moment.

Along with a full absorption, these people described a set of experiences that, taken together, suggest an altered state of consciousness. These include a distortion in the sense of time, so that events seem to go either very quickly or very slowly; an altered sense of one's bodily sensations or sensory perceptions; and a fine precision in gauging one's responses to a changing challenge.

This state of concentration needs to be distinguished from the strained concentration that is brought to bear when, for example, a person has little interest in the task at hand and must force attention. What is effortless and what is strained have been found to have distinctly different underlying patterns of brain function. Strained concentration involves greater activity of the brain, almost as if the brain were in the wrong gear for the work demanded.

# PICTURE YOURSELF
## (How to Improve Your Thinking)

| The Image: | The Image: |
|---|---|
| Dark, gloomy, disappointed; grief, failure, frustration; | Bright, hopeful, fun; successful, victorious, winning |

Here is something very basic that many people do not realize: We do not think in words or complete sentences. We think only in pictures and images.

I would always remind my players in a team meeting to "picture yourself making a big play." Then, to further illustrate that statement, I'd list every segment of the team, because some have fewer chances to make a big play. I didn't want to omit anyone, not even the kicking game.

I'd say, "It's very important to picture yourself making a great block. Picture yourself making a difficult catch for a first down or touchdown. Picture yourself throwing a touchdown pass." That covered the offense.

"Picture yourself intercepting a pass. Picture yourself intercepting one for a touchdown. Picture yourself recovering a fumble. Picture yourself sacking the quarterback and causing a fumble." That took care of the defense.

For the special teams: "Picture yourself kicking the game-winning field goal. Picture yourself blocking a field goal. Picture yourself making a perfect snap to the holder for a field goal. Picture yourself making a solid tackle on kick-off coverage or punt coverage."

I would do this more often after we lost a game, and I'd do it late in the week, closer to game time for better retention. I would also remind them to think about these mental pictures when they went to bed at night.

Picturing yourself in a given situation applies to every area in life—in business, in the home—not just in football.

Every time I took over a team, in both college and professional football, it was a rebuilding job. As a result, there were times when we were decided underdogs. I'd say, "We face a challenge and have a great opportunity this week." This creates in the player's mind a picture of success and fun, something rewarding and pleasant. I've heard others say, "We face a problem this week." Now, that creates an image of something difficult, confusing, and unpleasant to solve.

Most successful coaches I have known are specialists in creating positive, optimistic pictures in their own minds and in the minds of others. In football and in business, we must use words and phrases that produce big, positive mental images all the time. Lee Iacocca of Chrysler Corporation does this. So does Bob Beck at Prudential and John Carter at The Equitable. Donald Trump is always painting big pictures and delivering them to his people.

The late Ray Kroc employed this technique at McDonald's, and his wife, Joan, is doing it in both business and baseball. Bill Marriott, Jr., learned this from his father and has carried on successfully. Ed DeBartolo, Sr., and his son have been successful examples in the NFL. Jack Kent Cooke used this technique in building his empire in business and sports. Lamar Hunt, as the founding father of the American Football League, did this against great odds, along with Bud Adams, who joined him as the owner of the Houston franchise.

Al Davis, Sonny Werblin, Ralph Wilson, Billy Sullivan—all paint positive pictures. Joe Robbie does it with the Miami Dolphins. Baron Hilton has done the same in sports and with the Hilton chain of hotels.

I used the same approach in my film breakdowns. For example, if we had difficulty defending a screen pass, I would have our film expert, Nate Fine, splice together all our well-defensed screen passes, so the defensive players would see themselves only at their best against all types of screen passes by each offense. I always started the lecture talking about how to defense a screen pass and what our needs were to improve, by position and as a team.

"Picture yourself stopping every screen pass this week for minus yardage," I'd say. We did this at times when we played Dallas, because Tom Landry did the best job of screening against our defense.

I would also have another reel of poorly executed plays by our defense, and would use it after showing the successful film. Sometimes I would not even show this negative reel, because we improved just by showing the positive images and reviewing the basic rules. It shows you can teach by employing *only* positive techniques.

In the left-hand column below are fifteen examples that create small, negative, depressing thoughts. In the right-hand column, the same situation is discussed in a positive way. As you read these, ask yourself: What mind pictures do I see? This is what your employees see, your spouse sees, and your children see.

---

| *Statements that create small, negative mental images* | *Statements that create big, positive mental images* |
|---|---|
| 1. It's no use, we're whipped. They outman us at every position and they know it. | We're not whipped yet. Keep trying. Here's a new angle to confuse them and help us gain an advantage. |
| 2. It's raining and cold. We can't practice today. | Let's make this the best practice of the year. Anyone can have a good practice when the sun is shining. It takes pros to concentrate and have a good practice in the rain. |
| 3. I've tried to sign Jackson, but he doesn't want to sign with us. He doesn't like our franchise. | So far, I've not been able to sign Jackson, but I know he will. I'm going to keep trying until I succeed. |
| 4. The market is saturated. Imagine, 75 percent of the potential has been sold already. Better get out now. | Imagine, 25 percent of the market is still not sold. Count me in. This looks like a great opportunity. |
| 5. Their orders have been small. Cut them off. | Their orders have been small. Let's map out a plan for selling them more of *their* needs. |
| 6. Five more years is too long to spend before I can advance to possibly being a head coach. I've already spent nine years as an assistant. | Five more years is not really a long time. That leaves me at least fifteen years to be a head coach. |
| 7. The Dallas Cowboys have all the advantages. How do you expect "The Over-the-Hill Gang" to beat them? | The Cowboys are strong—there is no denying that. But no one has all the advantages. Let's figure out a way to beat them at their own game. |

| Statements that create small, negative mental images | Statements that create big, positive mental images |
|---|---|
| 8. Nobody will ever want to buy this home. | In its present form, it may not bring the best price, but let's consider painting and some modifications. Then it will sell. |
| 9. I'm too young (old) for the job. | Being young (old) is a distinct advantage in that job. |
| 10. Let's wait for a better time. | The future is now. Let's start action today, not tomorrow or next week. |
| 11. I was in business once and failed. Never again. | I failed in business because it was my own fault. I'm going to try again. |
| 12. We can't raise the money. This is not like the Olympics; this is a hard sell. People can't visualize a need for a United States Fitness Academy. | We *can* raise the money. People *can* visualize a Fitness Academy and there *is* a need. It's unique. Let me prove it. |
| 13. I'm too slow to return punts and kickoffs. Coach Allen wants someone who can go all the way for the touchdown. I'll be cut from the team. | Coach Allen wants someone who will always catch the ball, not drop it, and use good judgment. That's more important to him than speed. If I do that, I will make the team. |
| 14. It won't work. Let me prove it. | It will work. Let me prove it. |
| 15. It's too hot to play football in Arizona in the spring. It's going to be 117 again tomorrow. | There is no question, it's very hot and difficult to practice. Starting tomorrow we will practice at night under the lights, when it is cool. This change in practice organization will give us a big mental lift to win the Western Conference title in the USFL. |

## Concentration and Poise

It is easy to have poise and concentration when all is going well and you are running in front. The great athlete is the one who maintains that poise and concentration when he is staring defeat in the face.

The surest way to lose is to lose your composure, because then you also lose your mental edge. When you think the referee is against you, you will start battling him, not your opponent.

Think about the next play, not the last one. All your worrying and complaining are not going to change what just happened. You can only change what will happen.

If you committed an error in the field, think only about how you will field your next chance cleanly.

If you just made a turnover, think about how you're going to help your team get the ball back.

If you just dropped a pass, think about watching the ball drop into your hands the next time it comes your way, or making a great block to help one of your teammates score a touchdown.

Don't look back. Don't brood. Don't complain. Don't worry or wonder how you got yourself into the alligator swamp. Keep your cool and concentrate only on how you're going to get the heck out of the swamp.

Concentration in many sports may be something as simple as keeping your eye on the ball or doing what you have prepared to do. If you are in total control of yourself, you'll be oblivious of the crowd and the noise around you. Self-control and the proper response can give you the edge needed to win in many situations. What separates the perennial champions from the other athletes is the ability to perform up to their capabilities under stressful conditions. Super efforts are generally not needed—simply play up to your capabilities no matter how disturbing the things around you.

Finally, to lose your temper because of somebody else is to punish yourself for another's shortcomings. You are never out of a game until it's over. No matter what has gone wrong, don't lose your cool; don't lose your edge. If you maintain your composure, anything can happen. But if you lose it, nothing will happen.

Here are a few thoughts from some past and current winners on how to develop and keep your concentration:

**JIM BROWN, NFL hall of fame fullback:**

"The nine years I was in pro ball, I never quit trying to make my mind an encyclopedia of every possible detail—about my teammates, about players on other teams, about the plays we used, and about both our and other teams' collective and individual tendencies. Every play I ran, I had already run a thousand times in my mind. You get a jump on the game when you visualize beforehand not only the regular plays you run, but also the 101 other things that might happen unexpectedly. So when you're in the actual game, whatever happens, you've already seen it in your mind and plotted your countermoves —instantly and instinctively."

**FRANK GIFFORD, NFL halfback/end, sports broadcaster:**

"Most people think football is strictly a muscle game. In the pros, though, every club is loaded with so much power that sheer strength is cancelled out. You've got to outsmart the other team to win, and that takes enormous concentration on details."

**TOMMY HEARNS, professional boxer:**

"When I'm getting ready for a fight, I like to concentrate on what I have to do, and talking about it beforehand won't get the job done."

**REGGIE JACKSON, major league outfielder:**

"Hitting is concentration. Free your mind of everything. Study the flight of the baseball from the pitcher."

**TOM LANDRY, NFL defensive back, coach:**

"Concentration is when you're completely unaware of the crowd, the field, the score. The real secret to success as an athlete is control of yourself and concentration. Those are what make the difference once you get techniques down and training wrapped up. It comes down to the ability to control yourself in stress situations."

**CHRIS EVERT LLOYD, professional tennis player:**

"I won't even call a friend the day of a match—I'm scared of disrupting my concentration. I don't allow any competition with tennis.

When I play, I'm boiling inside. I just try not to show it because it's a lack of composure, and if you give in to your emotions after one loss, you're liable to have three or four in a row. Ninety percent of my game is mental. It's my concentration that has gotten me this far."

**EDWIN MOSES, hurdler, Olympic gold-medalist:**

"My concentration level blocks out everything. Concentration is why some athletes are better than others. You develop that concentration in training. You can't be lackadaisical in training and concentrate in a meet."

**GRAIG NETTLES, major league all-star third baseman:**

"A lot of people ask me if I work on my diving. That's something you can't work on. It has to be instinctive, because the first time you practice it you'll probably fracture your shoulder. When I dive for a ball, very rarely do I feel myself hit the ground, because there are so many things going through my mind. The key to fielding is total concentration."

**JACK NICKLAUS, golf's all-time leading money-winner:**

"Concentration is a fine antidote to anxiety. I have always felt that the sheer intensity Ben Hogan applied to the shot-making specifics was one of his greatest assets. It left no room in his mind for negative thoughts. The busier you can keep yourself with the particulars of shot assessment and execution, the less chance your mind has to dwell on the emotional 'if' and 'but' factors that breed anxiety."

**O.J. SIMPSON, NFL hall of fame halfback:**

"Keep your mind on the game. You can't get mentally lazy. When you do, you get hurt. You have to concentrate."

**DANNY WHITE, quarterback, Dallas Cowboys:**

"The way I look at football is, if you're going to beat me, you've got to beat everything I've got, everything I can do to you. You will have my total, complete concentration."

143

## The Nicklaus Method

The ability of Jack Nicklaus to concentrate on a single task is legendary. In 1969 he carried 215 pounds on a five-foot-eleven-inch frame. In those days he was vying with Arnold Palmer, and the contrast was startling.

"I didn't much look like an athlete," says Nicklaus. "I was too heavy. I didn't dress well and my appearance wasn't good. I was a fat guy who wore little porkpie hats."

That year Nicklaus, a man with a prodigious appetite, went on a diet, lost fifteen pounds in two weeks and then shed another ten pounds. The pudgy, bearlike man melted away, and a svelte Jack Nicklaus emerged. He has not gained weight since.

A few years ago, at age 40 and after playing a mediocre season, Nicklaus tore apart the famous golf swing he had been using for nearly thirty years and created one that better suited his latter-day physical capabilities. And he became a winner on the pro golf circuit again.

Another characteristic that sets him apart is his memory. After a match, Nicklaus can recount each hole in rapid-fire order—the distance of each shot, the club used, the break of each putt. He has the ability to concentrate on a topic and he listens well. He's not afraid of addressing difficult problems; he gets right to the heart of the situation and makes a decision. Nicklaus's concentration is well known to the millions who have seen him on the course via television.

"The ability to concentrate to the fullest on what I'm doing—I don't know where it came from—has helped me in life more than anything else," he says. "Once something is finished, I can switch off and go to something else without thinking about that again, or about what I have to do in the future."

# 8

# If You're Not in Shape, Everything Is too Much Work

▲

*Risks are fun if you're prepared and in shape. You'll come out in whatever way you must—when you are in shape.*

IF you are not in shape, it is too much work, literally, to mail a letter. You will wait until five o'clock, when you would normally leave, to drop off the letter instead of taking that extra step and going down to the box so it will be out at two instead of the next day.

If you are not in shape, your problems, no matter how small, will become major and eventually defeat you. This attitude starts, if not in the crib, close to it. I am frankly worried about America's children and their failure to get a proper daily workout.

I am thinking of the youngster ranging from kindergarten through the sixth grade. It is in this age group where health habits develop, and the United States, for all her reputation as a world leader, is not conditioning her kids as well as, say, Thailand.

A grade schooler can get a better workout in twenty other countries. Surveys show that in youth fitness we trail Poland, the Soviet Union, China, Japan, East Germany, West Germany, Czechoslovakia, Israel, Switzerland, Sweden, Finland, Norway, Bulgaria,

Belgium, Hungary, Yugoslavia, England, Australia, Cuba, and Canada.

How do we define being behind? You are behind when, in many parts of your country, children are getting only one hour of physical education a week. In other countries they get that much or more a day.

You are behind when your schools, for budgetary reasons, do not employ full-time physical education instructors. That one-hour workout a week may be supervised by a math or history teacher who is filling in. This is unheard of in many other countries. The Eastern bloc offers not only school programs, but extensive neighborhood programs with competent instruction.

The upshot is that in physical testing, our children are scoring lower than they should in a health-conscious land. We are one of the few countries that doesn't even have a national fitness academy. The Chinese, the Russians, the Belgians, the Germans, the Swedes, the Israelis have marvelous academies. Physical education instructors attend them for seminars, lectures, and studies, and then return home with advanced teaching ideas, much like doctors attending medical conventions. We have nothing.

In every country except ours, national fitness is state supported. With money raised from the private sector, we have built an academy at Colorado Springs for our Olympic athletes. Private health clubs flourish across the map, and American adults stack up well with the rest of the world. They are running, walking, doing aerobics; they have kept pace. But our children need help.

How good is the physical education program in your child's school? It is possible—even likely—that you have never asked yourself that question before. Some parents tend to take physical education for granted; others simply don't consider it important enough to merit concern. They are vitally concerned about the three Rs—reading, 'riting and 'rithmatic—but they don't realize that the fourth R, regular physical activity, is just as important.

That attitude is reflected in the poor physical condition of much of today's youth. Recent reports indicate that American children and adolescents aren't getting enough vigorous activity to develop a healthy heart and lungs, and fewer young people are able to achieve minimum standards of fitness than in past surveys.

The problem is twofold:

1) Only one child in three participates in a daily program of physical education (at least one school period of vigorous physical activity) as recommended by the President's Council on Physical Fitness and Sports and leading medical authorities; some children have no programs at all.

2) Some schools place little emphasis on activities that develop physical fitness and useful skills.

What about your children? Are they getting the kind of physical education they need? The answer is important to their future; physically fit young people are likely to be physically fit adults.

Regular, vigorous exercise is essential to physical and emotional development, and studies show that children's self-confidence and self-mastery grow as their fitness level rises. Childhood experiences also help shape adult behavior. The boy or girl who develops skills and learns to enjoy physical activity has a head start on good health and happiness throughout life.

Physical education has been called "the other half of education." Most school subjects are designed to train the mind, but physical education helps students develop and learn to use their bodies. Since physical education is the only subject that concerns itself with the complex organism that houses and supports the mind, its importance should be evident.

Basically, physical education in the school has three objectives:

1) To produce physically fit youth.

2) To educate young people concerning the essential nature of physical activity and its relationship to health; physical fitness; and a more dynamic, productive life.

3) To give students the skills, knowledge, and motivation to remain fit.

Not all good physical education programs are alike, but experience has shown that those that fulfill the three objectives described above tend to have certain features in common. These are reflected in the checklist that follows.

## A Performance Checklist

ANSWER YES or NO:

Physical fitness is not a part-time thing. Does your school provide at least one period per day of instruction in vigorous physical activity?

Play alone won't develop physical fitness. Is a part of each physical education period devoted to activities like running, calisthenics, agility drills, and weight training?

Skill in sport is a valuable social and health asset. Does your school program offer instruction in lifetime sports like tennis, swimming, golf, skiing, and jogging?

Most physical problems can be alleviated if discovered early enough. Does the school give a screening test to identify those students who are weak, inflexible, overweight, or lacking in coordination?

All children can improve with help. Are there special physical education programs for students with special problems, such as the retarded, the handicapped, and the underdeveloped?

Testing is important to measure achievement. Are all students tested in physical fitness at least twice a year?

## How to Change the No's to Yes's

First: Make sure you know what your local school code says about physical education, and what is specified in state laws or regulations.
Then:

1) Speak to the physical education instructor in your child's school. You will find him or her very cooperative and willing to answer your questions.
2) If the physical education instructor can't help, speak to the school principal.
3) If significant changes are needed in the school's priorities or scheduling, try to encourage your parent/teacher organization to support a regular physical education program with an adequate emphasis on physical fitness.
4) If your problem is one of policy in the entire school district, take up the issue with your local board of education.

5) If your school is doing all it can at this time, make certain your child gets at least a half hour of vigorous physical activity every day before or after school.

## MODEL YOUTH-FITNESS SUMMER CAMP

One of the things I'm proudest of in my career is that I set a goal to develop a model youth-fitness summer camp. It took me three years to reach the goal, but on July 9, 1986, we did it. President Reagan sent us a telegram and we had an excellent opening day. It was history in the making because it was a first. The General Foods Corporation provided the funding for filming the camp, so we have everything on record. John Cates, executive vice president of the National Fitness Foundation, was camp director. After being around professional football players, it was a unique experience for me to see these kindergarten-to-sixth-grade kids work out.

The National Fitness Foundation and the President's Council on Physical Fitness and Sports have identified youth fitness as their No. 1 priority. The camp consisted of two two-week sessions. Each session accommodated one hundred K-6 campers and fifty Orange County, California, elementary classroom teachers. The main goals of the model youth-fitness summer camp was to improve the fitness of the participants and "teach the teachers" the latest techniques in physical education, so they took what they learned back to their schools and improve the fitness of their students.

When the United States Fitness Academy is built, with support from the National Fitness Foundation, programs like this camp will take place all year round. Students and teachers from across the nation will be able to participate.

The youth fitness summer camp professional teaching staff will consist of nationally recognized experts on all aspects of youth health and fitness. Camp-staff-to-campers ratio will be 1-10. The camp curriculum will emphasize total fitness education, sports skills development and fun-related recreational activities. Campers will receive the best possible fitness education, to include: nutrition, exercise, substance-abuse awareness, stress management, self-esteem, behavior modification, individual/team lifetime sports, personal hygiene, injury care and prevention, and other pertinent health and fitness topics.

Try making a checklist entitled, "Evaluating Children's Play." Parents and teachers can learn tremendously just by preparing and completing the list. I've always believed in checklists but never realized how effective they can be even at the kindergarten through sixth grade age level. They can be a motivating factor for student, teacher, and parent. Try it on your children—it will be effective for you.

# BASIC YOUTH FITNESS PROGRAM

## What Is Physical Fitness?

Being physically fit means more than just being healthy. It means being able to withstand stress and not become exhausted from unexpected, demanding physical exertion. It also means being able to endure a day's activities without getting run-down.

Don't make the mistake of thinking that because you're active you are physically fit. Physical fitness involves strength, endurance, and flexibility. These qualities can only be gained from a wide range of exercises and activities.

Physical fitness also involves your heart and your lungs (cardio-respiratory endurance). All parts of your body benefit from exercise. But being sound of body is more than just a physical state; the benefits include mental alertness and a more energetic approach to life, as well as a sense of accomplishment. It's an investment in being the best you can be.

# HOW DO I PREPARE?

The exercises below are basic activities designed to increase your fitness. I've also included ideas on the best way to exercise and how to eat right to fuel yourself to a healthier body.

## Motivation

Make exercise fun. Exercise to your favorite music. Work out outdoors. Start a fitness club with your friends. Or get mom or dad to join you.

Set goals for yourself; challenge yourself to do a little more every week.

Get a book on fitness or on the human body from the library and read about how your muscles work.

Little things you do every day make a big difference. If you can walk someplace instead of ride, do it. Climb stairs. Try not to spend too much time watching TV.

## Technique

How you do these exercises is as important as whether you do them at all. Start into the program slowly and increase the number of times you do the exercise as you go along. Follow exercise directions carefully so you do them correctly.

Push yourself until you feel your muscles resist, but not until you feel pain. Work hard enough so that you feel it in your muscles, so that you breathe more deeply and work up a sweat. Be sure to do the warm-up and cool-down as well as the exercises. Try to exercise every day, every other day at least.

Wear loose, comfortable clothes that are suited for how hot or how cold it is.

Wait at least a half hour after eating before you exercise.

Do the sitting or lying-down exercises on a firm, soft surface such as grass, carpeting or a mat.

Don't be discouraged if you can't do all the exercises right away. If there's one that wears you out, do what you can and go on to the next.

Also, don't push yourself too hard. Don't try to get fit all at once by doing as many as you can of all the exercises. You could injure yourself, and the benefits will be lost.

## WARM UP

Preparing your body for a workout means you'll get the most out of the exercises, and warming up helps prevent injuries to "startled" muscles.

Begin your exercise routine with brisk walking, arm swings, and shoulder swings. Do several upper-body twists and standing leg lifts. This increases your circulation and loosens your joints and muscles in preparation for stretching.

Warm-up exercises stretch muscles in preparation for the workout and help increase your flexibility, or range of motion. For example, you'll be able to lift your leg higher because the muscles in your hips and legs will have a better range of motion after doing these stretching exercises.

While you stretch, relax (but don't go limp) and breathe slowly and deeply. Breathe out when bending, breathe in when holding the stretch position. Stretch as far as you can. Don't bounce and don't hold your breath.

## Upper Body Rolls

Stand up straight with hands on hips and feet shoulder-width apart. Slowly lean forward and roll your upper body around in a circle. Keep your back and shoulders straight; don't let your hips move. Roll to the left, then to the right. Repeat five times in each direction.

## Leg Stretch

Sit with your feet a comfortable, wide distance apart. Keeping your back straight, slowly lean forward. Put your hands in front of you for balance. Hold for twenty seconds. Then put your legs together and bend forward, reaching for your toes. Remember to keep your back straight and don't bounce. Make sure your knees and toes are pointing toward the ceiling. Hold for twenty seconds.

## Arm Stretch

Stand up straight. Hold your arms above your head, palms toward the ceiling. Push your palms up as if you were trying to touch the ceiling. Push your arms back slowly, but don't bend your waist. Hold for fifteen seconds.

# THE WORKOUT

Now you're ready to do exercises that increase your muscle strength and endurance. This will help you perform activities of speed and coordination more effectively.

## Jumping Jacks

Stand at attention. Position (1) Jump up and land so that feet are shoulder-width apart while swinging arms up to shoulder level (no higher). Position (2) Jump to attention. Position (3) Jump up and land with feet shoulder-width apart and clap hands above your head. Position (4) Jump back to attention.

## Head and Shoulder Curls

Position (1) Lie on your back with hands at your sides and palms on the floor. Position (2) Lift your head and shoulders off the floor and hold for four counts. Keep your back as straight as possible. Repeat five times.

## Crab Walk

Squat on your heels and place your hands behind you on the floor. Raise your body up and walk forward on hands and heels for five steps, then backward for five steps. Add one step each way every week.

## Running in Place

Jog slowly in place for thirty seconds, then run in place for thirty seconds, lifting your knees and pumping your arms vigorously. Remember to keep your feet pointed straight ahead. Don't lean forward. Jog five times, run five times. Gradually increase both the time in jogging and running and the number of times you do the combination.

## Push-ups

Lying face down, place hands on the ground slightly wider than the shoulders, back and legs straight, toes curled toward body on the ground.

Position (1) Boys: extend your arms until your body is straight, balancing on your hands and toes. Position (1) Girls: extend your arms until your body is straight, balancing on your hands and knees. Position (2) Bend your elbows and touch your chest to the floor. Make sure not to bend your back. Repeat five times.

## Coffee Grinder

Support your body (turned sideways) on your right hand and arm and both feet, with arm and legs fully extended and feet slightly apart. "Walk" your feet around in a circle so that you pivot on your right hand and arm. Repeat using the left hand and arm. You may not be able to make complete circles right away, but keep working at it.

## Gorilla Walk

Stand with your feet shoulder-width apart. Bend over and grab your ankles, keeping your legs and back straight. Walk forward five steps.

## One-Foot Balancing

Position (1) Stand at attention. Slowly stretch your left leg backward while bending forward and lifting your arms out to your sides. Keep your head up and lift your leg until your leg and body are parallel to the floor. Point your toes and keep your right leg straight. Position (2) Hold for five seconds. Slowly return to starting position. Repeat, standing on your left leg.

## Cool Down

Just as you have to warm up your muscles and joints, you also have to let them return to rest slowly. A cool-down period means your muscles will be less sore and stiff, too. Repeat the exercises you did for warm-up. Don't rush through them. When you're finished, lie flat for a minute or two until your breathing returns to normal.

# HOW TO WIN THE PHYSICAL FITNESS AWARD

These are the activities you will be required to perform on the National Physical Fitness Test for Adults. Passing the test means you have a very good level of fitness.

## HOW TO WIN THE NATIONAL FITNESS FOUNDATION AWARD

Fitness is only one word. It can mean different things to different people. Fitness for an athlete is not the same concept as fitness for a coach or fitness for an adult. For you, fitness means several things. Flexibility, strength, endurance, cardiovascular efficiency, and agility are all components of fitness.

### Flexibility

The first component to test is *flexibility*. Flexibility is important because it helps to keep the muscles in tone and helps prevent injuries. Many years ago, it was thought that bouncing or ballistic stretching was the most beneficial form of stretching, but research has proven that bouncing does not properly stretch the muscles and can actually cause you injuries.

Safe stretching is slow stretching or static stretching. Any and all body stretches should be held for about thirty seconds to achieve real benefit. And to build further flexibility, deep breathing is extremely important while you stretch. It helps you concentrate, and further relaxes your muscles.

Why are we testing flexibility? All exercises should begin and end with long, slow stretching. It helps warm your muscles up and also helps cool your muscles when you are finished with any activity.

### Endurance

The second component of the test is *endurance*. Endurance activities exercise your heart and lungs. Heart and lung fitness is important as a healthy heart and lungs help deliver oxygen to the cells of the body. Bringing nutrients and oxygen in and taking waste products out helps

155

to retard fatigue and premature aging. Regular, systematic breathing enhances the results you can achieve with your fitness program.

## Strength

The third component is *strength*. Strength is important because it enables your body to function at its most efficient level. Strong muscles help prevent injuries and also maintain your body shape and posture. And a body with strong muscles more efficiently utilizes calories, thus making it more difficult to gain excess weight because healthy muscle cells require nutrition provided from your calories.

# THERE ARE 12 TESTS

If you score in the gold:
> on any 9 of 12 you receive the gold card award.
> on any 7 of 12 you receive the silver card award.
> on any 5 of 12 you receive the bronze card award.

1. Sit and Reach (your feet)
2. Push Ups (50)
3. Pull Ups (8)
4. Sit Ups (60)
5. Standing Long Jump (Equal to your height)
6. Hanging (90 seconds)
7. 12 Inch Step Test (Increase in heart rate is less than ten)
8. Three Mile Walk (38 minutes)
9. One Quarter Mile Swim (9 minutes)
10. Two Mile Run (14 minutes)
11. One Hour Bicycle Ride (20 miles non-stop)
12. Stationary Bike (30 minutes)

Scoring is simple. Have your friend, parents, husband/wife, teacher, or coach lend a helping hand while you take the test.

# EATING RIGHT

Physical fitness requires good nutrition. Your body has to have good fuel to run on or it doesn't run as well. Eat a variety of foods every day from each of the following food groups:

*Grain group:*

Includes bread, cereal, pasta (noodles and spaghetti), baked goods and rice. Eat more whole-grain breads and cereals.

*Fruit and vegetable group:*

Eat a variety of fruits and vegetables each day. Be sure to include adequate amounts of citrus fruits (oranges and grapefruit), melons, berries and tomatoes for vitamin C and dark green and yellow vegetables for vitamin A.

*Milk products group:*

Milk, cheese, yogurt and ice cream contain important nutrients for good health and fitness.

*Protein group:*

Eat a variety of meats, poultry (chicken and turkey), fish, eggs, nuts and dried legumes (beans and peas).

While fats and oils are not included in any of the four food groups, they are a part of most individuals' diets. Your body needs only a small amount of fat. Avoid getting too much by choosing lean meats and limiting your intake of items such as butter, margarine, mayonnaise and fried foods.

Help plan good-for-you meals that you will enjoy. And remember to eat the amount of food that lets you stay at your proper weight.

Also, try to eat a good breakfast. Your body needs it to fire up for the day. Eating something from at least three of the four food groups gets your body off to a good start that will last longer.

# THROUGH A CHILD'S EYES

I came across this essay and fell in love with it. Here is a child's commandments to parents. It should be motivational for every parent.

## A Child's Commandments to Parents

My hands are small; please don't expect perfection whenever I make a bed, draw a picture, or throw a ball. My legs are short; please slow down so that I can keep up with you. My eyes have not seen the world as you have. Please let me explore safely; don't restrict me unnecessarily.

My feelings are tender; please be sensitive to my needs; don't nag me all day long. You wouldn't want to be nagged for your inquisitiveness.

I need your encouragement and praise to grow. Please go easy on the criticism; remember, you can criticize the things I do without criticizing me.

Please don't do things over for me. Somehow that makes me feel that my efforts didn't quite measure up to your expectations. I know it's hard, but please don't try to compare me with my brother or my sister.

# 9

# How to Cope
# with Stress

▲

BASED on my own experience over three decades of coaching, I have found that anyone who is motivated, anyone who is an over-achiever, is going to be stressed. As I said earlier in this book, individuals who are motivated have some disadvantages.

My method of combating stress has been to work out. I prefer running and lifting weights. Next comes swimming and basketball, with walking last. I try to vary these activities with a heavy punching bag that hangs in my combination gymnasium/garage. Believe me, it can be therapeutic to put on gloves and strike a bag and pretend you're airing out your frustrations on someone. Lately, I have taken up biking and entered some thirty-mile bikeathons. I find any form of exercise relaxing, except when I take a spill by having too many bikes around.

Now that I'm not coaching, exercise is more important than ever to me because I have excess energy to burn.

When I have a stressful day, I will come home and run at night. I have to relax before eating and sleeping.

One day I was asked to do a TV show with Roy Firestone, Deacon Jones, Cathy Rigby, Doug DeCinces, and Jerry Reuss. I got to the studio at 8:15 A.M. and left at 4 P.M. The computer broke down. I was supposed to be through by noon and missed two other appointments. Everything went wrong. I even asked one of my appointments to meet me at the studio and he grew tired of waiting and left.

To counter that experience, the next morning I got up at 6 A.M. and went over to the Rolling Hills High School and ran seven miles, did 101 sit-ups and thirty push-ups, and then went back home to lift weights. I felt like a new man.

I am at my best when I work out seven days a week. If you feel tight and bloated, have a workout: go for a long walk; get out in the fresh air.

Here are some pointers everyone should know about stress; I had to learn them the hard way.

# DON'T LET STRESS GET YOU DOWN

Are you tired of your friends or the people you work with? Are you suspicious of people? Do minor problems throw you into a frenzy? If so, watch your "pressure gauge." Too much pressure can spoil your life and your health.

## Definition and Causes

Stress is the reaction of the body to any demand made upon it. Stressors are the situations that cause this response. Any and every situation you encounter may cause stress.

## Stress Recognition

We all have stress, but its intensity and duration vary greatly depending on the events that trigger it and on the way individuals manage their own feelings.

No matter what happens, most people experience hurt, anger, guilt, envy, fear, sadness, joy, and love. Your feelings indicate how you are reacting to your surroundings.

Nothing influences your life as much as the way you feel. So whenever possible, you should try to identify your moods. Take time to notice if you are really happy with yourself.

When stress increases, the body starts preparing for action. Changes occur: the heart beats faster, breathing becomes more rapid, and adrenalin is dumped into the bloodstream. These and other changes are the old "fight or flight" mechanism taking over for your protection. If you were put behind a screen and your body functions were monitored, the observer could not tell whether you were very happy, sad, or scared; your physical reactions would be the same for each situation.

A good basic guide to determining when you need help in managing your stress is to ask yourself, "Do my feelings get in the way of doing my best work or my ability to love and be loved?" If the answer is yes, the extent to which feelings interfere is the extent to which they need to be managed. Let your discomfort with yourself be your guide.

## Stress: Good or Bad?

Your attitude determines whether stress works to your plus or minus side. A situation not stressful to you may be stressful to someone else. This is a result of what you interpret to be threatening to you, and this changes with the situation.

As you dress in the morning, you usually do not think about tying your shoes. In this situation it is obvious that stress is not present. Now place yourself in a burning building, where you must put on and tie your shoes before you can escape. Stress now occurs, and that simple act becomes hard.

## Personal Stress

We know that stress prepares the body for action. What you do next determines if stress is good or bad for you. Think back to the last time you were happy and remember what your actions were. Most likely you became engaged in some activity; when you are happy and feel good, you tend to be active.

Now think back to the last time you were sad or angry and remember what your actions were. The most likely reaction to either feeling is inactivity.

When the body is ready for action, it needs an outlet for the emotion and energy present. Happy people are usually outgoing and active. This activity expends the energy and relieves emotions that have accumulated. But anger or sadness tends to make people withdraw, focusing their energy and emotion inward. This is a little like running a car engine at full throttle with the car in gear and the emergency brake on. Your body is prepared for action, but you do not do anything, and all that energy must be used. Repeated situations involving unused or bottled energy can cause ulcers, burnout, or breakdowns.

## Degrees of Stress

Your attitude and your perception of the situation determine to what degree the situation becomes stressful. Remember, the occurrence that may be handled without any problem most of the time may be extremely stressful when the right conditions prevail. Also, stress seems to be addictive; it builds up. If you normally handle problems as they arise, you may not be stressed. When you allow problems to pile up, however, you may become stressed by normally small occurrences. A broken shoelace is not a calamity unless it occurs when you are running late, or three other annoying incidents have already happened to you.

## Stress and the Family

Some evening you and your family should sit down at the kitchen table and start brainstorming. Make a list of all the stressful events in your lives. Write everything down; what does not seem stressful to you may be stressful to someone else.

Then each member should select three events that were listed; as a family, rank these events in the order of their importance.

Once the order has been established, set aside the minor ones. Then ask yourselves, "How will we know when we have minimized our stress?" While you have the family talking, make a family program chart, listing the three most stressful events. On this chart answer the following questions for each event:

**What will be done to remedy this problem?**

**Who will do it?**

**By what date will our objectives of minimizing stressful events be accomplished?**

Decide how often to have a short family meeting. When you do meet, the first question should be, "Are we keeping pace with our goals?" The purpose of these meetings is to motivate one another to continue the direction.

This type of activity can offer some positive interaction among family members. Most of us wish to learn and talk about ourselves; perhaps at times each of us would like to be the best member of the family or gain approval from our parents. At other times, however, we show angry reactions toward others. Families do not talk or share ideas or problems often enough. Asking others to describe what is causing them personal stress helps reduce that exact tension.

## Stress and Physical Fitness

Mental stress can show on us physically. Think about this: An emotionally uptight person may often appear physically tight and rigid. One who is psychologically vulnerable is likely to present a body that reflects that; that is, the shoulders are slumped and the head is lowered.

People who are unfit have many physical and mental problems. When you are unfit you have aches and pains; various parts of the body may also malfunction. If you are unfit, you avoid exercise because it is too hard. If you do not exercise, you become more unfit and find it even harder to exercise. This is a vicious cycle that helps to add to your stress level. Being unfit probably is an indication that you are inactive and that your feelings are directed inward.

Studies have shown that physical activity reduces stress. Each time you work out, you can reduce stress instead of letting it build up. If you exercise, you use pent-up energy and are more outgoing than if you direct all your energy and emotion inward.

You have not become the person you are overnight. Your beliefs have been developed over a period of time. You have a deep-seated need to preserve the ideas about yourself, and you would probably like to improve your self-image. When you develop a more positive self-image, you will feel more able to handle stressful situations.

Not all stress is negative. If you look back on your life and think of the negative things that have occurred, you will probably discover that most of them turned out to be positive, since you learned from them. People who build themselves up perform better. Positive thoughts are not destructive to your mind and body; negative thoughts promote illness.

Since the body adapts to the level of activity demanded of it, you will have more energy and accomplish more at your job if you exercise.

The key, as in all preventive programs, is early detection and intervention, before stress levels lead to stress-related diseases such as alcoholism and emotional disorders.

## Keep the Faith—Spiritually

The emotional component of health often affects the physical component. Strain, stress, and tension inside and outside the home lead us to seek help from others to maintain our total health.

Spiritual faith creates for us a strength, a hope, and a power that give us the courage to cope with many of the major difficulties that strike at family life. The family with faith is a family with strength.

In times of serious illness and in other periods in our lives when tragedy occurs, our family and faith are important. Faith gives us patience in long illness and suffering, courage to face the unknown, and confidence in our care and treatment.

The home should be a place where we can relax, discover how to get along with one another, learn to care, and find peace from the pressures of life. Within the family everyone should learn about spiritual health; right and wrong; the importance of honesty, self-respect, hard work; and other traditional values. The family should provide support when crises strike and rejoice together when things go well.

The peace and harmony of society rest on the spiritual health of the family. The family is too important to our needs ever to be abandoned, for it is in these intimate family relationships that meanings are found, human values are nourished, and personal worth is affirmed.

Do not deny yourself the spontaneity and joy in life that come from disciplining your body, performing physical activities, and being healthy. Once you take the first step toward fitness, your life will never be the same. The first thing you will notice is a better self-image.

Your health and your total well-being depend much more on what you do or don't do for yourself than on what health professionals can do for you. Of the variables that affect your health, only heredity cannot be controlled by exercise and diet. So if you want to live a happier, healthier life, the choice is yours.

## HOW TO GET TIRED
### (How Not to Be Motivated)

1. *Do things you don't like*. Not everyone can have a job that's inspiring and rewarding, but this type of subsistence is tiring.
2. *Be overweight*. It's like carrying two suitcases around all day.
3. *Don't work out*. Do nothing physical.
4. *Be indoors all day*. Breathe air conditioning.
5. *Eat junk foods*. Adds weight.
6. *Drink alcohol*. Adds weight.
7. *Smoke*. Takes away your cardiovascular fitness.
8. *Don't have any goals*. Short-range goals or long-range goals.

## LAUGHTER

Most coaches don't get an opportunity to laugh that much. Even when you win, you're always getting ready for the next game. I always said you're only allowed twenty-four hours to enjoy the victory.

Laughter to me is a form of motivation because laughter is agreement, it is cooperation, it is fun. It allows people to work better together because it is happiness.

Jealousy is motivating, as are fear and anger when you feel someone is getting ahead of you. If you are a competitor, this becomes motivating.

### Good Medicine for the Mind

A hearty laugh is a form of internal jogging, a mini-workout that produces many of the same mood-elevating and tension-reducing effects of exercise. (Laughing burns about two calories a minute, so don't expect to lose much weight when you chuckle.)

First, when you anticipate a funny situation, your muscles tense. Then, when you laugh, the diaphragm, thorax, and abdomen contract. (If you really crack up, even your arms and legs get a workout.) In addition, your face contorts as laughing activates the muscles in the cheeks, at the sides of the eyes, and around the corners of the mouth.

With a belly laugh, both your heart rate and blood pressure soar and, because you are gasping, the lungs rapidly inhale and exhale air. When you stop laughing, your pulse and blood pressure drop below normal levels and your muscles relax. If you've ever fallen out of a chair laughing, you know just how loose you can get when you laugh. Because of its relaxing effects, laughter can combat certain headaches (so-called tension headaches) that are caused by muscle contractions.

Laughter derives in large part from painful emotions. When you retell an embarrassing story, you are "playing with pain," confronting a distressing moment head on. In effect, you're acknowledging the discrepancy between the you who has it all together and the you who goofs, who is less than perfect—in other words, the you who is human. When we can admit that we are not quite who we pretend to be—and reveal it to others, laughter results, and we are purged of the pain of those most embarrassing moments.

## The Best Medicine

Doctors are increasingly recognizing that laughter can heal physical ailments as well as relieve emotional hurts. The idea that laughter is the best medicine had little currency until Norman Cousins, a writer and former editor of the *Saturday Review*, showed that laughter is indeed hazardous to illness. Cousins was suffering from a degenerative spinal condition that many doctors said gave him a 1-in-500 chance for survival. Believing that his illness stemmed from adrenal exhaustion, an endocrine imbalance that can be brought on by negative emotions (such as tension and suppressed rage), Cousins wondered if the positive emotions—love, faith and laughter—had any therapeutic value.

Bucking medical orthodoxy, Cousins started taking his "medicine": viewing Marx Brothers movies and "Candid Camera" episodes. Soon he was laughing so much he had to be relocated to a hotel room.

Laughter was an anesthetic that helped him sleep. Within a few years, he recovered completely.

Chemically speaking, laughter stimulates the brain to produce catecholamines, the "alertness hormones" that include epinephrine, norepinephrine, and dopamine. While the data is not conclusive, there is some evidence that the catecholamines in turn trigger the release of betaendorphines, the body's natural painkillers ("Runner's high" has been linked to the endorphins). The endorphins may account for that overall good feeling you have when you laugh and also help explain how laughter can deaden the pain of serious illness, such as Cousins's.

In addition, some studies have shown that the increased levels of catecholamines in the blood reduce inflammation, which particularly benefits people with arthritis or other inflammatory diseases. Arthritis has a large emotional component (part of the personality profile of the arthritic is unreleased anger), and laughter helps reduce that tension.

## Humor Rooms, Humor Libraries

The humor–health connection is catching on. A growing number of hospitals have opened humor rooms, where their patients can view funny movies on a large-screen TV or select books from a humor library. A group called Nurses for Laughter uses a variety of techniques to introduce mirth into the somber environment that permeates hospitals. And many therapists are now using humor to treat cancer victims, drug addicts, and other seriously ill patients.

Your fitness agenda should include healthy doses of laughter. Here are some guidelines.

1. **Share your embarrassing moments with others.** This relieves the tension and pain associated with the incident. Basically, you want to develop the ability to detach yourself from a situation, to step back and get a different perspective on it.
2. **Seek out people you can laugh with.** Laughing with others creates a tremendous sense of closeness.
3. **The healthiest laugh is the all-out, sidesplitting, roll-on-the-floor variety.** But if you did that frequently, they'd probably put you away. Laugh parties are a possibility. Invite friends over and swap em-

barrassing moments. In the privacy of your home, you can laugh unreservedly. (Don't serve alcohol. It induces a kind of laughter that is not cathartic.)

4. Open business meetings with laughter. This will reduce tension and promote relaxation. People think more clearly when they are relaxed, so the meetings will move smoothly.

5. If you're having an argument with a spouse or friend, focus on a time you've laughed together. For example, I worked with a couple who agreed to say the words "lawn chair" every time they had a fight. It was a password that conjured up a hilarious episode in which a lawn chair had folded up in the middle of their lovemaking.

6. Avoid telling jokes. Most jokes involve ridicule and inflict pain in order to provoke laughter.

7. Develop the habit of saying "tee-hee" after what's important in your life. For example, "I owe Visa X amount of dollars—tee-hee." This sets up an incongruity between the light and the serious and helps to defuse the anxiety you feel about your problem.

## Developing Your Sense of Humor

1. Adopt an attitude of playfulness. Be willing to be silly and absurd.

2. Be a nonconformist. Develop an independent stance. Think: nothing is sacred. Don't censor yourself to conform to the mores of the group.

3. Appreciate the paradoxes of life. Lust often masquerades as love; altruism may be a front for egotism; humility is a form of pride.

4. Laugh at yourself, not in bitterness but with a spirit of bemused humility. Accept yourself, with all your flaws.

5. Look for incongruities in life's situations.

6. Develop your humor profile. Understand what makes you and others laugh. Start a collection of humor-related material. Then tear it up, because your sense of humor must reside in your head, not in your scrapbook.

# 10

# Over-the-Hill
# Fitness

▲

THE fighter Willie Pep was the authority who spelled out the signs
that tell a great athlete he is no longer at the top of his form.
"First your legs go," said Willie. "Then your reflexes go. Then your
friends go."

Okay, one more boxing reference. Do you remember this scene
from the original "Rocky" movie, when a half-punchy club fighter
begins his roadwork for a bout with the heavyweight champion of the
world? The morning sky is still dark as tar. We see him wheezing as
he drags himself up the steps at the Philadelphia Museum of Art.

But if you believe in dreams, you knew what was going to happen:
by the time the improbable fight drew near he would be soaring,
taking the steps three at a time and throwing his arms in the air at
the top as the music swelled.

Do you remember the last time—any time—that you succeeded
at some physical task and came away with that fly-like-an-eagle feeling?
Great, wasn't it?

Rocky had a goal. He didn't expect to win. He knew he couldn't beat the champion. But he wanted to go the distance, to last the full fifteen rounds and prove he wasn't "just another bum from the neighborhood."

Now let's switch gears and survey another neighborhood. In gathering the material for this chapter, I received a timely letter with an interesting viewpoint from Gene Blechman, the editor of *Senior World Magazine*. Gene wrote, "I believe that life should be lived simply and with enthusiasm and curiosity. I grew up in the Amish country of Eastern Pennsylvania. It has always intrigued me how these people, who adhere to a simple way of life, seem to enjoy nature to the fullest, while their more modern neighbors' lives are filled with frustration and consequential ill health. As for me, I'll take the Amish approach to living—the natural way of life."

The point is, there are slow and diligent and more hurried ways to senior health, and most of them work. Just be sure that you pick one of them. I refer to it as Over-the-Hill fitness in honor of my old troops in Washington, who were contenders when many of them were pushing what some considered the retirement age in the NFL. So when I pull out that phrase, you know it is meant as a compliment, not a put-down.

We just about revived the Over-the-Hill principle when I helped form the Chicago Blitz in 1983, then came back the next year to form the Arizona Wranglers. I enjoyed working with free agents and a few veterans I knew such as Eddie Brown, Karl Lorch, Greg Landy, Stan White, Joe Ehrman, Luther Bradley, Lenny Willis, Gerry Sullivan, Doug Dennison, Frank Corral, and Virgil Livers. These dedicated athletes and their enthusiasm gave me a novel experience. We had two great years together.

I am coaching a somewhat bigger team now as the chairman of the President's Council on Physical Fitness and Sports. Here again I have a unique opportunity to work with fitness leaders all over America as well as the entire world. To achieve something significant for the council is more motivating and difficult than coaching a team.

When we are in our 20s, finishing college or breaking into the job market, we don't see any limits, only an endless horizon. We don't think there will come a time when we won't do things as swiftly or as effortlessly as we do now.

At Morningside College in Sioux City, Iowa, we played four

Dakota schools and the likes of Nebraska University of Omaha, North Iowa, Augustana University, and Bowling Green University.

We bused 500 miles one way to play North Dakota University and then took the bus right back another 500 miles after the game. I taught real courses, among them anatomy, kinesiology, and personal health, and coached the track team. I sold season tickets, planted grass seed on the practice field, provided snow fencing from the highway department to keep students off the field, issued equipment, and taped ankles.

I rode a bicycle to the business office because I couldn't afford a car, worked seven days a week fourteen to sixteen hours a day and thought it was normal, and did all the recruiting and speaking around Northwest Iowa to promote the college. In 1948 I constructed weights for the team by pouring cement into empty Maxwell House Coffee cans. I persuaded local merchants to provide film and to take pictures of the team league games, and I bought my own projector to show them. I ate all my meals in the student cafeteria and visited Sioux City Stockyard to promote jobs for the players. My salary for the above duties was $3,900 per year. I never took a vacation.

The problems we had, including a budget so limited we did not have enough uniforms for everyone in the fall, didn't bother me. I just wanted to prove that I could coach or couldn't. I even tried to include Iowa State University and Drake University on our schedule. Morningside had not won a conference game in the two years prior to my joining the staff. I wouldn't trade my three years there for a million dollars.

## FOOD AND AGING

Aging: We can't escape it. We begin to age the day we're born. Throughout our lives, aging causes continuous changes. But why do some people age more than others? We don't really know. Longevity appears to be more closely related to genetics than to any other factor. Long-lived parents tend to have long-lived children.

Man's search for the "fountain of youth" has included the hope of finding a diet or food that prevents aging. This idea is not unreasonable, since the food we eat provides the raw materials out of which our body cells are made. But so far, no such magic potion has been found. We know of no way to prevent aging through diet.

But we do know that the kind of nourishment we provide our bodies throughout life can trigger or delay the onset of the disease of old age and may help retard the aging process. Nutritional preparation for old age begins in childhood and continues all our lives.

Some characteristics of senility, thought to be due to old age, may instead be caused by nutritional failure. For example, researchers found that poor nutrition was a major underlying cause of abnormal behavior of elderly Medicare patients hospitalized for psychiatric reasons in Philadelphia. Placing these patients on a good diet was an important factor in the success of treatment programs.

Older people need the same kinds and amounts of nutrients—vitamins, minerals, protein—as younger adults, but they need fewer calories. Since they need less food (in order to get fewer calories), older people actually need a higher-quality diet than younger people.

They need to eat a variety of foods from the four food groups: meat, fish, poultry, eggs, legumes; fruits and vegetables; milk and cheese; bread and cereals. And they need to limit empty-calorie foods such as fats and sugar that have few nutrients other than calories.

## Do Older People Have Good Diets?

Surveys show that people over 65, as a group, have poorer diets than younger people:

Their diets are often overloaded with carbohydrates—sugars and starches. Foods such as bread, crackers, doughnuts, breakfast cereals, rolls, and cookies may make up the bulk of their diets because these foods are less expensive, require little preparation, keep without refrigeration, and are easy to chew.

Even though older people need to control their weight, their diets are often lacking in the lower-calorie vegetables and fruits. Underconsumption of these foods results in low dietary levels of vitamins C and A and not enough roughage or bulk to prevent constipation.

Milk and dairy products are often neglected. As a result, older persons may lack calcium and riboflavin (a B vitamin). A longterm lack of calcium is believed to be a contributing cause of the bone disease osteoporosis, which is common among older women.

Low iron intake is also common and is probably the result of reduced consumption of meat, organ meats (like liver), eggs, nuts, fruits, and vegetables. Lack of protein is sometimes a problem, too.

Older people, because they tend to worry about health, are more susceptible to the false claims and misinformation of food faddists and sellers of "health foods." They are prone to trying questionable dietary treatments for disease (like sea water to cure arthritis) and often waste money on unneeded food supplements.

## Why Don't Older People Eat Well?

- Apathy and lack of motivation: It's too much bother to prepare food.
- Singleness and loneliness: "It's no fun eating alone." "I can't get used to cooking for one." "Foods aren't sold in quantities convenient for singles. Fresh foods spoil before I eat them." "I can't stand eating leftovers all the time."
- Physical disabilities that may affect ability to prepare food or to eat it, such as crippling effects of arthritis or stroke, dental problems that make chewing difficult, and digestive problems.
- Poor appetite resulting from lack of exercise, grief, loneliness, or illness.
- Lack of money. The incomes of over one-third of all Americans over the age of 65 is below the poverty level. Rising food prices have made the problem worse for people on fixed incomes.
- Lack of transportation and the inability of individuals to walk to the store and carry purchases home.
- Lack of cooking facilities or know-how. An elderly person may live in a single room with no range or refrigerator, may never have learned how to cook, or may not be able to cope with a special diet.

## How Can Diets of Older People Be Improved?

In rest homes and group care facilities where good food is provided and eating is a social experience, lack of interest in eating is not a problem for most older people. So one of the ways to improve the diets of older people is to provide a well-balanced meal in a social setting.

# WALK, DON'T RUN

Next to swimming, walking is the most popular exercise in the country, with more than 55 million regular participants. It is not only a more common form of exercise than running, it is, in the long haul, more beneficial and less injurious. It burns calories, builds strong bodies, increases circulation, and even reduces the risk of heart attack. Its proponents expect walking to be a regular form of exercise for as many as 80 million people by the end of the decade.

Exercise-walking is not just another fitness fad. As the population ages and as activities such as running and aerobics prove to be injury-laden (of 31 million runners in the U.S., more than 60 percent report related injuries), people are seeking alternatives. And while some are actually turning to faster, harder sports pursuits such as triathlons and ultramarathons, the number of runners is declining at a rate of 3 percent a year. Walking is proving to be a most popular option.

When most people think of exercise-walking, they imagine awkward motions, exaggerated stride, and pumping arms. But there are at least six different walking styles, including strolling at one-to-two miles per hour, which burns about 100 calories per mile but doesn't get the heart rate up; functional walking at two-to-four miles per hour, which is what we do when we walk to the store or to work; and brisk walking at three-to-six miles per hour (also known as aerobic walking), which burns as much as 160 calories per mile and can get your pulse to a high rate for fifteen to sixty minutes at a time.

True exercise-walking involves resistance. This can be achieved in different ways: there's weight-loaded walking, using a day pack or hand, ankle and body weights; hiking, which is perhaps the most pleasurable form of walking and burns from 120 to 170 calories per mile; and climbing—up hills, over mountains and upstairs—which can burn as many as 300 calories per mile.

Walking is a smooth, low-impact exercise that the medical community has lauded for years. Dr. James Rippe, a cardiologist at the University of Massachusetts Center for Health and Fitness, reports, "Jim Fixx's death showed us that running is not a panacea for all ills, nor is it true, as many people once believed, that by completing a marathon you will never have a heart attack. By turning to walking, Americans are getting more sophisticated about how to stay well over the long term."

# OSTEOPOROSIS: THE SILENT DISEASE

Osteoporosis, literally "porous bones," is a crippling, painful affliction that affects one in four women over the age of 60. The condition is characterized by dramatic bone loss throughout the skeletal system. Complications from the disease, particularly fractures of the hip, make osteoporosis the twelveth leading cause of death in America.

Often called the "silent disease," osteoporosis usually goes unnoticed until late adulthood, around the age of 50 to 65, when the damage is irreversible. Symptoms include painful bones, arthritic joints, and a weak, brittle skeleton. In advanced cases, bones become so fragile that they may fracture at the slightest abrupt movement, such as getting out of bed or answering the phone. In addition, the vertebrae may not be able to support the body's weight; with the collapse of several vertebrae, the spine can curve into a "dowager's hump" deformity.

One of the leading factors linked to osteoporosis is prolonged calcium deficiency, most frequently found in women. Our bodies need daily calcium for bone growth and for the regulation of muscle contraction (including heartbeat), blood coagulation, and nerve impulse transmission. When too little calcium is provided by the diet, the body draws calcium reserves from the bones, the body's "calcium bank." Over time the bones become weaker with each calcium withdrawal and eventually become porous. This is osteoporosis.

Unfortunately, osteoporosis is incurable. The good news, however, is that doctors believe we may prevent the onset of the disease by eating a diet rich in calcium and maintaining a daily exercise regimen. A calcium-rich diet and daily exercise are also important for those already afflicted with osteoporosis, as it will help arrest further damage to the skeletal system.

Milk and other dairy foods are the best and most easily absorbed sources of dietary calcium. Two and three-quarter glasses of milk, for example, provide the complete recommended daily dietary allowance of calcium for adults. Other calcium-rich foods include yogurt, cheese, ice cream, and sour cream. Non-dairy foods such as sardines and salmon (with edible bones), dried beans, and leafy green vegetables such as kale and collard greens are also sources of calcium.

Exercise also helps fight the battle of brittle bones. The best types of exercise to help strengthen bones are weight-bearing exercises. Activities such as walking, jogging, bicycling, and skiing all stress the long bones of the body against the pull of gravity, thus strengthening the bone structure.

The time to start the fight against osteoporosis is now. The earlier one starts a calcium-rich eating pattern, the stronger the bones will be in later life.

Osteoporosis is eight times more common in women than in men. There are several reasons for the difference:

- Women are generally smaller than men and have less bone mass.
- Women are much more likely to follow weight-reducing diets than men, restricting their calcium intake along with their calorie intake. Even those women who do not diet are likely to eat less than their male counterparts and therefore consume less calcium.
- Women tend to be less physically active than men and may not participate in bone-strengthening exercises.
- Unlike men, women reach two critical periods in their lives when their calcium requirements rise dramatically: pregnancy and lactation. Being unaware of, and therefore unintentionally neglecting, the body's increased needs during these times can lead to serious calcium deficiencies.
- Women's ability to absorb dietary calcium decreases during menopause, around age 45 to 50, as their need for calcium increases. Men, on the other hand, do not experience calcium absorption decreases until approximately age 60.

Because women are the population group most likely to suffer from osteoporosis, it is important that they know the facts and work to build up calcium reserves throughout their lives.

This does not mean that men can ignore the threats of osteoporosis. Some men do in fact get osteoporosis. They are a minority and are usually somewhat older than their female osteoporotic counterparts. Doctors believe that the same nutritional and exercise factors that influence the risk of osteoporosis in women also influence men, but to a different degree.

# YOUR WORK MAY IMPROVE
# AS YOU GET OLDER

Workers may get better at their jobs as they get older, refuting the notion that job performance declines with age. In an analysis of thirteen studies conducted between 1940 and 1983, it was found that performance increased with age when rated by productivity, and declined with age when rated by supervisors. Workers who take on challenging jobs as they age may improve or maintain performance. The older worker who appears dull may have become so due to years of accumulated boredom. Offering older workers renewed stimulation may help to maintain high levels of productivity.

# LONGEVITY

According to the National Center for Health, the best place to live to a ripe old age is Hawaii, where men reach an average age of 74.1 and women an amazing 80.3. The worst place is Washington, D.C., where the men average only 64.6 years and women 73.7. The national average for men is 70.1; for women, 77.6.

# 11

# Man at Work

▲

*Get in a field you will enjoy. If you don't like your work and find it laborious, you will dread going to the office, or wherever it is. If you hate your job, don't worry; you won't have it long.*

THERE is a story told about three bricklayers that describes, in a classic way, the importance of the attitude one brings to a job.

When asked what he was doing, the first mason replied, "I'm laying brick."

To the same question, the second answered, "I'm making $6.60 an hour."

And the third said, "Me? Why, I'm building the world's greatest cathedral."

We may use our own imaginations to decide what happened to those three bricklayers in the years ahead. Chances are, the first two remained just what they were: fellows taking home a paycheck in a job they did routinely. There was nothing inside to push them forward to greater success.

I can picture the third man becoming a foreman, or a contractor, or an architect. Perhaps he founded his own company. He had to move ahead because of his attitude. What could a man not accomplish who could look at bricks and mortar and see a cathedral?

It has been my experience that people with vision improve themselves and have the capacity to achieve great deeds. Basic to their attitude is one universal truth: they enjoy their work. How you think and feel about your job reveals your potential for larger responsibility.

This connection has been self-evident in football, and you need only look out the window of your home, your office, or your car to see other daily examples.

## SIGN OF THE TIMES

While doing my roadwork away from home, jogging through the streets and neighborhoods of different cities, I have a chance to observe the people whose labors allow the rest of us to function. I refer, of course, to the highway construction crews, the telephone repair people, the landscapers.

I have decided that the standard "Men at Work" sign, posted along with the orange cones and flags on America's roadways, is in need of modification. I suggest these changes:

**"Men Talking"**

**"Men Sitting"**

**"Men Standing"**

**"Men Listening"**

**"Men at Work"**

In short, it is my observation that one fellow is usually out there plugging away while the others are leaning on their shovels, putting in time. The crews I keep seeing need motivation. One man is working.

## LIVING

"Living is a business . . . a big business. Making a living, rearing a family, holding a job, making a contribution to the community, making friends, making enemies, succeeding, failing, stumbling, falling, working, playing, crying, understanding and being understood. To live is doing business . . ."—courtesy Hamilton Printing Company.

## A COMMON BOND

If part of your job involves management, then we have something in common—we are both coaches. I coach in one way, you in another, but we are still essentially coaches. We are out there to win, and not as individuals. We depend on others. We work as a team with those around us, below or above.

In 1971 the Redskins' team slogan was: "If we stick together, we can't lose." That could just as well be the slogan for any office where two or more people interact.

The toughest job I had as a coach, and I imagine the toughest for anyone in management, is to get people to think as a unit.

The most tiresome is to listen to another person's problems. I don't mean boring; I mean it is a physically fatiguing thing to do. But absolutely critical. I wanted my office door open at all times. I wanted to listen to those problems and, mercy, did they pour in.

But if you are unwilling or unable to solve those problems, you are not going to win—not as a coach or as a manager. The problems may seem small to you. But to the person trying to cope with them, they can be cancerous. So I listened and tried to help because I knew that if I let those personal problems linger or fester, one by one I would lose my team. Instead of forty men playing together, I would have five off in their own shells and five more sympathizing with them, and ten wondering what was going on.

To motivate a team, a group, a community, it is necessary to get it to channel its energy in one direction. If you have a team trying to reach several goals at once, you will wind up with confusion. Give them one goal and, when they reach that, give them another, but never more than one at a time. It is easier on them and easier on you.

As a coach, I found out that you can pay a man a lot of money, but that alone will never motivate him (Why should it? He already has the money). He must find a challenge in the job, and be recognized for his contribution to the team. Then he will be motivated.

There is another important part of your job that involves some reverse psychology. You want a team so involved that every individual suffers inside when the team loses; the only relief is to get in there and win. That is a great test for a coach: to make his team dread losing so much that winning is the only answer. Once they have tasted success and, like laboratory mice, have been conditioned to win, they will settle for nothing less.

I learned a long time ago that you can have just about anything you want in life, *if you want it more than someone else does.* Hold that thought for a moment. I don't care what the goal, if you stay after it you will fulfill your wish. The other guy will not be willing to work that hard—few people do. If you are one of those who refuses to give up, you can't lose. This is not a cliche or a pep talk or some sort of social propaganda. This is life.

The best way to assure your success as a coach or manager is through dedication. By that, I mean giving everything you have twenty-four hours a day. No one was ever a success who waited for the hour hand to point to five o'clock.

Do you remember the scene in the movie "Gone With the Wind" when the field hands were laboring at sunset and the big bell began to ring? One of the workers straightened up and shouted, "Quittin' time!" Whereupon Big Sam yelled, "Quittin' time? Who dat say quittin' time? I'se the one around here says, 'Quittin' time.'

"Quittin' time!!"

The funny thing is, if you really enjoy your job you won't worry about how many hours you log. It will be so important a part of your life you will be dissatisfied when you are away from it. And then you can't help but succeed.

Along with a love for your job, it is essential to have a love for your employees. Big word. But big people are not afraid to use it. To inspire people to do the work you want them to do, you have to love them, respect them and be happy for their individual success. When they succeed, so have you.

The coach has to be a spark plug for the entire team. If you are happy, so are they. If you have a cold, the team will sneeze. The coach or manager sets the pace, and can never afford the luxury of giving less than the best inside him.

Coaching offered me everything I wanted—challenge, goals, opportunities, rewards. This is what most of us want. It is that simple —for coaches or managers.

# THE NO-HOLIDAY CALENDAR

I may not recommend this business measure except in the case of a true emergency. But what I encountered when I took over the Washington Redskins in 1971 did meet that criterion.

The first day I walked into the business offices, my eye happened to land on a calendar on which every holiday had been marked off for the entire year. That hit me with the force of a two-by-four. Here was a franchise that had not been in the playoffs in twenty-nine years and had not managed one winning season in fifteen years.

Given that record, it was understandable that what the employees had to look forward to was getting the hell out of there. I decided right on the spot to provide the front office with a new motivation: there would be no more holidays until the Redskins won. The point was made quickly and the sacrifice was short-lived. We won the first season, and every year thereafter.

I know of one other case in which so harsh a method was used, but it was not exactly intentional.

In the early years of the American Football League, the principal owner of the team then known as the New York Titans was Harry Wismer, the sports announcer. A flamboyant fellow, Wismer operated the team on a shoestring; as the team struggled on the field and at the box office, each payday became a mad dash to get to the bank before the checks started to bounce. It was a race the players frequently lost.

When a group headed by Sonny Werblin bought the club, the team's fortunes changed dramatically, and so did a few other things. They renamed the team the Jets and began to operate in a first-class manner, which included the signing of a rookie quarterback from Alabama, Joe Namath.

At Thanksgiving, Werblin hosted a party for the players and their families. As they moved past a lavish buffet table, Werblin turned to one of the players, linebacker Larry Grantham, and said with a smile, "Well, Larry, I don't guess you had any Thanksgiving parties when Wismer had the club."

"Mr. Werblin," said Grantham, quite seriously, "when Wismer owned the club, we didn't have Thanksgiving."

*183*

## DE-MOTIVATION

I used to think that no job could be more difficult or demanding than to be a general manager and head coach in professional football. To me this was the ultimate test of one's ability, dedication, and patience.

Then in the mid-1970s I became involved with the President's Council on Sports and Physical Fitness and, through that agency, formed the new National Fitness Foundation. Coaching is still no walk in the park. But in trying to build a health and fitness program for an entire country, I have found that the goals we set are just as demanding and far more frustrating to achieve.

Day after day, little or no progress can be measured in the campaign to build a United States Fitness Academy. I have always known how crucial motivation is if we are to achieve all of our goals. But now I see it in another light, another challenge. It is called: overcoming *de-motivation*.

In coaching, no matter what the obstacles or the results, I could see progress nearly every day, in or out of season. It was tangible. It was visible. Now, instead of battling the Dallas Cowboys, we—on the President's Council and at the Fitness Foundation—are competing against the toughest defensive units ever devised: the bureaucracy. I would rather play the Cowboys twice a week. They are easier to prepare for, and your chances of winning are higher, than when you go up against a federal agency.

Now I know what Lee Iacocca went through in coping with various groups to accomplish something permanent in restoring the Statue of Liberty. The pity of all this is that the bureaucracy dampens the spirit of those willing to undertake these volunteer missions, attempting to do something for their country beyond the call of duty. It takes someone with guts and determination to make any yardage through the stacked defenses the bureacrats are so able, and too often so eager, to mount.

## NO TIME LIMIT ON QUALITY

In the summer of 1986 I had an occasion to drop a note to Bill Marriott, Jr., the son of the founder of the hotel chain. I could not help but recall an incident I once witnessed involving his father, and I passed it along:

"I had lunch with your dad at the Essex House (in New York) one day and he ordered a large glass of freshly squeezed orange juice for each of us. The waiter apologized, saying they had no fresh orange juice. Theirs was canned or frozen.

"Your dad told him, without raising his voice, to get some oranges and to squeeze them for his guest, Coach Allen. It took about twenty minutes, but the waiter appeared with a large pitcher of freshly squeezed orange juice. He told Mr. Willard Marriott, Sr., that he had to search the kitchen to locate the oranges, and that caused the delay.

"The point is, even at the age of 78, he felt there were no ways too small to improve the service at a Marriott Hotel, and he was out there looking for them."

## THE NEW BOSS

Business experts I know are inclined to credit the Japanese industrial invasion of the 1980s with the changes now taking place in the way Americans think and react to their role in the workplace.

I saved and filed an article from the *Chicago Sun-Times* dated August 14, 1983, that deals with this subject—and with my reaction to it. "The definition of boss is being revised," the story said. "On the way out is the autocratic model, full of rules and a devotion to the bureaucracy. Arriving is a more sensitive variety, interested in people and quality."

I do not mind hiding behind a newspaper clipping to get across a point. In the end, it seems more modest, and, in fact, people are more likely to remember what they have read.

The theme of this story, which was believable in 1983 and is now no longer even arguable, is consistent with the ideas I have already stressed.

Athletics provides strong examples of how good bosses can transfer their own purpose and infuse values into whatever task is at hand—even if that task is physically painful and "only a game."

I was then the coach and chairman of the board of the Chicago Blitz in the United States Football League, and the article identified me as "a confessed perfectionist . . . considered by many to be a boss with few peers. His track record of winning with players who are either over the hill or practically under it is legendary. . . ."

Now you see why I prefer to hide behind the conclusions of this story by Jim Quinlan as opposed to having to say these things about myself. I am not upset by the praise and much prefer it to criticism, with which I also have been familiar. But what matters to me is the approval of the methods I have long advocated and strongly feel will help you attain your goals.

So back to the future, as seen by the *Sun-Times*:

"An admitted workaholic, Allen qualifies as an all-star boss on and off the field because of his approach to the people around him. Let's take a look at George Allen's average workday.

"The Monday after the Blitz's recent disappointing post season loss to the Philadelphia Stars, he put in a 17-hour day in the team's Des Plaines office. During that busy day, Allen took time to meet with his office staff.

"It was during this informal gathering that he displayed some of the interpersonal talents required of the good boss. The meeting was a brief one, but he covered several areas and displayed one personal trait that sets him apart from the average boss. After thanking the staffers for their part in the team's success during the season, Allen asked for their ideas on how to improve the operation. He also told them that, like the team itself, everyone would have to work harder in the future if they were to be successful.

"The primary personal trait Allen displayed was sincerity. He meant what he was saying, and those at that meeting said they knew it. He told them he appreciated the help and loyalty they had provided . . . He was willing to hear suggestions."

In connection with this article, I was asked my definition of a good boss. Let me summarize my answer now in four parts:

1) **Be a serious listener.** If you expect your thoughts to be taken seriously, you must listen carefully in return.

2) **Believe in people enthusiastically.** Unity and family are the traditions that have made the Japanese organizations so strong. Between them there is an almost religious appreciation—by the workers for what the company is doing, and by the company toward the workers.

3) Work hard. I like people who work hard. No matter what their background or level of intelligence, if they are willing to work hard—and I mean purposeful work—then I like them.

4) Enjoy your work. A good boss must teach others how to win. Only those who have not won will accept losing. A letter I treasure came to me from Mike Hull, who played for me in Washington in the early 1970s. Hull wrote, "Your idea of developing your nature, improving yourself to the extent you are capable, kindled within me renewed attention to self-development."

There is nothing new or radical in any of these principles. The Japanese industrial miracle of the past twenty years is based on them, and it is really no miracle at all. Japan is a nation with few natural resources except the work ethic of its people. Japanese leaders recognized this fact, and the nation's workers were treated accordingly.

Just as a good football coach listens to his players, successful Japanese executives turned an ear to the workers. We have seen the results, and we need to duplicate, not envy, them.

# THE COMPARISON TEST

I always used a checklist to help me evaluate players, assistant coaches, and front office personnel. For example, in 1974, when I gave a first draft choice to Miami for the rights to Joe Theismann, I was thinking of the future.

When Joe came to the Redskins, I told him that Billy Kilmer and Sonny Jurgensen had done well and were my quarterbacks. Joe would have to sit on the bench and learn and not expect much playing time, even though he had an advantage over the veterans at that stage of his career: he had the mobility to avoid the rush.

Kilmer and Jurgensen had experience, success, a knowledge of the league, and leadership. They enjoyed the confidence and support of the fans, knew our offensive system, were good under pressure, and were proven winners.

Try this comparison test on yourself, with your spouse or a good friend. List what you consider your six major assets. Ask the other person to honestly evaluate your choices. It is also effective to ask someone you think is superior to you, whether he or she agrees with your choices. Call it Checkpoint No. 1.

For Checkpoint No. 2, you will need examples of common assets, such as:

(1) Attitude, (2) intelligence, (3) health, (4) personality, (5) education, (6) initiative, (7) background, (8) home life, (9) age, (10) experience, (11) technical skills, (12) vocabulary, (13) strength, (14) speed, (15) size, (16) quickness, (17) money, (18) contacts, (19) physical condition, (20) property, (21) relatives, (22) home, (23) friends, (24) competition. (Note: speed, strength, size, quickness and competition apply to athletes.)

Checkpoint #3: Under each asset, write the names of two people you know who have achieved a large amount of success but do not have this asset to as great a degree as you do.

Conclusion: When you have completed this drill, you will find that you outrank many successful people on more than one asset. There is only one conclusion you can reach: you are better than you think. So adjust your self-image to being better. Never sell yourself short.

## MOTTOES FOR MOTIVATION

You will never fail—if you keep the competition at your tail.

### How to Avoid Criticism:

**Do Nothing**

**Say Nothing**

**Be Nothing**

### Formula for a Good Life:

**Work like a dog.**

**Eat like a horse.**

**Think like a fox.**

**Play like a rabbit.**

When I am right, no one remembers. When I am wrong, no one forgets.

## WHAT BUSINESS ARE YOU IN?

Speeches, especially those given at a convention or a seminar, are not known as a form of entertainment. But they can be. When I find myself hearing a good one, filled with clear, crisp, no-nonsense advice, I can feel an excitement building within me that no sitcom on TV can equal.

I once heard Frank Sellinger, the president of the Joseph Schlitz Brewing Company, deliver a speech to a convention of his company's wholesalers at Long Beach, California. What he said impressed me and stayed on my mind. His words reflected the way I feel about football, but they applied to any business, any industry.

It was not merely that he challenged his audience to reconsider what business they were in. He brought it home to them on the most basic level, one on one. They were not out there moving bottles of beer. "I think you sometimes forget the business you're in," he said. "You're in the people business. The selling business. The friendship business."

He urged them to get out and see their accounts. He said the two best times to do so were when business was good and when business was poor.

After forty-three years of turning out the brewer's product, Sellinger still emphasizes the need for the personal touch. He tells of a time when he wandered into a package store in the West and noticed there were no Schlitz sign displays. He identified himself to the owner as a Schlitz employee.

The man asked him what he did.

"Oh, a little of this, a little of that."

"Well, you're the first Schlitz man I've had in here in months."

That remark troubled Sellinger and he asked why there were no Schlitz displays.

"Nobody asked me," the owner replied.

Sellinger had made it a point to find out a little of the owner's background. He said to him, "Don't you have a son who works for a Schlitz wholesaler?"

"Yes," the man said, "but they still have to ask."

The moral of the story was plain: nobody gets a free pass.

At the time of this convention, in 1979, Schlitz was struggling. Sellinger recalled how Anheuser-Busch, its foremost competitor, had fought back from a harmful labor strike in 1976. "The remedy they worked out," he said, "was to have every single wholesaler ride the trucks for nine long months. It was reported that one wholesaler said, 'If I got out with the trucks, my accounts will know something is wrong.'

"Don't you think they knew it already? It worked like magic," Sellinger reported. "Sales went higher than ever." In a subtle reference to his company's problems, he added, "If you're a Schlitz wholesaler, shouldn't you be on the trucks now?"

How effective was the speech? I can only say that for the next few months I thought about buying a beer distributorship.

# 12

# Classroom Motivation

▲

*Take work home. There is nothing wrong with doing homework. To get ahead you have to work hard and plan ahead. Condition yourself for the long run; the tested usually can take it.*

A case can be made, one suspects, that the one resource crucial to providing a quality education is good teachers.

That term, in fact, is almost redundant. The phrase "a bad teacher" is a contradiction in terms.

We sometimes tend to forget that teachers are real people; in fact, they are in every instance former students, products of the very educational system they now serve.

You may not have thought about it—many do not—but good teachers have a kind of toehold on immortality: they are remembered beyond the brief tick-tock of the years. You always remember the one or more who encouraged and pushed and moved you on to the next plateau. Some remain as vivid in your mind as a Norman Rockwell painting. A friend recalls an English teacher who, if your attention wandered, would zap you with an eraser in the chest. Pow, just like that. He said she had a fine arm.

Some teachers always had order in class. They never had to ask. They just had it. And some left lessons with you that were for life.

A teacher once said that history teaches us how new mankind is and how far we have come. History is the study of the mystery of time. She was right. Is right, rather. All good teachers stay forever in the present tense. And when we leave school we always mean to go back and visit the ones we liked and learned from. We seldom do. Fortunately, the good teachers always seem to understand.

## GRADING THE TEACHER

When I was working on my doctorate one summer at the University of Southern California, I made it a point to ask two questions:
1) Who were the best professors on campus, and
2) Which ones had received recognition for their lectures?

It did not matter to me what courses they taught, or even if I understood the material. I wanted simply to evaluate their methods. So I would obtain permission to sit in the last row of the class and observe the teacher in action. There would always be one the students regarded, at least unofficially, as their teacher of the year—similar to being coach of the year. I always signed up for that teacher's classes.

This is just about the opposite of the method Abe Lemons, the basketball coach, claims he uses in picking his future opponents. Abe says that when he speaks at a coaching clinic he always looks around the room to see which ones are taking notes. Those are the fellows he tries to get on his schedule the next year.

I have a list of ten characteristics I find in the best teachers:

1) Start on time.
2) Have an enthusiastic approach.
3) Have a businesslike manner.
4) Have a sense of humor.
5) Use quick, efficient movements.
6) Use charts, visual aids, films.
7) Keep a clean blackboard.
8) Have handwriting I can read.
9) Ask students to answer a few questions to keep everyone alert.
10) Announce at the conclusion of the class when the next session will be and what chapters will be covered.

After all these years, my conclusion is that good teachers are scarce and a precious resource. We should do everything in our power to keep the best and encourage them to stay in the classroom.

# THE PROBLEM PLAYER

Teachers are often faced with a question that confronts coaches: whether to take a chance on a so-called problem player and how far to go with him.

Over the years I have had a few players who were outspoken and undisciplined. Since I had taught in college for nine years as an associate professor, this type of individual was never hard to identify. First of all, he is often bitter and seems to be against everything. He is frequently disruptive in the classroom (or in the locker room) if not handled properly. He seldom wants to cooperate. The undisciplined student has two problems: he knows what he is against, but sometimes he is uncertain what he favors.

Most teachers, supervisors, and students regard him as a trouble-maker, but he doesn't usually see himself that way. This is important for the teacher or coach to remember in trying to help. A disobedient student rarely sees himself as others do. As a result, this behavior can go on for years and the student gets progressively worse because no one knows how to deal with him.

When I traded for Duane Thomas, the running back originally with the Dallas Cowboys, I knew he was hard to handle. I had already traded for one player with a so-called personality conflict, Roy Jefferson of the Baltimore Colts. Caroll Rosenbloom, then the team's owner, later told me that I was the only coach in the league who expressed an interest in Jefferson. He told me that one of the things that upset the Colt coaches was the fact that Roy ate with his hat on, though they had a rule against it. He was a free spirit who listened to no one.

Duane Thomas had a brief and sometimes brilliant pro career that was overshadowed by controversy. In Dallas, he called his coach, Tom Landry, a "plastic man." He described the general manager, Tex Schram, as "a liar, a cheat, and a racist." Schram dismissed it with a quip: "Two out of three isn't bad."

Thomas could run with the football, but with the possible exception of the late Howard Hughes, he received more publicity for not talking than anyone in America. Even before he made what became a public decision, he did not toss words around lightly. As a rookie, he helped lead the Cowboys to the Super Bowl, where a writer asked him, "Is this the ultimate game?"

Thomas replied, "If it's the ultimate game, why are they playing it again next year?"

For the rest of his career in Dallas, and pretty much wherever he went, he refused to talk to the press and said little more than necessary to his teammates. They milked it for a few laughs in Dallas after Duane was stopped one night by a highway patrolman and given a ticket for speeding. A writer wondered if the officer advised Thomas of his right to remain silent.

What I think every teacher and coach needs to do when counseling an individual of this type, one who is so clearly withdrawn, is to establish what he wants, what he rejects, and then, most importantly, *what you expect from him*. My rule was not to criticize. I learned the hard way that this was a waste of time. Talk to this individual in private. Care for him and let him know that he is usually tearing himself down, along with the class or team, but seldom building it up. You must do some compromising to allow him to change his attitude without losing his self-respect.

The key to handling this student is to let him know that you want him to be recognized for what he believes and not for what he is against. Once he is taught that this goal is what he needs, he will change to be a team player very quickly. The entire class will also help you in this transition if it is done properly.

In the case of Roy Jefferson, he was an outstanding football player for seven years and became a team leader. He and his wife and family are friends of mine today. The Baltimore Colts made a mistake, and the Washington Redskins gained a stand-out player when we decided we needed another quality wide receiver to team with Charlie Taylor.

In the case of Duane Thomas, I told him he did not have to talk to the media and I asked the reporters close to the team to respect his wishes. I offered to answer all their questions about him until he adjusted to his new environment. He played well for us and helped the Redskins beat Dallas.

After Harland Svare had released Thomas at San Diego, he told me he doubted that we would ever get Duane on the field. Duane is a friend of mine today, and I am flattered that he feels—as the following letter indicates—that we made a small contribution to his life:

Dear Coach Allen,

... I would like to thank you for being a positive guideline in my life and having a true faith in me, not only as a player but a person, too. May understanding keep us forever in harmony. Give my love and respect to your family.

Respectfully,

Duane Thomas

## Discipline Cuts Two Ways

It is easy to become frustrated and upset when you are working with students. One lesson to remember in disciplining a student is to do it in a constructive manner. When teachers lose self-control they lose their class, no matter how correct they are.

Now instead of one problem you have three: the student you are trying to discipline, yourself, and the respect of your class. Keep your patience and keep your poise. In all my years of teaching and coaching, I can recall losing my self-control once, and I was wrong to do so. In coaching or in teaching, the player or student needs discipline.

## The Withdrawal Method

I have known teachers and coaches who used the withdrawal of privileges as a punishment. But sometimes this approach will work in reverse and de-motivate a student, so care must be exercised in this area. I have found that it is better to assign work on special projects. Assigning added responsibility on a project that holds promise is simply more productive.

One NFL coach disciplined his players by taking away their lunch-time food service. It worked in the exact opposite way, and the team lost seven consecutive games. I can't say the losses were the direct result of their going without lunch or having to pay for their own food, but I think the players saw it as an act of pettiness. Once such a judgment is made, they seldom will respond well. It is better to work them harder and longer than to take away privileges.

## *Summary of How to Handle Discipline Cases*

1) **Find out what he wants.**
2) **Find out what he rejects.**
3) **Do not criticize him in front of others.**
4) **Give him private counseling to understand him.**
5) **Help him to find positive ways to express himself.**
6) **Be willing to compromise at the start.**
7) **Develop a sincere interest in helping the student.**
8) **Be patient and you will develop a leader.**

# THE PRESENTATION

If a teacher wants the student to enter the classroom and get right to work, then the teacher must have something prepared for them. It may be a message on the blackboard with an assignment in writing, but it is the responsibility of the teacher. It makes no sense to tell a student to get to work if no assignment has been made. This is like a head coach asking his staff to get busy before the meeting starts.

Every meeting I held with my team or class, I tried to prepare in myself in detail. Every meeting was such a challenge to me that I felt very nervous, would go to the bathroom, review my notes, and not allow anyone to distract my thinking. I wanted to make the meetings interesting enough that my enthusiasm would rub off on everyone there.

I started to prepare my notes the night before, if not earlier. I met with the team every day, even if just for ten minutes. When you do anything on a daily basis all season, it requires constant research and preparation.

I followed five factors in preparing myself for each meeting:

1) **I organized my material so that I knew exactly what I wanted to cover each day.**

2) I outlined the important points that needed to be stressed during the presentation.

3) I practiced the presentation, even to the inflection of my voice, in order to eliminate mistakes and rambling.

4) I attempted to reduce the amount of my talking by using charts, film, illustrations and slides, and by distributing written assignments to certain players.

5) I always allowed for flexibility in my lectures because I wanted the players to take part in setting up the daily practice program by making suggestions. Flexibility in meetings and on the practice field or classroom is essential.

## Helping Each Other

One of the ways a teacher can motivate a class is to commend a student who offers any kind of help to a fellow classmate. This type of recognition is a special motivator that encourages teamwork.

I was always on the alert for acts of support or consideration when my players did something to help each other. It might even have been a gesture after a costly mistake, when the individual's morale was low—this is when it is needed most. To drive home that point, I once made up an entire reel of film, 400 feet of clips, consisting of Redskins helping Redskins.

Let your students know that good behavior does not go unnoticed in your classroom. This type of leadership will provide a spirit of cooperation and become a strong source of motivation.

## Healthy Mind, Healthy Body

Once you begin to teach, there is a tendency to become so involved with your job that you gain weight and fall out of shape. How you feel physically has much to do with the way you react to the demands of teaching. It takes a tremendous amount of energy to keep up your enthusiasm as you relate to your students.

My daughter Jennifer had a professor in graduate school at New York University, Gordon Lish, who is in charge of creative writing. He wins the students over because of his energy and enthusiasm. He makes them want to compete with Hemingway. He tells them they may have the intelligence and the ability. The key question is, how badly do they want to succeed? In Jennifer's case, she said his method takes away the fear that you may not be able to perform and challenges not your talent but your spirit.

It is a gift for a teacher to instill confidence in a student that he or she can handle the work. It is harder, if not impossible, for a teacher to achieve this without a certain level of energy. Eat properly, avoid junk foods, and have good health habits. When you eat and exercise properly, the energy is there. When you feel tired because of a lack of sleep or poor diet, you simply will not have a good day. Getting yourself into good physical condition will allow you to reach your potential as a teacher and motivate your students by example.

## Democracy in Action

One activity I always tried to promote was classroom discussion. When I was in the United States Football League, it was difficult to get my players to carry out the kind of active team meetings we usually had in the NFL. The same problem exists in the early stages at all levels of classroom teaching.

A teacher can promote a gradual widening of the circle by starting with two or three students you know are not shy and who are capable of conducting an interesting talk. They will stimulate others.

I always felt that getting a class discussion rolling allowed me to think more clearly and developed everyone's interest. I encouraged everyone to speak and would ask questions of those who did not. The more thoughtful the question, the more likely the meeting was to be fun and the audience to be motivated. Even if they failed to answer, I found a compliment to pay them rather than put them down, so that the next time they would feel more free to speak up.

## The Art of Conversation

Signs and slogans—I harp on these often—are a form of communication, from "Have a nice day" on a T-shirt to "Baby Aboard" on the bumper of a car.

Most of us want to be able to carry on a conversation; we have a need or an urge for it. Let me give you two questions guaranteed to get a conversation going:

1) You turn to the other person and you say, casually, "I was just wondering how many people actually end up doing what they wanted to do when they were kids. What did you want to be when you were a kid?" It does not matter if you are at a party, a dinner or on an airplane. The shyest of people will respond.

2) You shake your head and say, in a sympathetic voice, "They made my uncle retire last week and he hasn't the foggiest notion what to do with himself." It doesn't matter if you have an uncle or not. The answer you get back instantly from anyone except possibly a statue in a park is, "How old is he?"

   The trick is to answer with an age not far from what you judge the other person to be (not recommended for people under 25). This one works like a charm, although it isn't clear why it does. Possibly I will ask a psychiatrist about that some day—right after I ask him what he wanted to be when he was a kid.

   When you are thrown in with people who do not know each other, or who do not make small talk easily, try to stay with subjects people are truly interested in: their past and their future. I don't mean that you should suddenly blurt out, "Ever want to be a cowboy instead of a musician, Mr. Bernstein?"

But it is a rare person who will not tell you about his or her job. A reporter once asked Vanna White, who I am told has gained some notoriety for turning the letters on the TV show "Wheel of Fortune," what the toughest thing about her job was.

"The alphabet, I guess," she said.

The reporter did a double take. "Knowing the alphabet is *hard*?"

"I mean the whole thing," explained Miss White.

Now there was the basis for a meaningful discussion.

## Specific Lesson Plans

No one should ever underestimate the value of a specific lesson plan. One of the reasons we were successful in the NFL is that we had an organized routine and did not deviate from it. The students (or players) knew what to expect. Knowing what to expect allows the student to come prepared.

However, some flexibility is always necessary. An opportunity may occur that will heighten their interest.

Telling students that an assignment is difficult and will require their total dedication is another way to stimulate curiosity. The more difficult tasks automatically bring about curiosity. They may groan, but they will react more quickly than usual.

## Design for Progress

Periodically changing the furniture in the classroom can help change the atmosphere. The teacher should move the desks to different locations; arrange them in a circle or in irregular rows. If the class is not too large, create a U-shaped row. A change in the environment can raise the spirits and motivate both the students and the teacher.

With the Redskins, I would change all the posters on the office and locker room walls every month. In addition, I asked Nate Fine, our film director, to change the blowups of action photos every two to three weeks.

Try it. After the new posters or pictures are in place, ask the students if anything is different. It will keep them alert and let them know you are looking for ways to improve.

Every year I made it a point to rearrange in some way our practice field at Redskins Park. It might be as simple as adding or moving a blocking or sled machine, or laying out another field strictly for the running game. The goal was twofold: (1) to strive to be more efficient, to prevent the loss of time going from one area to another; and (2) to stir the interest of the players.

## The Relationship

It used to be that you could bully students, but no more. Whenever possible, it is wise when correcting them to preface a negative comment with a positive one.

To use a football example, I would say to one of my players, "You usually make that block. What happened on this play?" Or: "You usually have all your lessons on time, what made you late today?"

It is easier for students to accept the teacher's guidance when they know you see their good points. Try to regard every corrective situation as an opportunity to build a better relationship with the students, not to widen the gap or destroy the lines altogether.

# GRADING THE TEACHERS

Something I have realized since my first coaching job, and which applies to every coach and his staff, is this fact of life:

When a teacher walks into the classroom the students are, consciously or subconsciously, asking these questions:

1. Do I like this teacher?
2. Do I respect this teacher?
3. Is he or she qualified?
4. Why should I study this lesson?
5. How is this going to help me?
6. What is my teacher doing for me personally?
7. Have I improved with this teacher?

These are just a few of many questions the students naturally have. They are searching for proof that their teacher is meeting their needs. The teacher is always being evaluated, every hour of every day.

All my players knew what was best for the coach, but I sometimes did not know what was best for them. The same applies to any classroom, which is one reason some students find the work uninteresting and sometimes boring.

## Fun Motivation

Being coach of the "Over-the-Hill Gang" was quite an experience. They were a handpicked group of veterans, and at times they took a fairly determined approach to having fun.

There was a good-natured rivalry between the offense and the defense. There was a period of one month when we had difficulty scoring. (In fact, because of the extraordinary togetherness on that team, our longest losing streak in seven years with the Redskins was two games in a row.) I always had several large bulletin boards that I changed constantly to keep up their interest. One morning when I visited the players' locker room, to my surprise, I came across a large poster tacked up, sixteen by twelve inches, in red and black letters, with my initials on the bottom as though I had signed it. I inquired around to find out who put up the poster; I think it was a defensive player who was still with the team as a coach in the 1980s, Richie Pettibon. I never knew for sure. But the giveaway was the word "OFFENSE" written in large capital letters above the message, which began: "The management regrets that it has come to their attention that employees dying on the job are failing to fall down . . ."

The reason I always suspected Pettibon was that a week before Thanksgiving he had placed a similar poster on the board listing free turkeys at the Food Giant stores. Al Miller of Food Giant, who felt our winning had helped unite the city, had been doing many favors for the entire organization. However, he had not planned on free turkeys that year.

I had an assistant coach named Charlie Winner who called his wife, Nancy, and told her to pick up one of the free turkeys. Of course, no one at the Food Giant stores knew anything about it. When Al Miller found out about the inquiries, he acted quickly and issued a memorandum to all the stores to honor the requests of Redskin players, to avoid embarrassment.

When Al called me, I explained to the team about the prank and that they could, in fact, pick up the complimentary turkeys. But I did not want this kind of episode to happen again. From then on, whenever a notice of a gift was posted, no one would make a move until we announced to the team that it was not a joke.

## The Parent–Teacher Relationship

From the experiences of my wife, Etty, and me with our sons George, Greg, and Bruce and our daughter, Jennifer, we have found that the teachers with whom we had a good relationship shared these characteristics:

1. They liked our children and enjoyed having them in class. They told us a story about one of the children that I knew had the ring of truth. We ate it up. Even though at times the kids would cause problems and embarrassment for a teacher, these teachers truly enjoyed having them in their classrooms. There was no doubt that they did; we could see it and feel it when Etty and I visited with them.

    We also could feel it when teachers did not like our children, or for whatever reason resented them. This type of feeling can spread to other students, so it is crucial for a teacher to try very hard to like or understand his or her students. Our children also knew when the teachers liked them, and that helped and was evident in the quality of their classwork. This empathy allows the teacher to be more successful, too.

As for the many football players I have coached, I can truthfully say I liked all of them. For many of them I felt a feeling close to love, and I liked some more than others. However, I never coached one I really disliked and I respected every one of them, even those I traded or released.

2. There is not enough time on either side to visit with teachers. Therefore, the conscientious teachers had a note system, a card system or a letter system to let us know how our children were doing in the classroom. It wasn't just a report card, but contained some written explanations. It was an effective method of communication and kept alive a relationship with the parents.

3. There was discipline in the classroom because the teacher was what I call professional. Students were on time and there was no talking. Everyone sat up with good posture. The teacher established this tone early. He or she did not have to talk about it every week. The students knew what the teacher demanded without words.

When a player entered a team meeting late, I did not have to say a thing. The player could see the reaction on my face. To come into my team meeting late was an insult to me and the squad. There wasn't a player in the room who was unaware of it. The tardy player was normally expected to see me after the meeting to explain his tardiness and to learn the amount of his fine. That was my rule— $50 a minute, $500 for the entire meeting.

## Teacher Adjustment

When I was in high school, teachers would put students down. In other words, the teacher was the winner and the student the loser. The teacher did not care to adjust very much. In some cases, the teacher would be physical with the student—sometimes with force, sometimes with a one-foot ruler.

The modern teacher realizes that no contest is going on in which the teacher must be proven right and the student wrong. This is no longer an acceptable philosophy; neither is losing one's temper. There is more concern now about adjusting to the situation. Also, the teacher cares enough for his or her students that there is no desire to embarrass them in front of the class. The concern is with trying to solve the problem, not with feeding one's ego at the expense of a youngster.

The modern teacher loves his students and wants to assist them. He feels they are a part of his family. He is secure enough to treat any situation in the classroom as an opportunity to help the class and strenghten the bonds.

## Student Participation

When I first started coaching and teaching in college, I was aware that I should do something to involve my players and students. I always wanted everyone to participate, whether it was on a team or in the classroom.

One of the things that I did was to bring a wooden suggestion box to the locker room. It was similar in size and shape to an old-time ballot box in a voting place. I encouraged my players or students to write short notes on how we could improve the practices or the classroom. I found this was an effective technique to get students who were timid about taking part in class to become more engaged. When I first started this, the box was full of suggestions. Nearly everyone wrote a note.

I would empty the box every night. I tried to answer each signed note by talking to the student—I thought that was important. After a month or so I had very few notes and after two months the notes were either inconsequential or showing off the writer's humor. Eventually I removed the box, but it had served its purpose: to create better communication between them and me.

Another innovation was to have my family plan and host a barbecue for the entire team. My wife and I purchased all the food, usually hot dogs, hamburgers, baked beans, milk, soft drinks and ice cream—nothing fancy. Since I was making only $4,800 a year, it was no small deal to buy food for sixty players. I would put on a chef's hat and apron and work the grill, usually at some recreation park where tables and facilities were available. My entire family was on hand, and that helped everyone relax. It was another attempt to show the players that I cared about them as people and wanted to keep working on our relationships.

Many of the players would still be thanking me weeks later. At first I was surprised to see the benefits. After several of these social gatherings, when the freshness wore off, we no longer needed them. They had helped a new teacher and coach to get acquainted.

## Summary of Student–Teacher Motivation

1) The professional teacher can always handle the undisciplined student.

2) Changing the environment in a classroom, if only moving a desk, is good for student motivation.

3) Having students write notes on how they feel about what is happening in class helps.

4) The teacher should stay in good physical condition to meet the demands of the students and to stay motivated.

5) The professional teacher does not lose self-control because that doubles his problem.

6) The good teacher gives the students choices and is not totally demanding. He realizes that this helps motivation, whereas a domineering teacher hinders motivation.

7) The good teacher is prepared for every class session and is ready for his students.

8) The good teacher promotes class discussion and realizes this is a learning proposition.

9) Withdrawing privileges as punishment is dangerous and can backfire on the teacher.

10) The good teacher realizes that it is very important to give the students specific lesson plans.

11) When correcting students, it is wise to make a positive statement before the correction.

12) The classroom is made up of many different types of students and more than one method of studying is required.

13) Modern teachers realize that you cannot put students down all the time, and that adjusting to the situation is more important.

They have confidence in their ability and judgment and sincerely want to help the students, not prove them wrong.

14) Professional teachers love their students. Their students' successes are part of the teacher's happiness.

# 13

# Around the World

▲

*Teamwork is the most difficult goal to achieve because people, like nations, think individually. Work for team victory without thought of individual reward.*

E VERY four years the Olympic spirit renews itself, in spite of the intrusion of politics and prejudices and historic hatreds. These scenes come to mind:

In 1968 at Mexico City, the authorities tried to limit each nation to five athletes in the closing promenade. The stadium was surrounded by a moat, and behind that a steel-spiked fence. But enterprising souls, the uninvited, found a section of the moat that was unfenced and began to pour across. They were met by Mexican security men wielding long poles. Some were caught and dragged away. Others struggled free, their clothes torn, one or both shoes missing.

A delegation from one of the African nations, tall men in flowing white robes, edged out to meet them. Literally, the gate crashers hid among the swirling gowns and dark bodies. This was an Olympic sanctuary, after all.

Four years later the Games at Munich ended under a man-made rainbow to the buoyant melody of "My Sweet Lord," while away from the TV cameras, soldiers bearing submachine guns patrolled the grounds.

The closing ceremony at each Olympiad is a bridge four years long.

And then came Los Angeles in 1984, and we saw the self-renewing spirit of America at work. These Games succeeded where no others had in this century, boycott or not. They really were the free-enterprise Olympics, proving that we are what we are: a country where a machine will shine your shoes for 50 cents; where sin is not condoned but most towns will have just enough to keep the tourists coming back; where nearly everyone knows who Carl Lewis and Mary Lou Retton are but nobody can name two physicists.

Yet I am prepared to say that here lies the best hope for the words and phrases we often use too lightly: fellowship . . . peace on earth, good will toward men . . . the fields of friendly strife.

As former chairman of the President's Council on Sports and Physical Fitness, I have traveled far and seen the evidence wherever I go. Let me share these experiences with you:

## IN ANY LANGUAGE

After a player from the Czechoslovakia national hockey team defected to America, this story made the rounds: The player was being given an eye exam and the doctor pointed to the next-to-last line and said, "Do you know this one?"

The player replied, "Know him? I played hockey with him!"

Given that country's record in the last season or so, it is important to note that we are laughing with them, not at them.

In 1986, returning home from a trip to the Soviet Union, I spent two and a half days in Czechoslovakia. In Prague, Dr. Antonin Himl, the president of their Olympic committee, asked me if there was any place in particular I wished to visit, anything special I cared to do.

I said my first choice would be to watch one of their hockey teams play or practice. There was no game that night, so the next morning at 10 o'clock I was driven to an indoor arena to watch the Sparta hockey club work out. With me were two coaches, Dr. Pavel Wohl, a professor of sports at the Physical Education Institute of

Prague and a former goalkeeper of the team, and Petra Brdicka, a former star player.

Even as I entered the arena, I heard the shriek of a whistle and I said, "That's exciting, hearing that whistle. They have a good man coaching this team."

One of my hosts said, "How can you know that?"

I said, "I can tell by the way he blows his whistle." They were not long, slow blows. They were short, precise, snappy and disciplined, just the way a coach should blow a whistle. The signal was: Attention! Move on quickly. His whistle had that connotation.

As the team began to practice, I asked for the name of one particular player and they said, "Why do you ask about him?"

I said, "Well, he looks to me like a real professional prospect."

And, again, my host appeared half amused and half startled. "He is the youngest player on the team," he said, "only 18. But what a talent."

Talent shows itself regardless of age or language, any place and any time.

The practice was well organized. Everything was precise, all business, no horseplay. It was a very productive practice, ending with the coach calling them up in ones and twos and threes until they were dismissed. They left the arena in the same manner.

I was so impressed, I later observed that if I owned a hockey team in the United States I would hire the coach whose practice I had watched in Prague. I wouldn't worry whether he could speak English or not. I'd hire an interpreter.

Later I learned that he had an outstanding record, had won several national championships and had helped the West Germans train their team.

This had been a very motivational morning for me. It also let me know why the Czechs can compete against the mighty Soviet hockey team. They are a small nation of only 17 million, but with the quality of coaching they get, their discipline, organization, and talent, they can compete against anybody.

I was pleased, but not surprised, when Sparta won the gold medal at the winter Olympics at Calgary in 1986.

Dr. Pavel Wohl, I learned later, was one of the top goalies in Czechoslovakia during his playing career.

As luck would have it, he came along in an era when the country had two legendary players at the goalie position, Jiri Holecek and Valdo Dsurilla. As a result, Pavel Wohl was never selected for the national team that represented Czechoslovakia in the world championships. This would be the equivalent of coming along as a centerfielder in baseball when Willie Mays, Mickey Mantle and Duke Snider were starring for the three New York teams.

But the recognition that eluded him as a player led Wohl to turn earlier to coaching. He worked several years in West Germany, where he built winning teams in that country's strongest league. He is described as an intelligent and deliberate coach as well as a perfectionist—a John Wooden model, I would think, if one were looking for an American comparison.

After I left Prague, a new second or assistant Sparta coach was hired, Josef Horesovsky, also a former star with the Sparta team. A spinal injury ended what had been a brilliant playing career—eight times a member of the national team, during which they won three world titles and Josef was twice named to the all-star team as a right defenseman.

The Czechs are extremely proud of this squad, and consider their Jiri Hrdina among the best offensive players in the world as a skater and shooter.

# THE INTERNATIONAL CONGRESS

I vividly recall that in the early days of World War II young Americans in uniform were often reminded that they were fighting for such things as "the right to play baseball on a sunny day." It did not occur to us that such rights, with some variation in the activity, applied to other countries as well, even those we might be fighting. The major change in international sports in the last ten to fifteen years has been the fact that U.S. coaches and athletes no longer lecture or explain. We now exchange tips and information.

In Frankfurt, Germany, in March of 1986, I was one of the speakers at the International Congress in Sports For All. In every respect it was a remarkable gathering, a collection of people who were among the best and brightest in the world at what they do or teach.

Cuba was represented by runner Alberto Juantorena, who won

two gold medals in the 400 and 800 meters in Montreal in 1976. Each morning at 7:15 we met in the lobby of the Park Hotel with anyone else who cared to show up and ran five meters along the Rhine River. We ran roughly seven-minute miles, not brisk but not exactly slow. One morning Jurgen Palm, the director of the German Sports Federation, ran with us and we picked up the pace.

As we ran I studied Alberto, who stayed on the grass—a smart decision that eased the pounding on the knees, hips and ankles. At six-foot-three and 184 pounds, the Cuban looked as though he could run forever—and he doesn't miss it by much, getting in his miles seven days a week. I could see why he was a great runner; he has extremely long legs and is very fluid and flexible. As we ran, he would encourage me with bulletins on our progress: "We are running faster than yesterday."

I was curious about Fidel Castro's fitness program. Alberto was not reluctant to talk about Castro, whom he said stayed in shape through regular exercise. Fidel likes all sports, Juantorena reported, but especially swimming, and is at his best under water. He said that Castro can swim the length of an Olympic pool without surfacing; that tells me he has a good cardiovascular rating. Castro also jogs, lifts weights, and plays softball.

Alberto added that Fidel never runs on hard surfaces in Cuba since he ruptured his Achilles tendon in Los Angeles in 1981. There was little of this that would interest the CIA, but it helped me to see the Cuban leader as a disciplined individual.

There were fifty-nine countries represented at the Congress in Frankfurt, with each speaker allowed thirty minutes for his presentation. I thought Antonin Himl gave the most interesting speech, and his film on the Spartakia was spectacular. I asked how his country developed such good hockey teams, and he said it was due to the fact that their best prospects started training at the age of 4. We talked about Stan Mikita and Peter Kilmra, two of Czechoslovakia's young stars who went on to careers in the National Hockey League.

When Himl gave his speech, he turned off the sound and let the film roll. To visualize the magnitude of their stadium, which seats 225,000, he compared it to American football: imagine a stadium the width of one football field and the length of six, and you have it. The place is so huge that the musicians must use amplifiers on their heads and a special apparatus to beam the music to the other side of the field.

The surface of the field has no grass, just dirt covered with light sand.

One morning I had breakfast with the Russians: Vladimir Nosov, the vice president of the Committee for Physical Culture and Sport in Moscow; Mr. P. Vinogradov, Mr. V. Stolinarov and Vassili Senatorov. Later, we continued our discussions at dinner in a German brewery and I diagramed American football plays for them on a tablecloth. I then had each of them sign it and I wrote above their names, "From President Ronald Reagan to Mr. Gramov, president of the Russian Sports Federation."

They went wild with laughter, saying they had never before seen anyone write on a tablecloth. I was once lost in thought in a restaurant, moving aside the dishes to scribble X's and O's, showing a writer the play that cost us a game, when a horrified headwaiter rushed up and cried, "What in the world are you doing?"

I looked up at him and said, "If the blocker takes out his man, this play goes for a touchdown."

That night in Frankfurt I had the proprietor take our picture and also a photo of the tablecloth. When the dinner was over, a Polish driver named Strundunski came over to our table and folded the cloth. I then presented it to the Russians on our way to the elevator to leave the restaurant.

The Soviets were so organized that Senatorov, their interpreter for Mr. Nosov, was also a journalist, the editor of a magazine called *International Sport*. That's like having a player who can also coach. Russia had the largest contingent at the Congress—four. The United States had one (me) and Canada had one, Russ Kisby of Toronto, whose talk was on financing and advertising.

I made it a point to visit with Juan Antonio Samaranch of Spain, the president of the International Olympic Committee. I was curious about how the man who oversees the world's greatest athletes keeps fit. Despite flying all over the world, he is able to maintain his fitness level, he told me, by skiing, riding, and playing golf.

It is irresistible to be among delegates from other nations and to study, measure, and compare. This can be a valuable process, enlightening, encouraging, and on occasion humbling. It is nearly always motivating.

One of the pleasantries of international exchange is the often ornate compliments members pay one another. I received a note from the deputy secretary for sports for India, Mr. Ranindvanath Gupta: "George Allen, Esq.—My heartiest felicitations on your scintillating, convincing and well-considered presentation today. It has been an education for me."

I offered to host the next Congress of Sports For All in 1990, and asked the Russians to do so in 1992. They nodded their heads as if they understood what I was saying. Time will tell if they got the message.

## MADE IN JAPAN

Tetuo Mesizuka is the professor emeritus of physical education at Japan's Yokohama National University and an expert on sports broadcasting. Do you wonder if the Japanese are stealing our thunder, not only in cars and television sets but on the athletic field as well?

Consider that in 1962 they enacted the Sports Promotion Law, which led to the creation of the Japanese Foundation for Health and Fitness. Today the number of young people in that tiny island nation who engage in physical training is close to 90 percent.

I asked Dr. Mesizuka to mail me a copy of a speech he had written. He had a translation sent to me with a modest note: ". . . You may freely edit it since English is not my mother tongue. Is this looking like what you would expected?"

His title was "Meandered Motivations Towards Fitness Preaching":

> "In a small farming hamlet located almost (at) the western end of the Japanese main island, a very clever but rather unhappy mother gave birth to the third boy of the clan Mesizuka on a warm summer night of Bon-festival day of August 21, back in 1921. The first such a move as called motivation was given by this mother when I was around six years old, and it remains still very clear and strong in my memory. She vigorously tried to let me believe (I could) become a blue-collar salaried man; for instance, a school

teacher, so that her son might be excluded from the mandated military service and could survive the wars smelling somewhat at that time. Then I went to a teachers' college, where the sporting club membership was enforced, and joined in the volleyball club ... lasting five years. This decision was also given by others, and can be named also one of my motivations when I was 15 years old.

"Even though the score of my entrance examination was in the top five at the beginning, the volleyball activity took everything I had, and when graduation came closer this rank was far lower down, to the bottom ten. But as captain of the team, we succeeded in a beating a decade-long enemy of our prefecture through my leadership, which included forty days of camp training through the summer vacation without any recess. We cried together at the moment of our victory at the final.

"This may be named 'Volleyball Motivation' with a sacrifice of my school records. Suddenly, then came a time I had to decide where to go, rather too late to choose a better way. At my age of 20, for the first time in my life, I had to motivate myself, and so I did to continue my volleyball career, not knowing any future at all, and started my study for the entrance examination into a normal university in Tokyo for another five years, until interrupted by dint of the Second World War. I, however, kept another motivation of my own, parallel to that given by my mother. It was to become able to talk with foreigners in English, and this possible availing (myself) of sporadic time-breaks among volleyball training sessions. To my surprise, English was forbidden to read or study because it was the enemy language.

"Volleyball was also stopped to play, only because it came from an enemy country, and I made a petition to an army officer so that we could continue our training ... a pledge written in blood on a sheet of paper, but in vain.

"I knew that the war was not in favor to Japan, and I used to carry an English-Japanese dictionary instead of my army handbook since the size was similar. As soon as the war was terminated, I volunteered to regain the volleyball stature among our university leagues, by digging and leveling the pumpkin field which was once our court in Tokyo. Then, again, my graduation time got closer without any preparation for my (future) placement, but I kept my interest going in volleyball.

"It was not at the time an activity that produced any food or income, but my young enthusiasm kept me in it with such a strenuous power, my motivation almost paranoiac, that I disregarded my any other career options. Naturally, there was nothing relative to my job; but still I desired to stay in Tokyo for the continuation of my sport, and so I did to take an offer to teach physical education at one of the Tokyo municipal senior high schools. Here, in comparison to other teaching subjects and teachers, I realized that mine was rather without any background materials for what I had to teach. But with just my own performance, and otherwise ordering my pupils to do what I performed, we began.

"With a baccalaureate degree of arts then, my regret finally caught me into shame and repentance to think that it seemed to be unworthy to devote my life to something without any background resources or science. Then my own motivation for my career began to form itself, and came to me at length, and it was to go to the United States to seek something missing in our profession at that time in Japan. For that I chose the Fulbright graduation students' program to try, and passed the examination to go to Columbia University in 1953, where there were professors such as Rathbone, Brownell, Scott and other well-known figures. Later, I attended the University of Iowa, where I discovered Professor McCloy, who had contributed very much to the postwar recovery in Japan. Without his advice, there would not be our physical education at our institutions of higher learning today. Together him, and his successor, Professor Alley, I owe much for my career (as) a scientist in sport and physical education for schools, as well as for the general society."

It seems to me that the story of Tetuo Mesizuka loses nothing in the translation. It is anyone's story who ever followed his heart, who started with little or nothing and built a future doing the one thing that was most important to him.

## DIFFERENT STROKES

Watching Yugoslavia play Australia in men's basketball in the 1984 Olympics, I was impressed by the contrast between the teams in their warm-up drills. Yugoslavia had eleven players and seven basketballs

215

in motion at one time. Nobody stood around. One player was shooting free throws while the others kept passing and moving.

Australia had just four basketballs for their eleven players.

As in Russia, Yugoslavia's players are state supported, some of them officers in the military. They seemed—well, seasoned. In fact they reminded me of my Washington Redskins in that they were an experienced, veteran team. I don't want to suggest that Yugoslavia was "over the hill," but that was the name they gave my team—and we still won 70 percent of our games.

# FROM RUSSIA, WITH SWEAT

Somehow I found an English edition of a small Russian sports book written for children. I believe it tells, in a very clear and simple way, a story our country cannot afford to ignore.

I quote from a chapter that describes a sports club for youngsters, called "Ogonyok":

"As time goes on, an ever-increasing number of ways of organizing mass sports present themselves. In recent years, sport has come to courtyards and reached those children who have never been to sports schools and sections. At many house-management committees, sports clubs started springing up like mushrooms.

"The Ogonyok Sports Club is an example. It has been established under the supervision of a house-management committee in one of the neighborhoods in Alma-Ata. This is how I (the author) found myself there: I heard, quite by chance, a group of boys arguing in the street, one of them insisting that he would chin himself up on the bar fifty times—more than any of his comrades.

"The youngster was as skinny as a rake. I asked the children, 'Are you gymnasts?' Several boys answered all together, 'No, we're wrestlers.'

"This came as a surprise to me, as they did not at all look like sturdy fellows going in for wrestling. But after talking to them, I learned that they were really members of the judo section of their courtyard club.

"I was curious to see what kind of a club it was, so I went there with the boys. Everything there was just as it would be at a real sports school. The boys were trying to perfect their judo holds and throws. Excited rather than tired after the training session, they still went to the (parallel) bar to settle their argument properly.

"To my surprise, the one who made the bet actually did fifty-six pull-ups, outstripping all the others.

". . . Before the sports club had been set up in the courtyard, many of its present members loitered about in the street after classes. Naturally they were up to some sort of mischief on occasion, and several times their parents used to get complaints about them.

(The author introduces a young coach, Serik Ashagbayev, who was actually recruited by friends and families in the neighborhood.)

"Two years ago he returned home after doing his army service. He is fond of sports. That is why he has taken up the job of instructor at the house-management committee, which has allotted a vacant flat in the block it operates to accommodate the teenagers' club. Kids from the whole neighborhood took part in fitting out their own gym, small though it was. They have another two rooms in the same block of flats: one has been fitted to accommodate a children's chess club; the other, the Skillful Hands circle. It may be that when the time comes some of them will participate in contests where the real Olympic flame will be lit. With this dream in mind, the boys named their sports club the "Ogonyok" (the little flame).

"Serik has proved himself to be quite a good organizer. Not only has he gathered children around him, he has not forgotten the parents, too. He has set up health-building groups for them. With the younger ones he goes on hiking tours. He has infected many with an enthusiasm for sports activities. He believes that sport brings people together and that, in the long run, both children and their parents will profit.

". . . At the city residential board, I learned that there are quite a few similar clubs in Alma-Ata. During my stay in Kazakhstan, the opening ceremony of the Spartakiad of Courtyard Sports Clubs, dedicated to the sixtieth anniversary of the formation of the USSR, was held at the stadium in the Gorky Recreation Park. It was a wonderful children's sports festival. There were gymnasts, boxers, fencers and wrestlers . . . And I thought, as I looked at the excited and happy faces of the contestants and of the fans, how good it is when children have a favorite pastime, especially when the pastime is sport—which brings them not only joy, but the highest blessing, health.''

No editorial comment is needed here. This is one time when, as they say in television, we will let the picture (in your mind) do the talking.

# 14

# All in the Family

▲

*Contentment is a form of rust. Discontent is not an
evil, it is a teammate of progress.*

IN the early spring of 1979, when the fortunes of the Chrysler Motor
Corporation were near a low point, I received an invitation that
both flattered and challenged me. Gar Laux, the assistant to Lee Iacocca, invited me to make a motivational speech to a convention of
their car dealers in Acapulco, Mexico.

Before I accepted, I asked my wife, Etty, for an opinion. All I
knew was football. What could I tell a group of car dealers?

She said, "Tell them what you tell your football teams when
times get hard."

That was the right answer and the only encouragement I needed.
When Etty and I flew into Acapulco, we spent the first few days
mingling with the dealers and the wives. I was still a little distracted,
not yet certain what I wanted to say. But I thought I knew people,
and I knew how to win.

Chrysler was open to all forms of encouragement. The stock was
trading that week below $3. Many in the government and among the
public were opposing a plan that would provide federal assistance—

the so-called bail-out. Plants were closing and dealers had shut down or dropped out in bunches.

Not until I walked to the microphone that morning did I make up my mind what I wanted to say. I looked out into the audience, at men and women representing the fifty or sixty surviving Chrysler dealerships across the country (out of a high of nearly 200), and I said:

"This is great! You have gotten rid of all the quitters and front runners and you are down to just the winners. The people in this room are the pros, the ones who won't fold." My hand swept across the audience. "These are the people you can count on . . . the ones who didn't get in because the car business looked like a way to make a quick buck. You can't help but succeed now. You're down to the people who will stick it out and turn things around."

Then I told them about my first coaching job, in 1949 at tiny Morningside College in Iowa. "That year I kept putting up notices and writing letters and telling everybody to come out for football. So we started out with 100 players and we didn't have uniforms for all of them. Some were coming out in shorts with no pads, and we couldn't even scrimmage them. But I put them on two-a-days for three straight weeks, and the players started dropping out, quitting. Soon I had plenty of uniforms to go around.

"The number got down to fifty and then forty. I began to worry that we wouldn't have enough players to open the season. We got down to twenty-seven from a squad that once numbered 100. And this was when you had two platoons, offense and defense. I had only five substitutes in case of injuries. To make matters worse, we had an eleven-game schedule, unusual for those days.

"What happened taught me a lasting lesson. We lost only three of those games. And the reason was simple: what we had remaining was the cream of the crop. These were the guys who should have been out there in the first place, who had the ability and wanted to play, not because it was the fashionable thing to do. And they were in great condition. They were in shape."

The point of the story was not lost on those in the room, who were putting their careers and the security of their families on the line. "The people in this room," I went on, "are the ones who probably belonged in the business in the first place. Not the ones who jumped on the bandwagon when it looked easy, or before the Japanese began to make things tough. Maybe a lot of those who are gone now got in for the quick buck. They may not have been qualified, or committed to sticking it out. It means something when you can look around a room and know that you are seeing people who will be there in the hard times. That's why we made it at Morningside, and that's why Chrysler will make it back. You're going to have a good year."

Of course, they did, and the comeback of Chrysler was one of the dramatic success stories of any era. The government loan, $2 billion, was paid off with interest in less than three years. The pep talk I gave them had nothing to do with that recovery, but I did predict it and I am proud of having shown those dealers a truth that has been tested time and again.

When the tough times come, you circle the wagons, and that is when you must be able to rely on the people around you. That is why I have included this story in a chapter on family motivation rather than in the business section.

The people who really matter in life may be few, but they are all your family. There is a special kind of help, of strength, that we draw from our parents, our brothers and sisters, a husband, a wife, our children. At times, those feelings apply to teammates or the people you work with.

It is no accident and no work of fiction that a great baseball team, the Pittsburgh Pirates of the 1970s, used as its theme the popular song "We Are Family." My guess is that the people who stuck with Chrysler share that sentiment.

In a funny way, I was almost one of them. My first job after I finished high school was at the Chrysler plant in Jefferson, as a messenger boy working for $80 a month. This was not long after the Depression, when full-time jobs were scarce.

I had two bosses, a Mr. Maguire and a Mr. Merritt, and I was assigned to the planning department. One of the things I learned was that by using the stairs and not taking the elevators, I could deliver the daily schedules throughout the Jefferson plant and the Kercheval Body Plant across the street about forty-five minutes faster. When Mr. McGuire became aware of this, he was impressed enough to give me a $20-a-month raise—to $100. After two years, I took a hard look around me and asked myself if this was what

I wanted my future to be. I resigned, took the $1,100 I had saved and went off to college.

Amid all the hardships of those years, it was often necessary to rely only on yourself to break the cycle of dead-end jobs and little money. That was the making of many a successful figure—in business, in science, in politics, in sports, in life.

But let me tell you, it is easier when you have the emotional resources of your family to fall back on. A wife can be a mighty motivational force, as Etty Allen has demonstrated time and time again. She has motivated me with affection and with words. The latter, at least, I can share with you.

## LETTERS FROM ETTY

This one reached me in the first weeks of building a new USFL football franchise in Chicago.

**Friday, 8:50 A.M.**

**Dear G. P.,**

It was nice talking with you this morning to start the day right. I am writing you while Dixie and Wahoo (our dogs) are looking at me with piercing eyes through the window in the balcony. It's a beautiful day in our neighborhood. Sorry it's snowing in Chicago, though.

I can hardly wait to see Jennifer. She is supposed to spend the weekend with me. Oh boy, she is going to like the goodies I got her in Paris.

You will enjoy the Illinois football game, I am sure, once you are there. I hope you brought some clothing to keep yourself *warm*. Please eat properly and don't get all riled up over details. It is normal to find things disorganized. It's like moving into a new house. You cannot expect things to be perfect, at first. It takes time and with "equanimity" (my favorite word) and good planning and patience, it will be more to your standards. It WILL be successful and you cannot give up. I really believe the Blitz is going to be a very good organization and venture. Keep your poise and *esprit de corps*. Remember your favorite slogans!

Love U, all my life,<br>Etty

# The Empty Nest

This next letter is one I classify as parental motivation. Etty wrote it to both of us, really, after the children had gradually left home. Jennifer was the last, a graduate of the University of California at La Jolla who wrote feature articles for the *Los Angeles Herald-Examiner* before enrolling in New York University's graduate school. Our sons are George, a successful attorney and now a member of the House of Delegates in Virginia; Greg, a graduate of the University of Delaware with a doctorate in psychology now practicing in the Los Angeles area; and Bruce, a graduate of the University of Richmond, holder of the school record for punting, third in the nation in that category his senior year, and voted all-Southern Coast Conference. He was an assistant coach at Arizona State, the head coach at Occidental College and the general manager of two USFL teams. Bruce now heads his own sports agency firm in Phoenix.

Any time you describe your children, there is a sense of breaking out the old snapshots and putting the people around you into a coma. But I wanted to include this background for a reason that ought to be obvious. Every mother and father will someday go through this experience in life: the empty nest syndrome. This is what children do—or should do: they grow up and leave home. In this letter, I believe, is a peek at the process of self-motivation by a couple with much to be thankful for, and the adjustments in their future.

Sunday, March 2, 1986

All of a sudden it is quiet! Only the sound of a ticking clock. The hum of a distant motor coming down the road. No more yells. No more rumblings down the staircase. No more laughter. No more arguments. No more banging doors. No more tracking red mud in and out. No more refrigerator doors left open.

All is quiet—all stays in the same place. The cars are waiting in the driveway. No one is fighting over them or who is going to drive where.

All is quiet—all is orderly. The crickets become louder as their sound takes the place of the ear-blasting stereo.

The children are gone. Each on their way, in the direction they chose for themselves. It is now just the two of us—tired, polite. We are not quite resigned to the fact that this is how it will be from now on.

What is the alternative? We have to get over the shock of reality first before we can organize our new thoughts, find new reasons, new directions. We are no longer needed in the same demanding, forceful, frenzied manner by our children. They want us where our place is, in our own world—which is not theirs.

The bananas are feeling too ripe. No one is ravaging through them. Market baskets do not need to be filled to the top for our moderate needs.

The last twenty-six years have lifted us up and up and around and down like a tornado, and left us limp, not knowing exactly how or where it hit us. A tremendous void—the lack of your children's presence, voices. Turmoil, but ohhh, what warmth! What action! So busy living, we are not aware of it.

Now it has all quieted down. The crickets are louder. The bark of the dogs . . . My heart pounds, or is it just breaking? Now what? What is the plan for the future? Or has the future just passed by like a moth to the light?

Love U, Etty

Etty was called to Paris in the summer of 1986 when her mother was hospitalized after a mugging. She left behind this note on the kitchen table.

Dearest Georgie Porgy,

I am leaving for Paris tonight and before I go I wanted to tell you how much I appreciate your love and support and your calls and the flowers and evvvverything.

Please don't worry about me. I can handle myself and whatever I have to do. I am a big girl, you know. Just take care of yourself. Get enough rest and food so you can be enthusiastic and energetic and poised so you can be the good leader you are. A fished-up season is coming, and I have to say *Mabouk*!

I hope Bruce's contract will be taken care of soon. I'll write and let you know when I can bring Momma back. Hopefully in time for the first game.

When you have time, call Jen at work sometime. I am so proud of her and my whole family.

Love you all my life, rain or shine,

Etty

## From The Mouths of Babes

I was with the Redskins when I found this note on my desk, scribbled on one of my notepads.

Good morning, Clutch Coach!
It's a beautiful day in our neighborhood.
You two are Number 1's.
Keep smiling.

Jennifer, Bruce, Greg, and George
(also Dixie and Hilda, the dogs)

After I had moved on to Los Angeles, I invited Bruce to spend a few days at our training camp. Later, he wrote this thank-you note. The date was August 19, 1970.

Thank you for letting me stay here. I had lots of fun and it helped me, too. Thank you for the helmet. I will miss you.

Thank you,
Bruce

P.S.—I love you.

By 1979, George was beginning his legal career in Virginia, after having been elected president of his senior class at the university and making the all-academic team as a quarterback.

Feb. 16, 1979
Charlottesville

Hey, my poor family:

It's a terrible life you all are living. I can see why you, Pa, would rather be straining and worrying and agonizing and coaching than enjoying the fruits of a lifetime of work and stress. Stop whining, as I know you are.

As for the rest of you, except Dixie Lee, you are missing out on some beautiful weather down in Virginia. Everything is covered with clean, pure, white snow. The mountains and the countryside are just like a Christmas card. The sun in the blue skies has melted the snow off of General Lee and Traveler.

Of course, some people, as with you, have to be pent up in hot, humid, tropical weather that never ceases.

Gol dang, we don't even have to worry about air conditioning and there you all are in Mawee (Maui, Hawaii), sweating and in water without ice on the banks and trees without limbs, much less snow, on them. Don't you realize that such an environment will thin your blood and you will end up with guava nectar running down your earlobes onto your shirts? Of course, the shirts getting stained won't matter because the style of shirts you tourists are wearing undoubtedly look as if some Polynesian sumo rassler has squashed pineapple, guava, papaya, strawberries, blueberries, blackberries and oranges on a solid-colored shirt oversized for the wearer.

Oh, well, I'll just keep my feet propped up on the radiator and think of you floundering flunkies feasting as if famished on french fries and fried fish.

I've enclosed the article on my almost hopeless case with the bank robber. He is a good ole boy. The teller that gave him the money is the wife of a teammate of mine at U. of Virginia. The other girl in the bank was the daughter of Dean Smith (the North Carolina basketball coach). Ain't all that something?

Aloha,
Festus

P.S.—wish you were here, the weather's great!

# THE TELEPHONE EXERCISE

By my telephone in the family room of our home in Southern California I keep a handgrip. I use it, alternating my hands, every time I'm on the phone, which is fairly often. If I can press the component parts together, I have a grip strength of 49 pounds. There are seven springs, each with a resistance of seven pounds.

If I didn't do this exercise, my hand strength would diminish. Since I spend so much of my day on the telephone, it gives me an opportunity to do more than one thing and not waste my time. This is an example of how you can take any ordinary situation and use it to improve and motivate yourself.

The results were so encouraging that I gave President Reagan a handgrip inscribed with this message: "Keep a strong grip on the nation."

# MOTIVATIONAL SOUP

What spinach did for Popeye, certain foods will do for the rest of us: provide energy and a healthy attitude. Once a week our evening meal consists of a soup Etty prepares entirely from fresh vegetables. High in all the nutrients, the recipe is Etty's own, and I have always described it as my motivational soup:

Begin with one-quarter cup instant oatmeal; one cup broccoli, spinach and parsley; one cup each turnips and zucchini; two cups each potatoes, carrots, celery. Add variable amounts of radish leaf tops, ciliento and leek. Optional ingredients: tomatoes and barley.

Fill half an eight-quart pot with water and boil. Toss in a sprinkling of salt. Add the cut-up vegetables and cook until tender. Sprinkle about one-quarter cup of instant oatmeal on top to tenderize.

Enjoy.

# THE CASE OF THE MISSING DICTIONARY

Persistence pays off.

In 1982 I wanted to give Jennifer a leather-bound dictionary, the finest money could buy, as her Christmas gift. I wanted her to have something useful, as opposed to the gifts we so often receive on special occasions that are either ornamental or perishable. As an aspiring writer and a New York University graduate student, she would find the dictionary of particular value, I was sure.

(I wanted to have one made for Bruce, as well, but it was for Jennifer that the gift would have real meaning.)

Knowing that my friend Milt Fromer of the Los Angeles Rams had a talent for finding unusual items no matter how out of the ordinary or bizarre, I asked him to find a supplier and order the special dictionaries. A couple of months later I called Milt and asked him when I could expect the books. He said he had kept them in the trunk of his car, then misplaced them and was still looking. So I never saw the dictionaries in 1982.

A few months before the holidays in 1983, I phoned Milt and asked if he would renew his search for the books. I refused to give up. He said he thought they might be at his home in the desert, somewhere in the garage. He offered to look for them the next trip he made. The next time we talked, he regretted that his efforts had been in vain. So the books were a no-show for another Christmas.

Early in 1984, I insisted that Milt stay on the case and keep looking. Even after he told me he had nowhere else to look, I wouldn't drop the idea. Of course, the books might have been stolen, or Milt might not have ordered them in the first place. But they had become real to me, and I refused to give up the chase. The books had become my version of the Lost Ark.

One summer day in 1985 I bumped into Milt at a sportscasters' luncheon for Chuck Benedict. I told him I still had not given up on them even thought two years had passed since my original order. Milt reminded me that it had been three years, not two.

One week before Christmas of 1985 I had lunch with Milt and received those dictionaries. I still needed them as presents for Jennifer and Bruce, and I think it is fair to say that the delivery of the leather-bound books was the highlight of my family's year—the highlight of the past three years, actually.

# PROFIT-SHARING

Any of us can sit down and recall funny quotes and stories about our children that tug at the heart strings. But the point is, there really is a wonderful and convenient support system for anyone willing and wise enough to use it. Children can learn from their parents. And grown-ups can surely be inspired by the young.

They are the dearest and most valuable resources we have. When our daughter and three sons were young and our summer vacations were always by car—the only way we could afford to travel (and then, barely)—we swore every year we would not take them the next time. No more fights in the back seat and arguments over who did what to whom, and someone always needing to stop to use the rest room.

But a peculiar thing happened. Every time we took a trip without them, we were so bored or lonely that we always cut our plans short and went home early.

# TIMELY REMINDERS

I am already on record as believing that wives are great motivators. Not only do they encourage us when we are down and lead our cheering sections, but they can often lift us with wit out of an otherwise depressing situation.

Ralph Branca, the onetime Brooklyn Dodger pitcher, has been reminded all his life about the home run he served up to Bobby Thomson of the Giants that clinched the 1951 pennant in the season that became baseball's most historic.

On the twenty-fifth anniversary of the home run, a writer asked Branca how often references are made to that moment. "Every day," he replied.

The writer asked if he could recall when he first thought about it that day.

"This morning," Branca said. "When my wife woke me up, she said, 'Happy anniversary, dear.' "

# Epilogue

▲

ALL of America thrilled to the victory of Dennis Connor and his crew in recapturing the America's Cup from Australia in 1987. For me, the triumph of Connor, who worked and struggled and sacrificed eight years to vindicate his earlier loss, renewed the memory of one of the most interesting and motivating experiences I ever had.

I spent two days with Connor in Honolulu, Hawaii, in a meeting arranged by John Kilroy, Sr., a yachtsman who thought I might be able to offer some suggestions on teamwork. It was just one idea, one possible edge, for a skipper who exhausted a lot of them in his quest to avenge his defeat as the last U.S. skipper to lose the Cup to the Aussies.

I was thrilled to have this opportunity to meet Dennis and his fine crew. Connor had selected the waters of Hawaii as a training base because the currents and the winds were similar to those he would encounter in Fremantle, Australia. I had a speaking engagement in Honolulu at the same time, so this setting was ideal. It pleases me to be able to say that I took the first sail *Stars and Stripes* ever made on the ocean.

On our first attempt we didn't get very far, unfortunately. The mast broke and we had to return to shore. Dennis asked me if I had ever sailed before and I had to reply truthfully, "Only on an ice boat."

He advised me to look out for the boom because it could kill you, which I accepted as a valid reason for staying alert. In the past, I was always the one who would get seasick or go to sleep when we went out to sea on a yacht. This was the one time I didn't do either one—I was too nervous.

We spent the entire day at it and the seas were rough and choppy, the air blustery. The way Dennis Connor commanded his crew and how they all responded impressed me. Dennis knew everyone's job and used an approach that I always preached: no detail is too small.

His style is so attentive, so sweeping, that he doesn't miss a thing. One day I went inside the trailer on shore and wrote the following on his blackboard and signed it: "DO SOMETHING TO IMPROVE EVERY DAY." It was the fourth item on a list of motivational points, and Dennis said it was the one most difficult for him and his crew to achieve.

I enjoyed meeting and visiting with Tom Whindom and exchanging ideas with the crew. One suggestion I made to Dennis was to have a weight room right at the shore, near the boat, where it would be convenient for everyone to work out at any time during the long days and nights. He liked the suggestion; they had been working out early in the morning at the hotel and then driving to the harbor. This change would allow his crew to work out twice a day. By having weights nearby, a crewman could have a short workout at any time he chose. I left after three days, and whether they worked out more often or not I don't know. But I think Connor knew and understood the value of a workout after long, unbroken hours of tension.

Dennis motivated his crew and everyone around him by being firm, knowing everyone personally, and dealing with them with a sense of humor. He clearly enjoyed what he was doing, and that attitude rubbed off on everybody. He told me that very first day that *Stars and Stripes* had raced *Liberty*, and that his new ship was much the faster. He was very excited about what he had going for him.

History proved him to be correct, as *Stars and Stripes* went on to defeat *Kookabura III* in four consecutive races to bring back the Cup to America.

# Editor's Note

▲

"GEORGE ALLEN RETURNS TO COACHING." That was the heading on a press release that moved around the country in the early summer of 1989. The headline was even reprinted on the outside of the envelope, prompting one writer to observe, "I bet this is one letter the Post Office was tempted to open."

Inside appeared the following news release:

"SIOUX CITY, Iowa—George Allen, one of the winningest coaches in National Football League History, will be returning to active coaching—back at the place that gave him his start in college football.

"In what may be an unprecedented move, Allen will once again get out the clipboard and blow the practice whistle for two weeks this August as he returns to Morningside College, an NCAA Division II school in Sioux City.

"It was forty-one years ago that Morningside hired Allen, out of the University of Michigan, to direct the school's football program. Allen spent three successful years (1948–1950) at Morningside, moved through the coaching ranks and eventually became one of the NFL's greats as a coach of the Los Angeles Rams and the Washington Redskins.

"Allen's 116-47-5 NFL remains the highest winning percentage, 70.5, in the league's history among coaches with more than ten years' experience.

"He is returning to Morningside to help revive the school's football program, lending his name, expertise and talent both on the practice field and in the community.

"Allen's work at Morningside starts August 21st and concludes with the school's season opener at Northwestern College on September 2nd. Allen will focus on defense and special teams, where he earned his reputation as one of the NLF's best in those areas."

" 'I want to help them turn the program around,' said Allen, 'beginning with a victory in the first game. I've been lucky in my career that we won the opener thirteen out of fourteen years in the NFL and seven out of nine in college.'

"A small private college of 1200 students, Morningside's football program has fallen on hard times lately. The Maroon Chiefs lost eleven games last year and take a 15-game losing streak into the 1989 season . . .

How could he resist? His revisit to his first coaching stop, one observer noted, has echoes of "Rocky," "Hoosiers" and "Field of Dreams". In a program that dates back to 1901, only five Morningside teams ever won seven or more games in a season and Allen coached two of those squads—in 1949 and '50.

George Allen doesn't need money or exposure, but he still needs football—five years after his last coaching job, in the USFL, and eleven years after the Rams fired him after two preseason games. And though several inquired, no team in the NFL would touch him, this man who never knew a losing season as a coach, the finest rebuilder pro football has ever known. It was bizarre then and a mystery still.